Books by John Einarson

Gene Clark: Tambourine Man (2004)

Desperados: The Roots of Country Rock (2001)

Randy Bachman: Takin' Care of Business,
with Randy Bachman (2000)

American Woman: The Story of the Guess Who (1995)

Magic Carpet Ride: The Autobiography of John Kay and Steppenwolf,
with John Kay (1994)

A Journey through the Past (1994)

Neil Young: Don't Be Denied (1992)

Aurora: The Story of Neil Young and the Squires (1991)

Shakin' All Over: The Winnipeg Sixties Rock Scene (1987)

There's Something Happening Here

The Story of

BUFFALO SPRINGFIELD

For What It's Worth

by John Einarson
with Richie Furay

Cooper Square Press

Published by Cooper Square Press
An imprint of The Rowman & Littlefield Publishing Group, Inc.
200 Park Avenue South, Suite 1109
New York, New York 10003-1503
www.coopersquarepress.com

Distributed by National Book Network

Design by Susan Hannah

Library of Congress Cataloging-in-Publication Data
Einarson, John, 1952–
    For what it's worth : the story of Buffalo Springfield / by
John Einarson with Richie Furay.—1st Cooper Square Press ed.
2004.
        p. cm.
    Discography: p.
    ISBN 0-8154-1281-9 (pbk. : alk. paper)
    1. Buffalo Springfield (Musical group) 2. Rock musicians—
United States—Biography. I. Furay, Richie. II. Title.
    ML421.B84E458 2004
    782.42166'092'2—dc22   2004004882

Manufactured in the United States of America.

♾ ™The paper used in this publication meets the minimum requirements of American National Standard for Information Sciences—Permanence of Paper for Printed Library Materials, ANSI/NISO Z39.48-1992.

CONTENTS

Buffalo Springfield: (clockwise) Neil Young, Bruce Palmer, Richie Furay, Dewey Martin, Stephen Stills

PREFACE

A s John Einarson and I talked about the Buffalo Springfield during the winter of 1996, I was reminded of things that had been stored away in some part of my heart a long time ago. For the most part, they are good memories, maybe a sad memory or two. Not many people get to live out dreams they'd been nurturing from childhood. When I was growing up in Yellow Springs, Ohio, all I ever wanted to be was a singer-songwriter-musician and that this wish ever came true is still amazing to me. I had the opportunity to make music with and become friends of some of the most creative musicians in North America. We weren't friends who grew up together in the same town playing music at school dances. We didn't even grow up in the same country, for that matter. And yet, on each of our individual journeys through life, we came together for a short time in Los Angeles in 1966 to satisfy the drive to release the music in our hearts. At times this seems almost like yesterday, then at other times, it's like another life. Thanks guys. I'm glad we had the chance to share this part of our lives together, to have had so many people care, and to have made such a mark in history.

Nobody could have made up this story, nobody! You can't plan a story like this. Thanks John Einarson for wanting to tell the story, for diligently seeking out the facts from the people who were there — what a reunion that would be! — and for putting them accurately into this book for us to reflect upon. For those who want to know what was going on in our lives 30 years ago, this book tells the story. I don't know how it could have been written any better.

Richie Furay
Boulder, Colorado

Back cover from the album BUFFALO SPRINGFIELD.

§

There's Something Happening Here

There's something happening here,
What it is ain't exactly clear.
There's a man with a gun over there,
Tellin' me I've got to beware.
I think it's time we stop,
Hey, what's that sound,
Everybody look what's going down.

For What It's Worth (Stephen Stills)

t would have been virtually impossible not to have noticed it amid the rush hour traffic edging its way up Sunset Boulevard on a muggy Friday afternoon in early April. The dark 1953 Pontiac hearse, battered and dusty from a manic two week odyssey across America, transmission worn out and rumbling underneath, could hardly have been missed; its occupants, two weary, hungry, long haired types, no different in appearance from the Sunset Strip denizens strolling the nearby sidewalks oblivious to the history about to be made in that line of traffic. Frustrated after several days searching in vain for a compatriot last seen a year earlier up in northern Canada, the two travelers had arrived in LA, appropriately enough, on April 1 and spent the last five days trudging from club to club, scene to scene, party to party, sleeping at nights in the hearse. "Anyone here know Steve Stills?" Dejected, the two determined to head north to San Francisco in the hope of finding kindred spirits for their musical dream. And there they sat, inching along in the home-ward bound procession of newer, cleaner, nondescript cars. Even the license plate was a dead giveaway that this was no ordinary vehicle: Ontario, Canada.

But miss it they almost did. The three occupants of the white van heading southbound could just as easily been distracted to the right, perhaps at one of the many fresh faced young girls along the Strip, rather than looking left. That they were looking around at all is fortuitous, preoccupied as they were with their own stalled careers. They, too, were frustrated over an inability to find sympathetic ears for their unique music aspirations.

What transpired next is no longer considered simply a chance encounter. Transcending mere fact, the events of the next few minutes have taken on mythic proportions to become, in the annals of popular culture, legendary. More than pure luck, coincidence or serendipity, at that very moment the planets aligned, stars crossed, everyone's karma turned positive, divine intervention interceded, the hand of fate revealed itself — whatever you subscribe to in order to explain the unexplained. Though each of the five participants in that moment in time tell it slightly differently, the fact remains that the occupants of the white van, individually or collectively, depending on who's retelling it, noticed the black hearse with the foreign plate heading the other direction. Once the light of recognition came on, the van hastily pulled an illegal, and likely difficult in rush hour, U-turn, maneuvering its way through the line of northbound cars, horn honking frantically all the while, to pull up behind the hearse. One of the passengers lept out, ran up and pounded on the driver's side window of the strange vehicle, yelling to the startled travelers inside who had taken no notice of the blaring car horn directly behind them. "Hey Neil, it's me, Steve Stills! Pull over, man!"

The drivers of the two vehicles managed to find curb space, or a vacant store parking lot, again depending on whose version is being related, and the five piled out to embrace and introduce one another. Standing together for the first time were four fifths of what literally in a matter of hours would become seminal California folk-country-rock pioneers the Buffalo Springfield: Stephen Stills and Richie Furay, two American ex-Greenwich Village folk singers relocated to LA for several months struggling to get a folk rock group going; and Neil Young and Bruce Palmer, Canadian rock'n'rollers fleeing the limited confines of Toronto's Yorkville music scene in search of Stephen Stills and a wider audience for their musical vision. With Stephen and Richie was Barry Friedman, the owner and pilot of that fated white van, the man who would put the four together and give them the wings to fly. On April 6, 1966, in that late afternoon line of traffic, the course of popular music was forever altered.

"It's the most remarkable karmic event ever," Bruce Palmer comments, still astonished 30 years later at the recollection of that encounter. "It's hard to even imagine. We passed parallel to one another and imagine if they had been looking the other way? You wonder about kismet and fate and all that when you consider this. Each of us was looking for the same thing: a band. We had each been looking for the other. Truly amazing. The band formed right there on the spot." What is further staggering about that encounter is that the two Americans proceeded to play to their awestruck Canadian friends a song that one of the Canadians, Neil Young, had composed six months earlier up in Toronto. Unbeknownst to Neil, Richie had brought Neil's intensely personal song of angst and frustration, *Nowadays Clancy Can't Even Sing*, out to LA, where he and Stephen had worked up their own arrangement, complete with sweet harmonies and shifting time signature. Hearing his own creation performed so well by these two talented singers sealed the deal; they would form a group then and there. It was that simple.

Reading like some Hollywood script, the story should have a happy ending: our heroes find a drummer (Canadian Dewey Martin), begin performing within a week of that meeting, find fame, fortune, adulation and gold records, retire successful, satisfied, and respected. It should have been. That's what the five headstrong young men envisioned when they came together. Drawing on a diversity of musical experiences — Greenwich Village and Yorkville folk, Nashville country, rural southern blues, Beatles rock'n'roll, Latin American rhythms, Detroit R'n'B — and boasting the talents of three uniquely individual singer/songwriters within one group determined to play only their own material, the Buffalo Springfield had everything going for them. They had an identifiable image collectively and individually, managerial and record label clout behind them, as well as the overwhelming endorsement of the music world elite. What could possibly go wrong? "Everything else that was coming from LA in the later Sixties, like Love and The Doors, was dark," recalls Richie Furay. "We had a sunnier side to us. There was something about us that wanted to be English, the Beatles thing, the way we looked. But we came from all over. I mean there were three Canadians in the band."

From their debut a mere week later on April 15, 1966 opening for folk rock pioneers The Byrds, the Buffalo Springfield was seen as a potentially major act in the pop music world. "We were so confident of what we were doing and the sound we had that we saw ourselves as having no competition other than the Beatles or the Stones," boasts Neil Young on those heady early days. "It was that good in the beginning. We thought we were going to be together for about 15 years because we knew how good it was." Following their impressive debut with The Byrds, the group began a groundbreaking six-week stand at the hottest club on Sunset Strip, the Whisky-A-Go Go. There the band's reputation was forged and a dozen record labels bid for their signatures. As well, their individual identities emerged on the Whisky stage — Stephen Stills, the impetuous, impatient cowboy; Neil Young, the dark, brooding self-styled 'Hollywood Indian'; Richie Furay, the ebullient boy-next-door; Bruce Palmer, deep, mysterious, back turned to the audience; and Dewey Martin, the personable, outgoing clown. They were Americana personified.

All the members seem to agree that the band may have peaked in performance at the Whisky and never succeeded in translating their vibrant live show to vinyl. "My fondest memory remains the Whisky-A-Go Go," states Richie. "It was the best the band ever was, and the most united. The photograph of the Springfield in my mind was that stint at the Whisky. That was the Buffalo Springfield; everything that came after it is like a blur. That's where the memories are. I visualize the band and hear the music from that period at the Whisky, not in a recording studio or on a particular television show. That's when we were what we were. Everybody else only had a glimpse of what we were from various television shows singing *For What It's Worth*." Neil laments the fact that the early Buffalo Springfield sound was never adequately captured on record. "When we got into the studio, the groove just wasn't the same. And we couldn't figure out why. This was the major frustration for me as a young musician. Buffalo Springfield should have been recorded live from the very beginning."

Road manager and longtime band confidante Dickie Davis remembers how the Buffalo Springfield not only created the "image" of the quintessential LA band, but also the LA "sound" of the late 1960s. "Being in a band was your ticket to success back then. The guys in the Buffalo Springfield expected nothing less than to make it, have hit records and be millionaires. They were impatient and saw no peers or competition." Compromising for no one, refusing to emulate their mentors or rivals, and eschewing current psychedelic trends, the band chose instead to chart their own course and follow their own guiding lights.

Regretably, the universe did not unfold as it should. The Buffalo Springfield story is one of tremendous promise and potential, perhaps more than any other group in rock music history. But if fate cast them together, creative differences, petty rivalries, personality conflicts, and impatience tore them apart prematurely. Fraught with frustration, plagued by misdirection, and eventually undone by factions, egos, and spinning wheels, the group self-destructed two years after coming together. "Their career was one long parade of walkouts, drug busts, power plays and psychodramas that won the band as big a reputation for conflict as for their music," notes rock music historian Pete Doggett. Despite this turmoil — or even perhaps because of this tension — the Buffalo Springfield created some of the most evocative and original music of the late 1960s, including three critically acclaimed diverse albums and several exquisitely-crafted singles which stand as rock music masterpieces, *Bluebird*, *Rock And Roll Woman*, and *Mr. Soul*.

Innovators of a unique acoustic-electric folk-country-rock amalgam, the individual members of the Buffalo Springfield were, perhaps, too creative, too headstrong, too impatient for their own good. Suggests Springfield admirer David Geffen, "Lots of great music has come out of all of them. Maybe it was too much talent to be contained in one group," an opinion confirmed by Richie Furay. "I don't want to point any fingers," comments Richie on the problems that befell the group, "but I think management didn't really know exactly what to do with us. But to give them the benefit of the doubt, they had some of the same frustrations with the people in the band that we had. I think what happened was that there was no direction from the very beginning. No one knew what quite to do with us. They knew that we probably had a product, but they didn't know quite how to sell it. Everybody was telling us we were ahead of our time. It was hard to swallow because we were right in the middle of it. We really didn't know exactly what we were."

When asked in interviews, 'Who's the leader?' the pat response was always, 'Steve's the leader, but we all are.' Their apparent collegiality, however, masked a love-hate relationship between the two principle songwriters within the group, Stephen Stills and Neil Young. Their feuding extended from the concert stage to the recording studio such that near the end the two took to recording apart, submitting completed tapes for inclusion on their final album. "They'd still be together if it wasn't for Stephen's ego up against Neil, the two writers," postulates manager/producer Charlie Greene. "Had they grown together rather than grown apart they would have been *the* sensational band of the decade. They had that capability." Then again, they may not have blossomed as individual artists in the 1970s, as The Turtles Mark Volman, a close friend of the Springfield, suggests. "It was Charlie Greene's will to build that band around Stephen and Neil, they were the dynamic in the group. But when Stephen's star rose with *For What It's Worth*, Neil had problems with that. I think Neil's later career came out of defense of Stephen's success, almost like a challenge to Stephen Stills. Everybody kind of looked at Stephen as the Buffalo Springfield, and I don't think Neil was comfortable with that. But that's the way the Sixties was: find the one guy to focus on. That was the blueprint that everyone followed and they didn't fit into that. That's one of the reasons they couldn't last. They couldn't play the game. They wouldn't fit the 1960s model. As the 'lonesome boy, singer/songwriter Seventies' came along, mysterious was in, and Stephen and Neil fit into that much better. It allowed them both to blossom. They set the standard for that hip, Southern California singer/ songwriter image in the Seventies."

Each member of the band now has bitter-sweet memories of their time together. "For all the noise the Buffalo Springfield made at the time we were together," suggests Stephen, "we didn't sell that many records. There wasn't a big mass appeal, it was on its way. It was about to break when we were on the way to do the Johnny Carson show when Neil went the other way." Neil returned to the group soon after his abrupt exit on the eve of a television appearance that would have brought the Springfield widespread national attention, then defected twice more before the group finally broke up. With Bruce Palmer's several busts and deportations for drugs, the band became a revolving door of personnel. "There was a real lack of consistency in the band," Richie points out. "Every time we were making a move, there was another guy in the band, so we just couldn't get any momentum. There were nine guys in and out of the band over the two years." For Neil, memories of the Buffalo Springfield are also mixed. "We were good, even great. When we started out, we thought we would be together forever. But we were just too young to be patient and I was the worst. I'm not sure now that the way I felt and acted was mostly because of nerves. It got that I didn't care, that I didn't want to make it with them. I know I should have been happy but in some ways it was the worst time of my life. The success really didn't come very fast for us. The adulation did, but we really struggled for success and recognition for what we were trying to do, and we never really attained it. When people heard the band live, they loved us but that never came across on the records. Our music wasn't the kind that got accepted across the board. Our contemporaries were groups like The Doors. They were our peers at the time and they cleaned up on us as far as leaving their mark goes and getting hits. I was frustrated because we didn't do as well as I thought we were going to. Success always seemed evasive." Remarks Dickie Davis, "They were heartbroken that they did not achieve the acclaim they expected."

Despite the band members' reservations about their success, the Buffalo Springfield did significantly influence the sound and image of rock music, and with one song the Springfield left an indelible mark on American culture. *"For What It's Worth,* that's what people know of us,'' stresses Richie Furay. ''It's the anthem of the Sixties because it summed up the feelings of the Sixties, the restlessness. You can say to people, 'Maybe you remember our big song *For What It's Worth'* and they'll say, 'No.' But if you say, 'Stop, hey, what's that sound' or 'There's something happening here,' instantly they know it.'' The lyrics from this song have indeed come to symbolize the turbulent decade that was the 1960s. Employed in virtually every documentary, television special, and feature film (including *Forrest Gump* and Oliver Stone's *Born On The Fourth Of July*) chronicling that period in America, *For What It's Worth* has transcended the pop charts to become an anthem, a touchstone to an entire era. In 1967, the Buffalo Springfield captured the restless, confrontational mood of a generation railing against the establishment with that song.

The Buffalo Springfield legacy remains firmly intact. *The Rolling Stone Encyclopedia of Rock'n'Roll* cites the band among a handful of seminal rock pioneers. Hailed as the quintessential Sixties California pop group, the Buffalo Springfield helped spawn several rock music genres, including folk rock and country rock, with no lesser luminaries than The Byrds, Flying Burrito Brothers, and Eagles openly acknowledging their Springfield influences. Though together a mere two years, the Springfield managed in that short space of time to achieve a major impact on the rock scene. Their unique folk-country-rock sound was like nothing heard before or since. ''I think we're one of the most popular, mysterious American bands,'' suggests Richie. ''Our legacy speaks for itself: Crosby, Stills and Nash, Neil Young, Poco, Loggins and Messina, Souther, Hillman and Furay. The trail is there. Look at the success of the bands and the musicians and the songs that came out of the Springfield. And it's still going on to this day. Just listen. I don't have to go out and prove there is a legacy; it's there. The stake we smacked into the ground was claimed by bands like The Eagles and the other California bands that came after us.'' There truly was something happening in the history of rock music and pop culture when the Buffalo Springfield came together in 1966.

‷

ONE

Gotta Travel On

Done laid around, done played around,
This old town too long.
Summer's almost gone, and winter's coming on.
Done laid around, done played around,
This old town too long,
And I feel like I gotta travel on.

Gotta Travel On (Clayton, Ehrlich, Lazar, Six)

In the autumn of 1958, the polished harmonies of California singing group The Kingston Trio took a traditional folk number, *Tom Dooley*, a calypso ballad of racial murder and execution, to the very top of the pop charts, thus inaugurating the American folk music revival. Although traditional American acoustic roots music had been revived during the 1930s and often held politically left leanings embodied by latter day troubadours like dust bowl minstrel Woody Guthrie and 1950s activist Pete Seeger, folk music had taken root in the bohemian coffeehouses of urban artistic and intellectual centers like New York, San Francisco, Chicago, and Boston, where it remained through to the early 1960s. Folkies snubbed their noses at the mindless themes of Fifties rock'n'roll, seeing a far loftier purpose in their muse. Folk music had a message often presented in the protest or topical song which found favor as civil rights, ban-the-bomb, and Vietnam War protests grew to public attention. Folk singers were expected to have a conscience, an opinion, something to say that their fans wanted to hear.

Though die-hard folk purists shunned them as squeaky clean sell outs, the impact of The Kingston Trio on turning traditional folk music into a popular genre for the masses cannot be denied. With their ascent, sales of acoustic guitars and banjos to young men eager to emulate their striped-shirted mentors soared, perhaps even more so than upon the arrival three years earlier of Elvis Presley. At least folk singers actually played their instruments rather than using them as props to gyrate behind. Besides, the entire folk catalog rarely deviated beyond three chord progressions, making it appealing to the novice musician. Folk music was grassroots music easily playable at informal social gatherings. What could be more fun than singing *Michael Rowed The Boat Ashore* with all your friends around the campfire? For thousands of young people in the late 1950s and early 1960s, The Kingston Trio offered their initiation into music. In their wake came hundreds of Kingston Trio wanna-be's, capable groups like the Chad Mitchell Trio, The Highwaymen, The Rooftop Singers, as well as innumerable generic Rambling Four's and Roving Five's, hummin' and a strummin.'

With the first of the baby boomers arriving on American college campuses by the fall of 1963, the folk music boom hit full stride. What had begun as a genre largely dedicated to preserving and reproducing the authentic roots music of the American South and adaptations of traditional American acoustic songs of a century before had come to embrace original composition within its ranks. The paragon of the singer/songwriter folk artist was , of course, Bob Dylan, who by the end of 1963 was performing his own material almost exclusively. Even The Kingston Trio, having recruited capable songwriter John Stewart to its ranks, was beginning to self-generate material. The protest song was at the forefront of the folk music movement as 1964 arrived, with Dylan's *The Times They Are A-Changin'* and *Chimes of Freedom*, Buffy Ste.-Marie's *Universal Soldier*, Tom Paxton's *I Can't Help But Wonder Where I'm Bound*, and Phil Ochs' *Too Many Martyrs* setting the tone.

Taking its cue from the wholesome image of The Kingston Trio, folk music became sanitized, packaged, and sold to the masses in groups like the New Christy Minstrels and Peter, Paul and Mary. *Walk Right In* by the Rooftop Singers, Peter, Paul and Mary's *Puff the Magic Dragon* and *Blowin' In The Wind*, *Green Green* from the New Christy Minstrels, and *If I Had A Hammer* by Trini Lopez were all Top Ten hit records by mid-1963. No longer the exclusive domain of specialty record labels like Folkways and Elektra, the major leaguers like Capitol and Columbia clambered aboard the bandwagon to sign up folk artists. The prime time television extravaganza *Hootenanny* offered millions of viewers their favorite folk artists each week. Even established supper club entertainers such as Bobby Darin found favor on the pop charts dabbling in the folk ballads of Tim Hardin. Folk music was no longer strictly the preserve of predominately white, urban, middle to upper class, educated, elitist college crowds. Now it was Top Forty hit parade fare, though it continued to hold little appeal to teenyboppers. Nor did it offer anything of substance to blacks, even though its roots are in black country blues and even though folk music became the soundtrack to the civil rights movement.

Despite the mass market appeal of folk music by 1963, its roots remained in the coffeehouses of New York's colorful arts community, Greenwich Village. For all aspiring folkies, neophyte or otherwise, it was their Mecca. This bohemian enclave in Lower Manhattan, a popular haven and residence for college students in the older walkups, was dotted with tiny nightclubs and even tinier coffeehouses and basket joints, where entertainers earned their keep passing a basket for donations following each set. Bounded to the north by 14th Street and to the south by Houston Street, the focus of the folk music scene centered around MacDougal and Bleeker Streets, where dimly lit dens like the Gaslight, Commons, Bitter End, Café Wha, and Village Vanguard presented established as well as up-and-coming folk fare. Basket houses like the Four Winds and the aptly named Café Why Not exploited each new crop of hopeful young "folkniks," and there were plenty of those for the pickin'. It had been widely reported that Bob Dylan had been discovered at Gerde's Folk City, thereby making it a magnet for devotees. Dylan was, by 1963, the most illustrious graduate of the Greenwich Village scene, but several comparably talented singer/songwriters toiled away for years amid the clubs, local heroes who remained largely obscure to the wider music audience, such as Fred Neil, Dave Van Ronk, and Ramblin' Jack Elliott. More than merely offering a venue for novice folkies, Greenwich Village represented a sense of community, an alternative lifestyle, and a sanctuary. Woody Guthrie had lived in the Village in the 1940s, as had Pete Seeger and Dylan himself. As such, Greenwich Village drew thousands of aspiring folk singers to its streets, guitars slung over their shoulders, from all over the continent, young artists like Richie Furay and Stephen Stills.

In Ohio, Richie Furay had already fallen under the sway of the folk boom by the time he entered his freshman year at Otterbein College in Westerville, just north of Columbus, in the fall of 1962. And it was folk music that would inspire him with the dream of pursuing a musical career, a dream that, like so many others, would ultimately draw him to Greenwich Village. Born May 9, 1944 in Dayton but raised in Yellow Springs, the youngest of two children, Paul Richard Furay grew up listening to country music around the house as a boy. "My Dad liked country music," recalls Richie. "Back then I liked guys like Conway Twitty and Eddy Arnold." The family ran Furay's Drugstore in Yellow Springs until his father Paul's death when Richie was 13. After that his mother Naomi operated a gift shop.

Bitten by the music bug at the tender age of seven, Richie pestered his parents until they relented. "Finally my parents bought me a guitar for Christmas. It was one of those full-sized ones but it was cardboard. I picked it up on Christmas morning and said, 'I don't want it! It's not the real thing!' So, of course, that broke everybody's heart so after convincing them that I would practice and practice, I finally got a real guitar when I was eight years old. My guitar teacher tried to teach me lead and that's where I lost all imagination and it became dull. I played guitar for awhile and then in late grade school, musical instruments and stuff weren't really where it was at because all the other guys were out playing baseball and basketball. So I gave the guitar up for about five years."

During that time, the emergence of rock'n'roll caught Richie's attention but not enough to rekindle his early passion for the guitar, though he had already developed a powerful singing voice and a keen ear for harmony. "I loved Dion and the Belmonts. I liked the New York street music, the harmonies and vocals. The Dovells, the Del-Vikings, and all those harmony groups. When I first saw Ricky Nelson singing on Ozzie and Harriet, I said to myself, 'If he can do that, I can do that, too.' Ricky Nelson was a big influence on me. I loved Elvis and Ricky Nelson. I liked Buddy Holly, too. I also loved all those New York vocal groups. The Belmonts, Drifters, Ben E. King, Chuck Jackson and those guys. Anything with harmony singing."

Enrolled at Otterbein College, Richie soon switched his allegiance to folk music, notably The Kingston Trio's brand of pop folk harmony, and found his ample singing ability brought him attention on campus. "When I went to college, it was just when folk music was really starting to come on strong, so I went out and got myself another guitar. They had a freshman talent night, so I listened to my favorite Kingston Trio albums, learned all the top folk songs of the day, and went out and sang *They Call The Wind Mariah*." His rendition was enough to impress his fellow classmates.

One of those who took notice of Richie's clear tenor voice that night was another freshman, Bob Harmelink. "I was doing a barbershop quartet thing with three other freshman," recalls Bob fondly, "and Richie came onstage, just him and his guitar, and he brought the house down. He closed his eyes and was in another world singing out to the audience. He won the talent show and became a hit on campus instantly, becoming the star of the freshman class. We didn't become friends right away, though, because he lived in a different dorm and there were four or five hundred freshmen but I saw him around and knew who he was." It would take the intervention of a third college mate with an unusual request to instigate the formation of Richie's first folk group. "Nels Gustafson, a sophomore and upper class-man, had Richie and I come together with him to sing a birth-day song to his girlfriend over the phone back in Pennsylvania. The three of us harmonized well together and that was the start of The Monks."

Accompanied solely by Richie's guitar, the three found a nat-ural vocal blend, and before long The Monks were a popular attraction both on and off campus. "We did Kingston Trio, Peter, Paul and Mary songs and started writing our own songs, too," Richie enthuses. "That made us a little more unique, singing our own songs as well as other folk stuff." Continues Bob, "Richie brought the folk music influence to us. Nels and I were choir people, but Richie was a Kingston Trio fan. Most every song we sang was a song he knew how to play, so he determined the repertoire and the flavor of what we became. He became the leader and we became folkies. We started doing a lot of parties and college events. One of our favorite things was to go down to Ohio State University, knock on the door of a sorority house, and ask if we could come in and serenade. They'd be a little skeptical but they'd let us into the vestibule, maybe five or six of these sorority girls, Richie with his guitar and the three of us would start singing. Within three or four minutes here came about 15 or 20 girls down the stairs and we'd do a little concert right there in the foyer. It really stroked us, to go in cold and have these sorority girls swooning."

In their sophomore year, Richie and Bob joined Nels in the A Capella Choir, a college organized glee club-style vocal ensem-ble. But it may have been more than harmony singing that attracted Richie to the choir; a trip to New York was in the off-ing for spring break 1964 and Richie saw his opportunity to make the pilgrimage to Greenwich Village. However, he almost didn't go. Laid up with appendicitis over Christmas, Richie did not return to college for the second semester, instead remaining in Yellow Springs to recuperate, thus jeopardizing his participa-tion on the trip. After personally interceding with the choir mas-ter he was allowed to go along. "That was really something we were looking forward to," notes Richie, "because we actually thought we were pretty good and we'd go to New York and become The Kingston Trio just like that, overnight. We thought, 'We're going to be discovered in New York.'" Richie's sights were already firmly set on a career in music. The others weren't quite as determined. "Richie was driven," emphasizes Bob. "He had a goal for himself. Nels and I didn't have that. I was kind of along for the ride. I enjoyed it but I didn't see myself as a professional entertainer, which I think Richie saw himself as."

In early March 1964, the A Capella Choir arrived in the Big Apple, and as soon as they could the three Monks lit out for the Village. As Richie recalls, "We had a Saturday night off so Bob, Nels, and I decided that we were going to go down into Greenwich Village and play. We were really naive. We had no idea that these places had hired entertainment. I don't know how many places we knocked on the door of, places like the Bitter End, and got, 'Sorry.' But a couple of places let us in. One was the Café Wha, and we did a 30 minute set. This wasn't a basket joint, they had set entertainment, but Nels could sell you anything, and he sold the manager on us. We did two or three other basket joints also. When we saw the response, that's all it took for me to say to the other guys, 'We gotta come back this summer.' At one of the basket houses we played, the Four Winds Café over on West Fourth Street, the manager, John Hopkins, told us that if we came back in the summer we could pass the basket there. That sounded pretty good to me, so I talked Bob and Nels into going back that summer. I thought we could make a living there."

Returning to Yellow Springs, Richie impatiently bided his time in various labors until the opportunity to return to New York arrived. In early June, the three set out on their own to take the folk world by storm. It was a less than auspicious arrival. "We put our luggage in a locker at Grand Central Station and spent the first night at a hospice," smiles Bob, "just a flop house where we heard someone had been murdered a week before. And we spent a night in Central Park and another with a college friend in Brooklyn. Finally, we met Jake Jacobs, who was a singer working with a girl. They were going off to play somewhere else, so he sublet his apartment to us at the corner of Bedford and Grove on the sixth floor with no elevator. The three of us moved in."

"I was overwhelmed by New York," offers Richie on his move to the big city. "I came from a town of 4,500 people and there was that many people living on my street in New York.

The biggest city I had ever been to was Cincinnati to maybe see a baseball game. It was really out of character for me to just pack up a tape recorder, my guitar and a suitcase, drop out of school, leave home, and say to my Mom, 'I'm off to New York to be a folk singer.' I'm sure my Mom was wondering, 'Where did I go wrong?' But she didn't resist and actually helped me out when times got a little tough for me. She even gave me a book on how to live in New York on a dollar a day or something like that." Greenwich Village was still the folk music bastion, and in the coffeehouses and nightclubs, the three young singers from Ohio managed to catch some of the Village's best known artists, including Fred Neil, Tim Hardin, Vince Martin, Patrick Sky, Odetta, and Tom Paxton, as well as up-and-coming comedians like Richard Pryor and Flip Wilson. "There was a group at the Bitter End called the Bitter End Singers," recalls Bob, "with Lefty Baker on guitar, who later became Spanky and Our Gang, and we followed them around."

The trio managed to eke out a meager existence in the basket joints, where what you took home at the end of the evening was determined by the strength of your performance and your nerve. The premise to these clip joints was simple enough and aimed largely at the tourists. Shoe-horn as many customers as you can into these tiny clubs, sell them over-priced coffee and espresso, offer several folk acts, mostly rookies hungry for any attention, have each perform a half hour set, and while the next act prepares to go on, walk around passing the basket. Intimidation was part of the drill. If the patrons don't cough up, stand there and wait them out. Once the rotation of acts was completed, start over again with the same performers doing the exact same set so the patrons get the hint and vacate for the next sitting. "It had been about three or four weeks that we had been singing at the Four Winds and starving," remembers Bob. "I don't know how we paid the rent. We passed the basket and I found myself making up stories to the tourists, like 'We've got kids at home and this is our only means of support.' We started playing the game to get more money into the basket. You'd see a large group starting to move towards the door and you'd stop your set and immediately take an offering. 'Cause they were about to leave."

"The Village had changed between the time we were there from March to June," Richie points out. "There were still the guys in the jean jackets with guitars, but there were a lot more tourists now and, strangely, a lot of suits and ties. Business people would come into these little places, just sit there, throw their money into the baskets and leave. I remember Bob, Nels, and I getting a pot after working from eight in the evening til two or three in the morning, and there was barely enough to do anything, maybe ten bucks each after we split it three ways."

Though they didn't know it yet, the folk revival was already on its last legs by the time Richie and company hit town, the British Invasion having set up a firm beach head earlier that year. "By the time we got to Greenwich Village to do our folk music," confirms Richie in hindsight, "the folk scene was already over. I had already seen the Beatles on the Ed Sullivan Show and the British Invasion thing had already taken hold. The Lovin' Spoonful was about to happen, and here we were with our acoustic Martins and twelve strings walking through the Village and electric music was just ready to happen. By 1965 the folkies were having to look for places to play and things to do."

Nevertheless, Richie, Bob, and Nels pushed on unawares. Inspired by the heady surroundings, Richie began composing his own songs. Two such compositions, *The Ballad of Johnny Collins* and *Hear Our Song*, were copyrighted that summer. "Those were two of the very first songs I ever wrote. It was real hip to do Civil War type folk songs in those days, and *The Ballad of Johnny Collins* was my attempt at that. Bob, Nels, and I performed those songs, but I don't know what ever happened to them." With the Four Winds Café serving as their base, the trio worked sporadically through the summer, hanging out between engagements with the other novice folkies who congregated at the Four Winds. One such guitar-toting Four Winds habitue caught Richie's attention, a cocky, self-assured, short, blond-haired Southerner who literally bowled everyone over with his guitar skill and coffee grinder voice. The young man's name was Stephen Stills.

"I was impressed with Steve immediately," Richie recalls. "I thought he was a very good singer, his voice and his guitar work all connected together. I just liked the way he sang and played. He's an out-going guy, and we developed a rapport right away. I think he appreciated me and my singing, and we got along well. I thought he was really talented with a unique and interesting way of phrasing songs. He had more of a sense of direction than the three of us from Ohio. He was writing some then, but it wasn't until we got together later in California that his writing began to impress me. He could really belt out *High Flying Bird*, so I thought, 'Hey, I'd like to sing like this guy.'"

Born in Dallas, Texas on January 3, 1945 to William and Talitha Stills, Stephen Arthur Stills' roots are firmly planted in Southern soil. His family traces its history back to the plantations of the rural antebellum South. After the Union armies laid waste to much of the Southern farm economy, the family relocated to Illinois. Stephen's father William was somewhat of a soldier of fortune, an engineer, builder, and dreamer who frequently uprooted the family to follow his dreams and schemes. William's transient life would eventually take young Stephen through Illinois, Texas, Louisiana, Florida, and Central America.

It was in Florida where Stephen's love for music first took hold. While attending the private Admiral Farragut Military Academy, a strict environment that would leave a lasting impression on his disciplined approach to both music and his manner of dealing with others (and play no small part in his later nickname, The Sarge), Stephen took up the drums after an earlier false start on piano. With the advent of rock'n'roll he soon switched to guitar, drawing inspiration from the black blues players he witnessed on extended visits to the rural South.

A musical sponge, Stephen absorbed all forms of popular music from rock'n'roll and blues to folk and hit parade pop. "Because I wanted to play with everyone," notes Stephen to writer Dave Zimmer, "I learned to adapt myself to whatever styles were running around. I always wanted to fit in, so I was always, I guess, a fairly decent mimic." In Gainesville to attend school, Stephen joined his first band, The Radars, on drums. Never one to be kept from the limelight, he soon switched to guitar with his next group The Continentals. "I had a big blond guitar and played rhythm, mostly blues and folk stuff; we played fraternity parties around the campus in Gainesville." Joining Stephen on guitar was Don Felder, later to find fame with The Eagles. Together, Stephen and Don favored the manic surfing guitar stylings of Dick Dale and his Del-Tones, working up dual lead lines. "He was a little more wild and crazy than the rest of us guys in the band," related Don years later on his time with Stephen. "And he was already shedding off the Ivy League, early Sixties button-down collar stuff and going for the gusto. He had this drive.

He was going for it his way and be successful no matter what."

An unfortunate incident with the administration at his Tampa Bay high school resulted in Stephen's dismissal in 1961, after which he joined his wayward family now settled in Costa Rica. While checking out a San José lounge act consisting of Palá White on bass and Pibe Hine on keyboards, Stephen developed a love for Latin rhythms. Once again, the young musician picked up on the infectious Latin beats, storing them away for future reference. Drifting between Central America and Florida to finish school, Stephen landed in New Orleans in March of 1964, determined to make music his life. The folk boom was still going strong, so anyone with an acoustic guitar and a half decent voice could usually find a venue to perform. Not long after arriving, he hooked up with another young itinerant musician, Eugene 'Chris' Sarns, and the two formed an acoustic folk duo to play New Orleans' Bayou Room. As Chris told Dave Zimmer, "Stephen was into Dylan and I was into The Kingston Trio and Bud and Travis. So we managed to cook some stuff up. We'd do five sets a night until all hours of the morning and made somewhat of a living."

But like all aspiring folkies, New York's Greenwich Village beckoned, so like three Ohio college boys that summer, Stephen Stills, too, made the journey to New York, catching a lift with an East Coast folk ensemble heading home. There he breathed in the rarified air of the Village, and, like he had always done, absorbed the sights and sounds around him. "There were so many really creative people in the Village then, people like the Tarriers and the MFQ, who never made it. I was learning so much music I couldn't stop to sort it out. I used to love Timmy Hardin, and Freddy Neil taught me an incredible amount about playing rhythm guitar, about playing guitar at all. Freddy and Timmy Hardin and Richie Havens are probably more responsible for my style on guitar, along with Chet Atkins, than anybody else."

"I started working the basket houses," recalls Stephen, "sometimes with Chris, who had also hitched to New York, sometimes by myself. That's where I met Peter Tork. I was making pretty good money, believe it or not, but I was sort of confused by a lot of things. I was a Southern boy and had a whole different way of thinking." For a brief period, Stephen, Tork (or Thorkelson as he was known then), and John Hopkins formed an unnamed trio to work the basket joints before Hopkins, a native North Carolinian, split for Long Island to teach guitar. "I can remember the first time I met Peter Tork," relates Stephen. "For four days beforehand, I heard from everyone, 'Hey! Have you seen the kid down the street that looks just like you?!' And Peter told me later that he heard the same thing for approximately the same amount of time. We finally ran into each other at the Four Winds Café, and he said to me, 'Oh hi! You're the kid that looks just like me!' And that's how we met. I was singing by myself doing country blues and folk. Peter, of course, was playing his banjo around the Village." When their trio folded, Stephen remained in the Village hanging out at the Four Winds and scuffling for gigs; Peter migrated to Connecticut then Venezuela. The two would meet up again a year later in California. Around this time, Stephen and Richie struck up their friendship. "I met Richie and really liked his guitar and I really liked Richie."

"New York was still heavily folk influenced in 64," affirms Nurit Wilde, photographer, friend, and confidante to the Buffalo Springfield. "There was still acoustic instruments but some people were already experimenting with electric instruments. I knew of Stephen in New York. He was a friend of a friend of mine. I met Peter Tork there, too, when he was singing on the streets holding out a hat for money. I was going to school in Toronto and I would go to New York in the summer times to work in the coffeehouses. I worked at the Figaro, the Bitter End, and the Café Au Go-Go, and that's how I started hanging out with musicians. I had known Zal Yanovsky back in Toronto and knew the Lovin' Spoonful in New York. Zal and I were like brother and sister. I was good friends with Cass Elliot and Denny Doherty, [both of The Mamas and The Papas], and John Sebastian. Also the MFQ, Henry 'Tad' Diltz, and Cyrus Faryar." Like so many others, when electric folk rock superceded acoustic folk music in 1965, Nurit headed west, where she would become an integral member of the LA music scene.

By early July, Richie, Bob, Nels, and Stephen were at loose ends, the basket house circuit proving a dead end. The Four Winds remained their oasis. "Stephen was playing there," recalls Richie, "Charlie Chin was playing, Peter Tork might still have been there. There were several people we got to know there but we were all poor. And playing down the street was The Bay Singers." By comparison, The Bay Singers were veterans of

Greenwich Village, having migrated south from Boston in January 1964. Consisting of a quartet — Michael Scott on bass, Jean Gurney on vocals, Fred Geiger on guitar, and Roy Michaels on five string banjo — they had built a strong name for themselves in and around the college campuses in western Massachusetts and were featured on a weekly local radio show before trying their luck in New York. "In the latter part of my senior year in high school I started playing bass with The Bay Singers," remembers Michael Scott. "When I went to my first year of college, we had so many jobs that it was hard for me to get back to college. It was a lot more fun to go to Boston and play music. That was in September of 1963. That winter we decided to head out to the Village in New York. That's when we became the New Chautauquans. We did a single under that name. We all lived together on Thompson Street. Jean and I were going together. She lived at 171 and the band lived at 173. I would live with her but when her parents hit town I would move over to 173. We weren't long out of high school. We didn't have much money but we had a lot of fun. We hit the Village at a time when things were starting to go electric, near the end of the real heyday of folk music." The new moniker, taken from a river in upstate New York as well as a Depression-era social movement, proved too difficult for club owners to remember so the group soon reverted back to the more familiar Bay Singers.

"They were pros to us," says Bob Harmelink, "because they had been in the Village for maybe half a year and had a regular paying job." However by the summer of 1964, The Bay Singers, too, found they were spinning their wheels on the Village scene.

Enter aspiring folk music impresario and sometime songwriter Ed E. Miller. Ed, whose bread and butter was earned in the family garment business, dabbled in music, having written *Don't Let The Rain Come Down* for the Serendipity Singers. Something of a minor league visionary, Ed's dream was to assemble an off-Broadway revue tracing the evolution of American folk music through song and dance. As Richie tells it, "Eddie Miller had the idea of putting together a Back Porch Majority / Bitter End Singers kind of thing. Someone had heard the Bay Singers, had heard Bob, Nels and I, and heard Stephen sing and play and said, 'Wow, let's get this thing together.' Roy Michaels brought his girlfriend Kathy King in, so we had our two girls and seven guys, banjos, guitars, stand-up bass. We got black pants, gold lamé vests and some striped shirts and we were off and running. The whole thing was built to a formula: two girl singers, a deep bass voice, plunky banjos, tuneful folk standards and a little choreography thrown in, too."

"Eddie Miller didn't get us together specifically to make a group," suggests Bob Harmelink on the eventual formation of the Au Go-Go Singers in July of 1964, "although in the back of his mind I think that's what he wanted. He rented this little theater and brought us together with a musical director named Bert Carroll, who took the best of all our individual acts and created a revue that traced the history of folk music from Negro spirituals like *Go Down Moses* and brought it all the way up. Stephen did *High Flying Bird*, the three of us did *What Shall We Do With A Drunken Sailor*, we had costumes, choreography and acted it out. That was how the nine of us got together. We weren't the Au Go-Go Singers then, just a part of that off-Broadway show." The revue opened on July 21st at The Players Theater on MacDougal Street, billed as America Sings. Unfortunately America did not sing for long. The show opened and closed in two weeks. "We didn't know how bad it was," laughs Bob.

Despite America Sings' dismal run, Ed succeeded in convincing Roulette Records producers Hugo Peretti and Luigi Creatore to record the nine-piece group for a folk album. "They were looking for a New Christy Minstrels type recording group," Bob continues, "so they signed us to record an album. They paid us to record it, $500.00 a piece, and I couldn't believe it. That was the most money we'd seen all summer." Following the sessions, in an effort to keep the group alive, Ed managed to book them into a few borscht-belt nightclubs in upstate New York as warm up for established acts like Tony Bennett. They even performed at Gracie Mansion for an exclusive mayor's do. As Stephen recalls, "After the off-Broadway musical closed, we stayed together because we loved the music we were doing. But the time for big folk groups was already past."

Howard Solomon, owner of the Café Au Go-Go thought otherwise, and in an effort to recreate the Bitter End Singers, asked the group to perform at his renowned club opening for comedian Vaughn Meader and another Village enclave he had a piece of, the Café Bizarre. "That became our home base for awhile," claims Bob, "and we started working up an act. Howard got involved and took the group away from Eddie Miller and said, 'I'm gonna call you the Au Go-Go Singers, you're gonna perform here at the Café Au Go-Go, I'm gonna get you jobs, I know all the other club owners in America.'" Adds Jean Gurney, "There was a power struggle between Eddie Miller and Howard Solomon over the group. They had a big blow out, something about some underhanded dealings with Roulette Records." By the time the album finally appeared in November 1964, the troupe were now officially the Au Go-Go Singers.

Entitled THEY CALL US AU GO-GO SINGERS, the album presents a fairly pleasant if hardly inspiring dozen tracks of standard, wholesome, white-bread commercial folk fare in a similar vein to the New Christy Minstrels or Rooftop Singers, two aggregations the Au Go-Go's sought to emulate in terms of sound and presentation. None of the 12 tracks are group originals, most being more than competent arrangements of well-worn folk material like *This Train, Gotta Travel On*, and *Lonesome Traveler*. Richie and Kathy King appear as the principle soloists; however, there are few moments when individual voices stand alone. Richie's clear tenor rendition of Tom Paxton's *Where I'm Bound* and Stephen's blues-tinged take on country songwriter Billy Edd Wheeler's *High Flying Bird* offer the only sterling moments on the album, with Stephen managing some real grit with his gravely drawl. Although the few instrumental solos on the album belong mostly to banjoist Roy Michaels, Stephen takes a decent acoustic lead break in *Lonesome Traveler*, revealing that even in 1964 he was already an accomplished player. Both Stephen's solo efforts, *High Flying Bird* and *Miss Nellie*, a number by Eddie Miller about Indians attacking settlers, feature an early experiment in folk rock, incorporating electric bass and rhythm guitar as well as drums. Drums appear on several cuts throughout the album, hinting that the Au Go-Go Singers were not content to simply mine the traditional acoustic folk format and were aware of musical changes in the wind. Certainly Stephen was hip to the Beatles and the possibilities of plugging in by then.

Though the vocal harmonies are spot-on throughout the album with the accompaniment never getting in the way, taken overall the album lacks any sense of identity. The sound is faceless and generic. There is nothing on THEY CALL US AU GO-GO SINGERS to warrant sustaining a career, and by the time of its release, the folk ensemble format had already become passé. Had it been released a year earlier, the album might have fared much better. With the folk boom waning, sales were minimal and the album was quickly relegated to the delete bins. Folk ensembles were out; electric guitars, long hair, and British accents were in.

Roulette's efforts to promote the album were limited, placing it among 12 other releases in a *Billboard* ad, but they did release a single, the folk chestnut *San Francisco Bay Blues* backed by *Pink Polemoniums*. The Au Go-Go's arrangement of *San Francisco Bay Blues* owes more to Mitch Miller than composer Jesse Fuller or The Kingston Trio. As Bob recalls, "Richie sang *Pink Polemoniums*, which was a song that Roulette had for Jimmy Rodgers but he was fading by then so they gave it to us. They hoped that would catch on in a Jimmy Rodgers vein. It was Richie's big showstopper." The single sank without a trace.

Nevertheless, Howard Solomon managed to pull off a major coup by arranging for the group to appear on the nationally televised program *On Broadway Tonight*, hosted by Rudy Vallee and featuring popular chanteuse Diane Carroll. And Howard brought in veteran New York vocal arranger Jim Friedman to work with the group to present a more hip show. "It was near the end of summer of 1964," Friedman remembers about meeting the troupe. "I'm walking around the Village and I bump into Cass Elliot, Mama Cass, and she tells me that there's a bunch of kids in the Village Music Hall who are trying to put a sound together. 'Maybe you'd like to go hear them,' she suggested. When I walked into the place at Thompson and Sullivan, there were these nine kids, seven boys and two girls. They had no direction and were trying to sing this medley. It was 23 minutes long and it had all the phony folk songs of the era — *Charlie On The MTA*, *Tom Dooley* — all the current fake folk songs. They went on and on but there was something about them. They were on a very rickety stage and one of the girls was kind of heavy. When they did some choreography, I was afraid the stage was going to collapse and they were all gonna be killed. But what I heard was a miraculous sound coming outta these kids. They were singing harmonies that were incredible. First thing I said was, 'Number one, you're a singing group, not a dancing group. No more dancing.' And that's how we started. They were like my kids. And I loved them."

Friedman was then 37 years old and a noted songwriter, having composed *The Hills Of Shiloh* as well as collaborating with Shel Silverstein. He determined to revamp the nine-piece group to exploit their rich harmony potential to the fullest. Under his tutelage, the Au Go-Go Singers undertook a rigorous rehearsal regimen and dumped the bulk of their former repertoire. To this day, both Richie and Stephen credit Jim Friedman for much of their knowledge of harmony singing. They learned their lessons well; an integral component of the early Buffalo Springfield sound was the harmony and unison lead singing of Richie and Stephen.

"We worked for about a month getting a set together," claims Jim. "The modus operandi was that we would sit down and I would pick a tune and we would agree on it. Richie, Steve, and Roy would then noodle around with it and somebody would come up with a phrase or a lick and we would start building from that, just head arrangements. We would play around with it then we would put on the voices. Most of the people in the group were church trained. They were singing nine-part harmonies, all kinds of different, complicated things. If they were written out in charts, they'd have looked like maps of mountains. I would say 'Sing this' and it would slot right in. There wasn't much trouble with any of them. They picked things up quickly."

Within the group, individual personalities and talents were already coming to the fore. "Kathy King had a beautiful soprano voice, but she was very temperamental," recalls Bob. "She was an ingenue from New York and had a real artistic temperament. She would walk out on a show or just sit in her dressing room if things didn't go right. Jean was the heart of the group. She was like Mama Cass. She put herself into every song. Onstage, Michael was the comedian in the group. He was the only one of us who was funny. Stephen tried to be funny but didn't quite come across. He would try to be cute or tell a joke but nobody got it. So we had to quiet him down from taking the mike. He was the guitar player and he had his parts to sing, but many times he'd get so involved in what he was doing instrumentally that he would forget to sing. There were nine of us so we didn't really miss him, but we'd say, 'Steve, this is a singing group not an instrumental group.'"

In Jim Friedman's eyes, "Stephen Stills was this wild, maniac from New Orleans, a real *enfant terrible* who just stuck his nose in a guitar and played dead serious. He was obsessive about music. Stephen fought everybody. He was like James Dean, nothing satisfied him. There were a lot of women coming around and

Stephen made it a point to go after any woman he saw me with. And he usually got her. And I didn't resent it because he was my kid. He was beautiful." But Jim also saw beyond the mercurial young musician's brash exterior. "Stephen's two people. There's a lonely little boy in there. Stephen was always trying to gain his father's acceptance."

Comments Jean Gurney, "Richie was like the brother I had always wanted, and Stephen and I were really close. He came from a fairly dysfunctional family, so he'd come home with me to Massachusetts quite frequently. I'd drag the whole group home for a week and my mother would cook for us all. We'd sit and rehearse songs. My father took a real shine to Stephen. He could be really hot tempered sometimes, whereas Richie was more laid back and easy going, Mr. Mellow. He and Stephen would get into some terrific fights. Stephen would be screaming and ranting at rehearsals and Richie would only take so much." But the young Southerner's talent was irrepressible. "Stephen was voracious in expanding his own skills," adds Jean. "He had a real whisky voice for being as young as he was."

Bob Harmelink roomed with Stephen and witnessed his frustration. "Steve said to me, 'Bob, I'm doing so many neat riffs on this guitar, if only they could hear.' And I told him, 'Someday, Steve, you might have an electric guitar or your own mike, but right now we're a singing group.' He was very driven. He knew where he was going and you didn't want to get in his way. If he saw a man on stage doing something that he didn't know how to do, he'd take his guitar and go back stage and ask. He was developing his style and learned from everybody. He had Latin and Bossa Nova influences in him back then. He liked to do different stuff like that. He was a party guy, too, who wanted to be where the action was all the time which was a little bit scary for someone like me who was real conservative in my upbringing. He was kind of wild, but I liked him, everybody did." Bob recalls Stephen's first tentative steps in songwriting which resulted in the sale of one of his earliest compositions to the Modern Folk Quartet. "That song was something about a bear going over the mountain," chuckles Bob.

A review of the group's set at the Café Au Go Go warming up for comedian Vaughn Meader appeared in the November 4th edition of *Variety*. Noting their more than abundant vocal skills, the reviewer went on to cite the ensemble's onstage exuberance and rapport with the young audience as its strength, and choice of material the group's principle weakness. "Folk groups have about had it with Civil War and protest songs and should add some lighter fare (or a later war). The only adverse impression is the disturbing effect of watching a beautiful girl [Kathy King] who looks like a Revlon ad singing about the hardships of being on a chain gang." In a holdover from the failed America Sings project, the group offered a novel stage entrance. Strolling from the wings in ones and twos to the tune of *Pick A Bale Of Cotton*, each new entrant would chime in overtop with another traditional folk number such as *Swing Low, Sweet Chariot, Nobody Knows The Trouble I've Seen*, even *Froggy Went A-Courtin'*, creating a colorful vocal collage of Americana that rarely failed to turn an ear. "By the time they're all on," noted the *Variety* review, "it's a miniature folk festival."

The following week, the Au Go-Go Singers, with Jim Friedman in tow, embarked on their one and only tour arranged by Howard: six weeks in Texas playing Beaumont, Houston, and Austin. "We did two weeks in Beaumont at the Petroleum Club, which was like something out of a film noir full of rich people and sleazebags," laughs Jim, "the kind of people who flew airplanes from Central America to Arkansas bringing contraband that you either smoked or injected. It was the kind of place that wherever you sat down you liked to make sure there was a wall behind your back. We then moved to the Tidelands Inn in Houston. By that time we were really starting to swing. Jackie Vernon was the headliner and we were the opening act. We copped all the reviews and Jackie Vernon hated us." In Houston, the group appeared on a local television show before moving on to the Club Caravan in Austin, where the tour quickly unraveled.

An argument over fees and tour expenses ensued between the group, represented by Jim, and Howard Solomon. The group received $500 per week, and from that each of the ten members had to pay meals, laundry, and travel expenses. Consequently, there was no money left. Accusing Jim of attempting to usurp control of the act, Howard washed his hands of the group, leaving them high and dry in Texas. "Our six week tour broke right in time for Christmas," Bob remembers, "but we had no money to fly home so we had to take a train. It was at that point that Jim Friedman convinced us to sign an agreement saying we were splitting from Howard. On December 2nd, we sent the letter off, signed by all of us, and Howard called — I took the call in my room — and he's yelling and cussing. 'I'll ruin you guys. You'll never sing in New York again.' Here I was a 19-year-old kid and I'm fearing lawsuits. But Jim took control of things and told us not to worry, he had some contacts back in New York.'' The group broke for Christmas with Richie, Bob, and Nels returning to Ohio. They all agreed to meet up in New York early in the new year to consider their options.

In January of 1965, together once more, the Au Go-Go Singers determined to carry on without the clout of Howard Solomon. Tapping his extensive network of connections in the business, Jim brought the group to Jack Rollins and Charlie Joffe, managers of both Woody Allen and Harry Belafonte, who were impressed enough to arrange auditions for a couple of television shows. But the word was out: there was plenty of folk music around and it was already dying out. According to Jim, "Jack and Charlie set us up with an audition with one of the biggest talent agencies. It was January 10, 1965. I'll never forget it. We did this audition for these guys — there were 12 of them — at Nova Studios on 57th Street, and these guys went apeshit over the group. One of them comes over to me and says, 'They're incredible! By the way, do you have a record contract?' And I didn't know. So I went over to one of the kids and asked and he said, 'Yeah, we did a record with Roulette.' I'd never heard of Roulette so I went back and told the guy, 'The kids did a record with Roulette.' So he walks over to the other guys, they whisper something, they put their coats on, and walk out. I couldn't believe it, so I went over to Charlie and asked, 'What's going on?' He says, 'Why didn't you tell me you were with Roulette, that's Mafia.' It was Morris Levy. I still get sick when I think about it today.'' Morris Levy was later indicted on various criminal charges related to his operations in the record business; however, at the time, only insiders knew of his connections. Certainly, nine naive young folk singers had no knowledge that they were under contract to a mobster.

Devastated, Jim was not down yet. Charlie Joffe held out an olive branch. If the group could get free of their contract with Roulette, he would again approach the agency. Jim undertook to meet Morris Levy face to face on January 25th to plead his case for the group and request a release from their contract. "He listened to what I had to say," sighs Jim, "and replied, 'Everything you got belongs to Roulette. Anything that don't belong to us, you throw out. We're gonna keep you on as the music director and write the songs that will belong to our publishing company. You will teach them everything and you'll get ten dollars a week.' Over his shoulder was a picture on the wall of Cardinal Spellman, the cardinal from hell, with an autograph 'To my dear friend, Morris Levy', and Morris continues, 'and if you don't like it you might find yourself walking around on the bottom of the river in a cement overcoat.' I went home and died. It really broke me."

The future looked grim for the Au Go-Go Singers. Not only was popular music passing them by but they were shackled to an ironclad contract. Although the group struggled on until the end of February, playing an assortment of low profile nightclub engagements, the spark was gone. "It had become a real struggle," notes Michael. "We were sort of on the tails of a couple of groups and there was only room for the Christy Minstrels and Serendipities and we were kind of copying them." It was a rather ignominious end. Richie laments the demise of the group coming when it did. "We were doing some amazing stuff before the group split up, some really unique harmonies. We had been working on songs with Jim for another album that never came out, stuff like *The Underground Railway* and different little folk things. Jim had this collage of songs we were working on. We used to go over to his apartment every day and work on all these arrangements."

B ad news always seems to come in threes. While the Au Go-Go Singers weighed their options, Nels Gustafson received his draft notice and hightailed it back to college to avoid having to serve. Richie, too, got the same letter from Uncle Sam but managed to avoid the call. "We were all of draft age," states Michael Scott, "and everybody had their story on how to beat it. Richie got a deferment fairly easily but almost wrecked his health. He got out on weirdness. He told me how to get out, but it didn't work, so I had to get a little more drastic after that."

With dreams of combining folk and rock in a smaller group, Stephen set about putting his plans into motion using the remnants of the Au Go-Go Singers. Bob recalls how he saw the writing on the wall. "There were six of us living in one apartment at 171 Thompson Street. Nels had left, Kathy King quit, and there was no money. We realized we couldn't go on this way. There was nothing happening. Steve heard of a chance to go to Canada on a tour. So he started singing with Richie, myself, and Freddy. We were singing in this apartment doing *That's What You Get For Lovin' Me*, Steve was playing guitar, and we were making beautiful music. We hit a chord that, to me, sounded beautiful. Now my background is barbershop quartets and this was kind of a barbershop chord. Steve looked at me like, 'Wow, is that hokey!' And I thought it was pretty good. But right there in his mind he was saying, 'Well, Harmelink's out.' I saw it in his eyes: 'This is not where I want to go musically.' It was all I knew and that was the last time we sang together. It was nothing derogatory, I just saw in his eyes that I wasn't cool. After that I got my draft notice and headed back to college, too."

Indeed, Stephen had already embraced the British Invasion sounds dominating the pop charts by late 1964. He and Bob Harmelink recorded several songs at an impromptu session in Modern Folk Quartet member Jerry Yester's Greenwich Village digs, the two harmonizing Beatles style on *You Can Be My Girl*, a pop number composed by Lefty Baker and Kenny Hodges of the Bitter End Singers. But if Stephen was chafing under the limited confines of the traditional folk form, his mates were not yet ready to ditch *If I had A Hammer* for *I Want To Hold Your Hand*.

In one last gesture of goodwill, Rollins and Joffe had come up with a mini-tour of the Fourth Dimension chain of coffeehouses in Canada, three weeks with stops in Fort William, Winnipeg, and Regina for whomever of the Au Go-Go's might be interested. Folk music was still alive and well in Canada, so there were abundant, if not terribly lucrative, opportunities for American folk artists to find receptive ears across the border. The four members of the Bay Singers jumped at the offer to pick up some money and recruited Stephen to join them. Stephen viewed the Canadian dates as more than an opportunity to pick up some quick cash and see the countryside. He had determined that New York was a dead end; California was the place to be. Moving up to the Gurney family residence in Massachusetts, the quintet — Jean, Michael, Roy, Fred, and Stephen — christened themselves The Company and rehearsed enough tunes for two sets, resurrecting several numbers from the defunct Au Go-Go's. Richie was not asked to participate, though he, too, wound up at the Gurney's soon after the five headed north. "The Company was the Bay Singers' deal and they needed a male lead singer so they took Steve. I was never asked and I can't blame them for taking him. That was Steve's ticket to get to California, where he wanted to go. They were going to go across Canada and down the West Coast." "The Company was Roy Michael's idea more than Stephen's," emphasizes Jean, scotching the long held belief that Stephen was the mastermind of the group. "After the whole Roulette Records fiasco happened, we came back to Massachusetts, sat around singing songs and making harmonies. We managed to score a contract for a series of coffeehouse gigs across Canada so we decided to go back on the road. That's how The Company came about. In that group we were starting to get away from pure folk music and were getting a bit more rocky. Richie wasn't invited to be in The Company because of a falling out between Stephen and him."

After briefly attending acting school and taking a fling at selling encyclopedias door to door, Richie contacted a cousin, an executive at Pratt and Whitney Aircraft in Connecticut, for a job. He had not abandoned his musical aspirations, merely shelving them until his financial affairs were on more solid footing. "I had to eat," asserts Richie. "So I called up my cousin and convinced him that I'd be there for 25 years and get my gold watch. I got the job and went up there and stayed with the Gurney's in Wilbraham, Massachusetts. I was seeing Jean's sister Anne at the time. But each Monday night, somehow or other, I'd drive down to make the hoot night at the Bitter End. I even auditioned for a couple of television shows." Richie also answered a call to replace Chad Mitchell in the Chad Mitchell Trio, making it as far as second runner up out of 250 hopefuls. The position went to a John Deutschendorf, who quickly changed his handle to John Denver. Richie remained at the Gurney's through the summer and fall of 1965, journeying to New York as frequently as possible where he helped maintain the apartment he had shared with Michael, Jean, and the others on Thompson Street. There he would meet an eager Neil Young a few months later, but first Neil Young and Stephen Stills would need to meet, quite by accident, in a small town in north Ontario, where their respective bands shared a gig at the Fourth Dimension Coffeehouse in Fort William for a week.

Au Go-Go Singers with Richie Furay (center) and Stephen Stills (right) on guitars and vocals.

THREE MONKS—This is one of the many groups that appeared during the Jaycees sponsored Music Festival, a part of the Fourth of July Celebration, on Saturday. The gentlemen are known as the Three Monks. (Photo by Don Gulley)

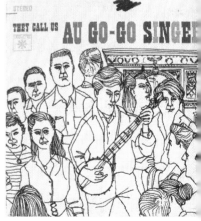

TWO

High Flying Birds

There's a high flying bird,
Way up in the sky.
And I wonder does he look down,
As he flies on by.
Just riding so free and easy,
In the sky.
But look at me,
I'm rooted like a tree, here.
I've got those sit down, can't fly,
Oh Lord, I'm gonna die blues.

High Flying Bird (Billy Edd Wheeler)

Nineteen sixty-five was a watershed year in the evolution of popular music, marking the point when American musicians mounted their counter-offensive against the British Invasion which had so overwhelmed the pop music charts the previous year. Indeed, the times they were a-changin', more than Bob Dylan ever envisioned once the Beatles landed in North America in February 1964, appearing before an audience numbering some 70 million on the *Ed Sullivan Show*. At the vanguard of this reclaiming of lost ground was The Byrds, a Los Angeles-based group of ex-folk musicians who combined the poetic lyricism and substance of folk music with the beat and instrumentation of British Invasion rock'n'-roll, a marriage that proved potent enough to launch an entire music genre, folk rock. But unlike the folk music revival, folk rock was not born out of East Coast basket joints and coffee-houses. Though many folk rock purveyors, such as John Phillips, Mama Cass, Jim McGuinn, and David Crosby, received their initiation into the folk milieu via Greenwich Village, folk rock was, with a few exceptions like the Lovin' Spoonful and Simon and Garfunkel, largely a West Coast phenomenon. By 1965, folk music, though managing to hang around on the periphery before evolving into the angst-driven solo singer/ songwriters of the early Seventies, had become passé. Folkies fell over themselves to plug in their guitars and grow their hair.

The Beatles opened the eyes of many a young folk musician to the possibilities of rock'n'roll that Fifties and early Sixties popular music, with its rather shallow themes, simplistic structure, and greasy teen idols, had been unable to offer. For New York folk musician Erik Jacobsen, later producer of the Lovin' Spoonful's recordings, hearing the Beatles' *I Want To Hold Your Hand* on a restaurant jukebox was sheer revelation. "I'd never heard anything like it before! It hit me so hard I just sat in that place and played it over and over again. I'd been arranging folk songs with the traditional acoustic instruments, but, until then, it hadn't occurred to me to use bass and drums. Hearing the Beatles not only put loads of ideas in my head, it made me start thinking about electric folk music . . . it suddenly seemed so simple." Another convert to the Beatles was ex-Chad Mitchell Trio accompanist, solo folk performer and Byrds' founder Jim McGuinn. "I realized that this was indeed electrified folk music.

I was never really a purist, but I did respect the people who liked acoustic music and didn't want to see it change. However, I realized the Beatles were incorporating a lot of folk music changes into their songs, folk music chord changes. They had played skiffle so that's a folk music influence on them."

The impact of the Beatles' first feature film, *A Hard Day's Night*, released in the summer of 1964, cannot be underestimated in this transformation. The rush to trade in acoustic guitars for electric models the next day must have been staggering. After witnessing that film, every young white musician wanted to be the Beatles. And no exception were the five young men out in Los Angeles who ultimately became The Byrds. David Crosby recalls the impact of that movie on the fledgling group: "One night we went to see *A Hard Day's Night*, and I can remember coming out of that movie so jazzed that I was swinging around stop sign poles at arm's length. I knew right then what my life was going to be. I wanted to be that. They were cool and we said, 'Yeah, that's it. We have to be a band. Who can we get to play drums?'" Noting George Harrison playing an electric twelve-string guitar in the film was incentive enough for Jim McGuinn to acquire one, too. "I looked at his guitar and said, 'He's got an electric twelve string! That's exactly what I need. That's that sound. So I went out the next day to a music store and traded in my banjo and my acoustic guitar and got a Rickenbacker twelve-string electric." His jingle-jangle sound, created on that same Rickenbacker, came to characterize not only The Byrds specifically but folk rock in general.

Folk music had always taken itself seriously. It was cerebral rather than hormonal. The Byrds brought that same tone to rock'n'roll, becoming one of the first examples of rock'n'roll musicians who saw themselves as serious artists. They were able to do this because none of them had emerged from the Fifties rock'n'roll stream, drawing their influences not from Chuck Berry or Elvis Presley, but from folk, jazz, and bluegrass, blending these diverse sources into their hybrid folk rock. Coming from exclusively folk backgrounds, Richie Furay and Stephen Stills would ultimately bring those sensibilities to the Buffalo Springfield. As Byrds' bassist Chris Hillman notes: "The Springfield came from the same background as The Byrds and the Lovin' Spoonful. These were three unique bands from that era because each of them did not come from rock'n'roll per se or from being in a teenage garage band. We all came from acoustic music, folk music. We all had this acoustic background so we approached electric music in a completely different way. We didn't know how to play rock'n'roll and it was trial and error. We didn't know how to play *Roll Over Beethoven*. We grew up listening to the music, but we got into acoustic folk music, so the slant was different. There was no rule book, we all just did it and it came out unique. We all copied the Beatles but subtly the other influences came out."

The birth of folk rock is generally dated in June 1965 when The Byrds' electrified version of *Mr. Tambourine Man* hit No. One, though the album the song first appeared on, Bob Dylan's BRINGING IT ALL BACK HOME, was released two months earlier, with the former king of the acoustic protest ballad playing several electric tracks on the album. His follow up release, HIGHWAY 61 REVISITED, released in September of that year, would find Dylan jumping head first into the rock form. As a popular phenomenon, folk rock lasted to the end of 1966, but it had a profound influence on the evolution of popular music, bringing a literate sense, an intelligence and poetry, to three chord rock'n'roll.

L ike many young folk musicians with feet not firmly planted in the Woody Guthrie-Pete Seeger tradition, Stephen Stills had begun to see the limitations of the acoustic folk form. Hardly a purist, he was restless to explore new avenues of folk using electric instruments. He was not alone. Already in the Village, John Sebastian and Zal Yanovsky, both late of the Mugwumps, were toying with the idea at the Night Owl Café in what would evolve into the Lovin' Spoonful. In San Francisco, Paul Kantner and Marty Balin, two inveterate folk singers, were turning on to the possibilities of what could be created with electric instrumentation, even working up their own electric arrangement of *High Flying Bird*, before forming the Jefferson Airplane. And in Winnipeg, a lanky rock'n'roll guitarist, Neil Young, with a penchant for freaking out during *Farmer John,* was making similar plans to merge traditional folk songs with a rock beat.

But if Stephen was feeling the constraints of the folk format by the spring of 1965, his compatriots were not. The Company's instrumentation and presentation remained acoustic folk music. On April 16th, the five members headed out from Massachusetts in a rented station wagon northward to Fort William, Ontario, at the top of Lake Superior in the rugged, tree-lined Canadian Shield. They arrived on the afternoon of April 18th for their first performance that evening. As Stephen recalls, "We were booked for a week at each stop. Fort William was our first gig, and on the night we arrived at the 4D, Neil Young and the Squires were playing."

On the tiny stage of the Fourth Dimension coffeehouse stood three young Winnipeggers called The Squires — Neil on guitar and vocals, Ken Koblun on bass, and Bob Clark on drums — having pulled in late after their vehicle, a 1948 Buick Roadmaster hearse named Mortimer Hearseburg, or Mort for short, had broken down somewhere along the way. There was a smattering of recognition from a few faces in the crowd, for The Squires had performed in Fort William several months earlier and were a known commodity among the small music fraternity, though they had earned their reputation as die-hard rockers specializing in surf instrumentals, Rolling Stones, and Kinks covers as well as a notorious extended jam of The Premiers' *Farmer John*. As they began to play, it was immediately evident to everyone that the group was attempting something quite different from *You Really Got Me*, a work in progress, an embryonic version of folk rock. Clearly, the group still had their work cut out for them, especially on the singer's high-pitched vocal delivery, but they won points for daring. Here was a unique concept in out-of-the-way Fort William. What wasn't clear to those assembled at the 4-D that evening was that history was being made. Neil Young was about to introduce himself to Stephen Stills.

Watching in the wings, the members of The Company were suitably smitten with Neil and his group. "I remember being impressed by what I was looking at on stage," recalls Michael Scott. "It was really fun to hear him, though I thought his singing style was really odd." Adds Jean Gurney, "They were amazing, a rock'n'roll folk group! We had been toying around with that idea, but Michael wasn't the kind of a bass player to be that driving and we didn't have a drummer. Steve, Michael, and I went over to meet Neil and his band. Neil came right up to talk to Steve about music."

Stephen, too, was fascinated with The Squires, seeing in them his own musical dreams. "Neil was playing folk rock before anybody else," Stephen recalls. "He had his Gretsch, a rock and roll band that had just recently turned from playing *Louie Louie* to playing the popular folk songs of the day with electric guitar, drums and bass. It was a funny band 'cause they could go right from *Cotton Fields* to *Farmer John*. And they'd just come back from Churchill, and Neil had written, I think, this song: 'Let me tell you about a thing called snow where it's 45 below,' and we had a great time running around in his hearse and drinking good strong Canadian beer and being young and having a good time. At first I thought, 'Well, I'm gonna quit this idiot group and go play with him right now."

Neil Young and Stephen Stills had more in common than music. Both had grown up in transient families, Neil's journalist father Scott uprooting his mother Edna "Rassy," Neil, and older brother Bob several times during Neil's first 15 years. Born in Toronto, on November 12, 1945, Neil Percival Kenneth Ragland Young developed an independent streak early on. An affable child whose off the wall sense of humor endeared him to friends, Neil was a loner. Self-driven to the point of obsession, he would set his own course and proceed full steam ahead. "I had to shit on a lot of people in one way or another and leave a lot of friends behind to get where I am now, especially in the beginning," Neil reflects on his journey to success. "There was no other way. I had almost no conscience for what I had to do. If I could justify it in terms of furthering my goal, I would just do it. And it's obvious when you look back at my early years, that's what I was like. I was so driven to make it."

Witnessing Elvis Presley on television in the late 1950s brought out in the boy a love for music which resulted in the purchase of a four-string Arthur Godfrey ukulele on which he practiced until his fingertips ached. By the summer of 1960 Neil had switched to an acoustic Harmony guitar, and, with the breakup of his parents' marriage and a forced relocation to Winnipeg, determined that music was both his passion and his salvation. "I knew when I was 13 or 14 that that was what I wanted to do," Neil affirms. "There was nothing else that interested me. There really wasn't anything more important in my life than playing music and you had to really want to do it and you had to make music first in your life."

Neil's first formal musical endeavor came within months of settling in Winnipeg's middle-class Fort Rouge district when he formed his first band, The Jades. It was a short lived effort, managing only one performance in Neil's neighborhood at Earl Grey Community Club in early January 1961. His next few musical aggregations were equally short lived until, over Christmas break 1962, he formed The Squires. "The Squires was the first band that I ever got anything happening with," notes Neil. "We were together a long time, even longer than the Buffalo Springfield. We were pretty young and just learning the business and we were pretty naive, but we had a lot of fun back then. They could have made it. I just wanted it more than they did." Right from its inception, The Squires was Neil's band; he was the leader; he set the direction. As the old saying goes, it was his way or the highway, and as a result, over the next three years a succession of players passed through the ranks of the group. "If somebody didn't fit in, I knew I had to tell him," states Neil. "Whereas if I hadn't have been so serious about music, I probably wouldn't have had to do that. But knowing what I knew, where I wanted to go, what I had to do, there was no way that I could put up with things that were going to stand in my way."

One player who stuck it out from the beginning was Ken Koblun. Already pushing six feet tall (his growth spurt would eventually peak out at six foot seven), Ken couldn't help but stand out at Earl Grey school where he first encountered Neil in their grade nine class. Impressed by Neil's abilities on the guitar, Ken, born May 7, 1946 in Winnipeg, convinced his foster family to acquire one for him. Not long afterwards, at Neil's urging, Ken switched to bass guitar, a role he would hold down throughout the various lineups of The Squires. Ken became Neil's partner on his musical journey over the next four years, content to remain in the background, consistently supportive, willing to follow him.

Within a matter of months The Squires had become a popular draw on the thriving Winnipeg teen dance circuit, specializing in guitar instrumentals by British group The Shadows. Unlike their contemporaries on the circuit, The Squires boasted an impressive number of original compositions in their sets, all from Neil's pen. "We'd get together at my parents' house to practice a couple of times a week," marvels Squires' drummer

Ken Smyth, "and Neil would show up each time with a new song or two. He had piles of songs. Songs that we never even played." A quick glance at a Squires' set list circa 1963 reveals, besides the typical cover tunes of the day like *Night Train, Walk Don't Run, Boney Moronie, Wild Weekend, Round And Round, Memphis,* and *Walking With My Angel,* more than a dozen original titles, such as *The Ghost, Banana Mashed, Summer Snow, The Shepherd, Swift Water, Green Velvet, Lonesome Town, Enchanted Sea, Comanche, Panic Button,* and *Red Eye.* Few of these have ever seen the light of day since and remain a memory in title only.

Illustrating the need at that time for a band to be versatile and cater to any and all requests, The Squires' set list also includes *Exodus, When The Saints Go Marching In, Greensleeves, Harbor Lites,* George Gershwin's *Summertime, Alley Cat, South Of The Border (Down Mexico Way),* and a country chestnut that later became a staple of Neil's 1970s acoustic country foray, *It Might Have Been.* The band also featured a healthy dose of Shadows instrumentals, including *Kon Tiki, Dance On, Torquay, Apache, FBI, Wonderful Land, Aladdin,* and *Spring Is Nearly Here.* The latter was recorded in 1996 by Neil and Winnipeg guitar mentor Randy Bachman for a Shadows tribute album. Having long since lost the original Shadows recording, the two had to piece together their rendition from memory.

On July 23, 1963, The Squires recorded two of Neil's instrumental compositions, *The Sultan,* backed with a version of *Image In Blue* retitled *Aurora,* released that fall on the local V Records label. But with the new year, the entire music world was thrown on its ear by the Beatles. Neil and his group were no exception, with Neil now assuming vocal duties, though his early attempts were less than appealing. At a church basement dance on January 3, 1964, The Squires debuted their new vocal numbers, to which one fan loudly responded, "Stick to instrumentals!" Undaunted, Neil persisted in his new role, drawing strength from the criticisms hurled his way. "People told me I couldn't sing," smiles Neil, "but I just kept at it. My voice is a little strange." His biggest boaster remained his mother Rassy. "Everybody said that Neil couldn't sing except me. I said, 'It's an interesting key but if that's your key, who cares.'" At a further recording session in April, 1964, Neil laid down his first vocal tracks, the producer cautioning, "You're a good guitar player kid, but you'll never make it as a singer." That summer, Neil was first diagnosed with epilepsy, having suffered minor seizures to that point. It would remain a secret shared with only a select few.

Neil was also a fan of folk music and by 1964 was a frequent visitor to the local Fourth Dimension coffeehouse in south Winnipeg, where, besides stretching his songwriting abilities to embrace acoustic folk songs, he also struck up a fleeting friendship with Joni Mitchell. Joni was working her way across the country, destined for Canada's version of Greenwich Village, Toronto's Yorkville. What appealed to Neil in folk music, once he had progressed beyond composing melodic guitar instrumentals, was its lyric content. A convert to Bob Dylan's early work, Neil embraced the poetry of his lyrics along with the lyrical efforts of other folk writers such as Ian Tyson, whose *Four Strong Winds* was Neil's favorite song. Rather than the 'boy meets girl and they fall in love' themes of rock'n'roll, folk music had substance, a message, an expression of inner feelings and deeper emotions. For an introspective young man who tended to hold his feelings in check, folk music offered Neil a release.

That autumn, Neil abandoned high school to pursue his musical aspirations full time. With his trusty hearse Mort at the ready, The Squires' first road trip in October 1964 took them to The Flamingo Club in Fort William, now Thunder Bay, some 500 miles east of Winnipeg. There, alone in his hotel room on his nineteenth birthday, Neil penned *Sugar Mountain*, his ode to eternal youth. Even that early in his songwriting career, *Sugar Mountain* reveals Neil understanding the lessons of folk music songwriters who emphasized a highly personal and insightful approach to their craft, a quality that would come to characterize much of his later writing. The band, now billed as Neil Young And The Squires, was a popular attraction in 'Fort Bill,' and arrangements were made to return in the spring of 1965 to play not the rock'n'roll Flamingo but the 4-D coffeehouse.

"Fort William was the beginning of this kind of folk rock that we played," Neil points out. "It was different from anything else I did before or after. It was a minor key, folk, punk, rock kind of thing. It was funky. We had a lot of songs that we were doing in that period that were kind of arrangements of other songs. We got into a thing in Fort William where we did classic folk songs with a rock'n'roll beat and changed the melody. We did a really weird version of *Tom Dooley*, which was like rock'n'roll but it was in minor keys. And then we did *Oh Susannah* based on an arrangement by a group called The Thorns. Tim Rose was in The Thorns. We saw them at the 4-D. And also we did *Clementine* and *She'll Be Coming Round The Mountain When She Comes.* I wrote all new melodies. We changed them totally with rock'n'roll arrangements. It was pretty interesting. It was different." Though the idea of folk rock was already in the minds of several musicians scattered across North America, no one had considered a marriage of The Kingston Trio to The Rolling Stones. In this, Neil Young And The Squires were truly original.

Tom Horricks, a member of Fort William favorites Donny and the Bonnevilles, recalls the impression Neil had on the local music scene. "Every band in this area was envious of The Squires in a way because Neil was different. He was from out of town so everyone thought he knew something they didn't know. He was totally different from anything else happening then. He had a style. Neil was experimenting with original ideas and he had a lot of courage. He took heavy criticism from some people because everybody was so straight musically and here was this guy with this strange high, reedy voice doing *Oh Susannah* with an electric guitar. Some people laughed at him, but he wasn't afraid to be an individual. It didn't matter what anyone thought because he believed in himself."

Not only was Stephen Stills impressed by Neil Young that night in Fort William but the feeling was mutual. "Stills' voice was phenomenal," Neil confirms. "His guitar playing was marginal. He was a rhythm guitarist, and he played a big red Guild acoustic guitar. He didn't really get into playing lead guitar until the Springfield. He was more of a singer. He had been with several singers in the Au Go-Go Singers and the whole hootenanny thing in New York so he was voice oriented, had voice training, and knew harmony." So taken was Neil with Stephen's performance of *High Flying Bird* that he added his own rendition to The Squires' repertoire. "The Company did an old folk song called *High Flying Bird*," Neil recalls fondly. "Stills sang it and he really sang it well. So we started doing our version of it. People started to tell us how well we did that song, so we started calling ourselves The High Flying Birds."

The two bands spent their days together at the Sea-Vue Motel. "We used to eat dinner together, both bands, at Dinty's," recalls Jean. "It was the first time I ever ate Kentucky Fried Chicken. I remember bombing around in Neil's hearse Mort. I have a picture of Kenny, his arms folded over his bass, leaning against Mort. I took photographs of Stephen, Neil, and Kenny running around Mort like the Beatles in *A Hard Day's Night*. I was so taken with Kenny Koblun. Here was this guy all dressed in black with boots on. I had never seen anybody dressed like that. God, he was so handsome. I remember Kenny more than I remember Neil."

Amid the youthful bonhomie, Stephen and Neil developed a rapport. "We got on quite well right away," states Neil. "We didn't talk about forming a band together then, but we knew we wanted to get together later. I knew he was going back to the States and I wanted to go to the States and now I knew a musician in the States." Before departing, Stephen gave Neil an address to go to if he ever made it to New York, an apartment at 171 Thompson Street.

While Stephen and Company headed west to Winnipeg, Neil, Ken, and Bob worked the Fort William area for a few more months before they, too, departed for greener pastures. On a road trip to Sudbury, Mort broke down in Blind River (later inspiring his song *Long May You Run*) and The Squires eventually straggled into Toronto in late June to pursue Neil's version of folk rock in Yorkville. "The most important thing for me back then," he muses, "was to keep moving so that I always had the advantage of being someone that people knew nothing about, the unknown factor." Unfortunately his plans fell on deaf ears and by fall he had abandoned the band for a career in folk music, trading his Gretsch electric for an acoustic twelve string, inspired by the heady folk scene amid the Yorkville coffeehouses.

Much like Greenwich Village, Yorkville was an artistic community nestled in the heart of downtown Toronto, a two square block district dotted with older brick Victorian homes whose front rooms had been converted into coffeehouses. Here folk music thrived even as it was declining in Greenwich Village. Among these coffeehouses were the Purple Onion, Chez Monique, the Penny Farthing, and the granddaddy of the Yorkville clubs, the Riverboat. Yorkville drew folkies from across Canada to its streets, communal pads, and flop houses to try their luck at launching a folk singing career. Ian and Sylvia,

Gordon Lightfoot, and Joni Mitchell got their first break in Yorkville. One person who tasted both scenes, Greenwich and Yorkville, was John Kay, later of Steppenwolf fame, who at the time was working as a folk blues singer. "The two had different flavors," notes John. "Greenwich Village was more aggressive, more New York hustle, while Yorkville was more innocent, more relaxed, friendlier, fresher." At the time, John was living in Yorkville with folk singer Vicky Taylor above the Night Owl coffeehouse; soon after Neil's arrival in Yorkville, John moved out and Neil moved in with Vicky.

While his former partner Ken Koblun immediately found himself in demand as an itinerant bass player for traveling folk acts, Neil's solo career never got off the ground. "My folk singing career didn't really go over well in Toronto," shrugs Neil. "There was a review of one of my shows in a newspaper and it said my songs were like a cliche. Toronto was a very humbling experience for me. I just couldn't get anything going." Out of that frustration emerged a string of songs, the most significant being *Baby That Don't Mean A Thing Because Clancy Can't Sing Anymore*, as it was originally scrawled on a sheet of looseleaf, complete with several crossed out attempts at spelling 'silhouette.' Clancy was Winnipeg school mate Ross "Clancy" Smith. "He was a kind of persecuted member of the community," explains Neil. "He used to be able to do something, sing or something, and then he wasn't able to do it anymore. The fact was that all the other problems or things that were seemingly important didn't mean anything anymore because he couldn't do what he wanted to do." Retitled *Nowadays Clancy Can't Even Sing*, the poignant, highly personal lyrics served as a metaphor for Neil's stalled career. Later, Neil revealed more about the song. "Clancy is just an image, a guy who gets come down on all the time. He was a strange cat, beautiful. Kids in school called him a weirdo because he would whistle and sing *Val De Ree, Val De Rah* in the halls. After awhile he got so self-conscious he couldn't do his thing anymore. When someone as beautiful as that and as different as that is actually killed by his fellow men, like taken and sorta chopped down, all the other things are nothing compared to this. In the song I'm just trying to communicate a feeling. Like the main part of Clancy is about my hang-ups with an old girlfriend in Winnipeg. Now I don't really want people to know my whole scene with that girl and another guy in Winnipeg. That's not important, that's just a story. You can read a story in *Time* magazine. I want them to get a feeling like when you see something bad go down, when you see a mother hit a kid for doing nothing. Or a frustration you see a girl at an airport watching her husband leave to go to war."

Hey, who's that stompin' all over my face?
Where's that silhouette I'm tryin' to trace?
Who's puttin' sponge in the bells I once rung,
And takin' my gypsy before she's begun?
Singing the meaning of what's in my mind,
Before I can take home what's rightfully mine.
Joining and listening and talking in rhyme,
Stopping the feeling to wait for the time.
And who's sayin' 'Baby that don't mean a thing,'
'Cause nowadays Clancy can't even sing.

Nowadays Clancy Can't Even Sing (Neil Young)

On November 1, 1965, following a disastrous one night stand at The Wobbly Barn, a bar in Killington, Vermont, Neil and Ken Koblun determined to journey to New York. Ken wanted to see Jean Gurney; Neil was looking for Stephen Stills. The Company's Canadian tour had come to an end on May 9th in Regina, Saskatchewan as a result of personal problems. "The plan had been to head across Canada then down the West Coast to San Francisco," confirms Jean Gurney. "But it didn't happen. Fred Geiger had some sort of emotional breakdown in Regina." Unable to continue on as Stephen had planned, the five musicians instead returned to New York with a brief pause in Chicago to open for Woody Allen at Mr. Kelly's club. Once back home, the group folded. Jean returned to Massachusetts, commuting to New York frequently over the next six months. Michael found work around New York, eventually going on the road with The Highwaymen and later the Serendipity Singers. Fred and Roy drifted into obscurity. Stephen wasted little time in pursuit of his own folk rock dream, though the results were less than satisfying. "I desperately wanted to be in the Lovin' Spoonful," relates Stephen. "They didn't know I could play electric guitar, bass, and drums. I wanted to be their bass player but they wouldn't give me the time of day. To them, I was just a kid wandering around the Village."

Attempts at locating Neil up in Canada and bringing him down to New York to form a group together proved futile. "When I finally did get a phone number in Toronto and called him, he'd quit the group, they'd split up, and he'd gone back to being a folk singer and was living with this folk singer chick, playing acoustic guitar in coffeehouses, something I'd already been doing for three years and which I decided I didn't want to do any more. So that was it, Neil wanted to be Bob Dylan, I wanted to be the Beatles."

Stephen then contacted Richie with the idea of forming their own folk rock group. Still working at Pratt and Whitney up in East Hartford, Connecticut, and living with the Gurney's in Wilbraham, Massachusetts, Richie agreed to give his friend a listen. "After Steve came back to New York we talked several times and I came down to see the group he was trying to put together. He was into electric music now and had seen the Lovin' Spoonful at the Night Owl on the corner of Bleeker Street. He told me, 'Man, I heard this group and they're great. We can be just like them.' I came down to hear them — I can't remember who the other people were but I think Gram Parsons was a part of it. I know there was a girl and I can't recall if she was Nancy Priddy, but I'm fairly sure it was. But it sounded awful, to my ears at least. We had worked with Jim Friedman, who was a genius at putting vocals and harmonies together, so I was used to something more refined, and when I came down to hear this group of Steve's it was bad. It was worse than a garage band, there was no direction. So I told Steve I didn't want to be a part of it and left."

In frustration, Stephen decided to abandon New York for California. "I was listening to the radio and heard The Byrds. The sound of their electric guitars and voices made me think that LA was the place to be if I wanted to rock'n'roll. I thought I had to get to LA and get a band together." In August, 1965 Stephen bid New York farewell.

Richie carried on at Pratt and Whitney through the autumn, making the trip down to New York sporadically where he would stay at the apartment on Thompson with Jean and Michael. He was there the day Neil and Ken came calling. As Neil recalls, "When we hunted around Greenwich Village for the people who'd been in the Au Go-Go Singers, Stephen was gone. Somebody said he'd gone to LA to try to put together a rock'n'roll group. That was funny because at exactly the same time I was getting more and more into folk. Anyway, Ken found the girl and we hung out there for a few days. That's when I met Richie Furay." As Jean recalls, "Kenny and I had been corresponding, torrid letters to each other. Neil and Kenny showed up at our door at our apartment in New York. It was my apartment and Richie stayed there when he was in the city. Kenny had called and told me he was heading for New York City so I wasn't surprised when they came over. They arrived and stayed with us a few days."

"I was back down to do some of these acting auditions for this television show," says Richie. "Steve had told Neil to come hang out at the apartment if he was ever in New York. So he came over and we sat around and he pulled out a guitar. Back then, guitars were the common denominator. So we all played awhile. I played him some songs and he played me some of his songs, and the next thing I heard was this song like nothing I had ever heard before. It was *Nowadays Clancy Can't Even Sing*. I thought the song was really unique. It had all these metaphors and allegories. Neil really struck me right from that moment as someone who was completely different. I was impressed because he was at another level from where I was. He was already writing introspective songs, not your typical songs like the kind I was used to hearing. I liked them and I liked him. I had this big tape recorder that my Dad had given my Mom and I brought it with me to New York. I had Neil record it and write out the words. Boy, if I had that tape now, that'd be like *Free As A Bird* or something. I performed *Clancy* at a couple of auditions as a solo folk singer at the Bitter End across the street from where we lived." During Christmas 1965, Bob Harmelink, back in Ohio, received a tape from Richie of the songs he was performing then and his version of *Clancy* was included.

"I remember hearing Richie learn *Clancy* from Neil," confirms Jean. "The song was wonderful even back then. It was still a work in progress — he had only recently started it and was still working on it. Neil was such a passionate man, wild mane of hair, scraggy face, dressed in flannel. Richie had him commit the song to tape because he was very particular and careful about doing things right. Richie did a very good job of that song. All things being equal, Richie was the preferred provider for that song. Neil's voice didn't lend itself well to such a complicate tune as that."

Dismayed at missing Stephen, Neil made the best of his brief visit to the Big Apple, checking out Greenwich Village, though he declined to try his hand in the basket houses. In the short time they spent together, Richie noticed something different about the determined young Canadian compared to Stephen. "Neil seemed very sure of himself, of where he was going, and was very intense. Steve had the desire to make it, but didn't know how to go about it; Neil had more of a focus on what he was going for. He knew what he was looking for. Neil had goals. He knew he had to take this step to get to the next step in order to get to where he wanted to go, whereas Steve's attitude was more of 'I'd like to get there but I don't know how I'm gonna get there but I'll just keep doing it.'" After three days, Neil and Ken returned to Toronto and promptly went their separate ways, Neil to resume his doomed folk singing career and Ken to join promising folk rock act Three's A Crowd.

By January 1966, Neil's solo folk aspirations had died stillborn. A hastily organized demo session in Elektra Record's tape library on a second jaunt to New York, where he committed Clancy, Sugar Mountain, and five other originals to tape, failed to kick start his career. At the end of his tether, a chance encounter with Bruce Palmer on Yorkville Avenue offered him a lifeline. "I met Neil walking down the street carrying his guitar in Yorkville," points out Bruce. "We were looking for a guitar player at that time in The Mynah Birds and he was there. He was looking for people to play with, so I asked him to join. Up until the point he met me, Neil's solo career was nothing, zilch. He met me and that was a turning point in his life musically."

Bruce Palmer was already well-known on the Toronto music scene when he stumbled upon the lonely Winnipegger. The son of a classically trained violinist and concert master father and artist mother, Bruce was born in Toronto on September 9, 1946 and grew up in the Leaside area of the city. With music virtually all about him, it was no surprise when Bruce took up the guitar before his teens, switching to bass guitar at age 14. He joined his first band, The Swinging Doors, soon after. "My first band was an all black band," notes Bruce, "saxophones and singers, everyone in mohair suits, doing R'n'B stuff. Wow, what a trip! Toronto was big on R'n'B." At the age of 17, Bruce had already evolved a style all his own, underpinning the solid R'n'B funk he learned from black players with a fluid feel that weaved intricate bass lines in and around the chord pattern, complementing but never distracting the melody.

Besides the hip Yorkville coffeehouses, Toronto also enjoyed a vibrant bar scene with many go-go clubs along Yonge Street featuring rock'n'roll and rhythm and blues groups. The most raucous of all was Ronnie Hawkins and the Hawks who tore up the Le Coq D'Or and Concord taverns with their transplanted Arkansas rockabilly in the early 1960s. The Hawks would later become The Band, but under Ronnie's tutelage they were the undisputed kingpins of Yonge Street, offering the rawest rhythm and blues north of the Mason-Dixon Line, becoming mentors to every young musician in Toronto. With its close proximity to both Detroit and Buffalo, Toronto had imported American R'n'B and sprouted its own practitioners, including The Majestics, The Disciples, and David Clayton Thomas and the Shays. Though the two scenes coexisted separately, by 1965 they were beginning to intermingle.

Bruce's next move was to jump on the British Invasion bandwagon with Jack London And The Sparrows. As Bruce recalls, the band went to great lengths to appear British. "Dennis and Jerry McCrohan came from Oshawa. Their dad had the Jubilee Auditorium there and that was very handy for a venue for us. I was from Toronto and Jack London had migrated from England in 1948. But he sure kept that accent. He not only affected it, we all had to. We'd go around Toronto with English accents. We'd have to talk to old friends with fake English accents and they would crack up. But that was the game plan because we were billed as being just in from England. It was a hoax played on the Toronto public. I thought it was nuts. I was sitting there talking to David Clayton Thomas — we were old friends — and we were playing with him at the Crane Plaza. And I had this phony accent, and he thought, 'What is this?!' And I think that's one of the reasons I eventually quit." One witness to this ruse was Stan Endersby, a local guitarist who would work with Bruce a decade later. "Jack London announced to the crowd in this heavy Liverpool accent, 'And now we're going to do a song called *If You Don't Want My Love*,' then he turns to the band and yells in his Canadian voice, 'Come on, Dennis, get it together.' And the crowd started booing and throwing things."

Featuring Jack London (a.k.a. Dave Marden) on vocals, keyboard player C.J. Feeney, Bruce, and the McCrohan brothers, Dennis on guitar and Jerry on drums, who changed their name to Edmonton to avoid conflicts with promoters over their father's venue, Jack London And The Sparrows scored a number one record in Toronto in late 1964 with their debut single, *If You Don't Want My Love*. By the time the record was released, Bruce had departed, replaced by Nick St. Nicholas from rival group The Mynah Birds. "It was like a hockey trade with The Mynah Birds," laughs Bruce, "but I initiated it. I was getting fed up with this phony English facade. I had seen Ricky James Matthews — or Rick James as he is now known — on stage in The Mynah Birds around that time, and even though they were doing all Rolling Stones stuff, there was a definite talent there, a spark, something that hooked me. I saw a fantastic performer, this little Stevie Wonder type person, so I decided right there to pack in this English phony-baloney, no soul music for Rick's group. So we just switched groups, Nick St. Nicholas and I." Over the next few months The Mynah Birds and Sparrows would engage in a cordial rivalry that would also see another Mynah Bird, Goldie McJohn, defect to The Sparrows. Nick, Goldie, and Jerry Edmonton would find success a few years later after the Sparrows dumped Jack London for John Kay, metamorphosing into Steppenwolf. Dennis McCrohan would once again change his name, this time to Mars Bonfire, and write Steppenwolf's biggest hit, the enduring rock anthem *Born To Be Wild*.

By the time Bruce joined The Mynah Birds in early 1965, rock'n'roll was already encroaching on Yorkville's turf. The Devil's Den, El Patio, and Purple Onion were testing the waters, alternating folk and rock each week. Bands like The Paupers were experimenting with their own brand of folk rock by mid 1965. The lines of differentiation were becoming obscured; rock'n'roll had a toehold in the once exclusively folk-oriented venues. It's no wonder Neil couldn't find work. Besides his unusual voice, there weren't many showcases left for a solo folk artist. The first of the go-go clubs to open in the Village, replete with a scantily clad go-go dancer in the upstairs window luring passersby, was The Mynah Bird Club. Operated by young entrepreneur Colin Kerr, this club was at first merely a vehicle to sell actual mynah birds, but the focus of attention soon changed. "Colin Kerr opened the first body painting club in Yorkville, with a girl in a glass window," recalls Bruce, grinning. "You'd go in and for 20 bucks or whatever he had the girl all decked out in sections and numbers and you could paint this part or that part. He was a real entrepreneur."

Enterprising huckster that he was, Colin decided to create a rock'n'roll group named The Mynah Birds, dress them up in mynah bird colors and have them back his prized possession, Rajah, a mynah bird who had been taught to say, 'Hello Ed Sullivan.' The master plan was for the group to gain a spot on Ed's Sunday night television show on the strength of the bird's pronouncement. To that end, The Mynah Birds' first recording, released with Nick St. Nicholas still in the group, was *The Mynah Bird Hop*, a silly little ditty in which the group plays pseudo-calypso accompaniment to Colin Kerr's narrative and Rajah's squawking. "We had to take that bird to all our gigs and the damn thing would be flapping around our heads in the van," recalls a bemused Nick St. Nicholas. "We'd get to the gig, set up our equipment, then it would be, 'Where's the hell's the bird?'" The Ed Sullivan gimmick failed but the band carried on, recruiting Bruce.

"Colin dressed us up in yellow boots, black leather jackets, and yellow turtlenecks so we looked like mynah birds," laughs Bruce. "That was the group before Neil joined. Colin actually wanted to shave a V in our hair because a mynah bird had a V on its head. The only pictures taken were of that lineup before it metamorphosed with Neil and I. We were doing mostly Rolling Stones material then and had two lead singers, Ricky and Jimmy Livingston. Ricky was like a black Mick Jagger, what Mick Jagger wanted to be." Those who witnessed Ricky James Matthews with The Mynah Birds attest to his riveting presence and dynamic performance.

Colin Kerr often resorted to staging his own publicity stunts. According to Bruce, "he would rent a limousine and pre-arrange for a gaggle of girls at a certain place, like right by Eaton's. He'd arrange for the limo to break down, the girls would spot us and rush the car. At that point we'd exit the car and run into Eaton's with the girls running behind us screaming. And he'd have the press standing nearby, and we'd get a little blurb in the papers the next day, 'Pop Group in Riot at Eaton's.'"

The band shifted its focus to Yorkville clubs in the fall of 1965, becoming a popular attraction at Chez Monique's and the El Patio, where they learned that millionaire retailer John Craig Eaton, of the Eaton's department store chain, was sniffing about for a rock band to finance. Having jettisoned Colin Kerr, The Mynah Birds determined to pursue and snare Eaton. Their rivals, The Sparrows, were also competing for his wallet. The Mynah Birds won. "We got John Craig Eaton as a financial backer along with Morley Shulman," notes Bruce. "John Craig was one of the wealthiest men in Canada. He had unlimited funds. That was the El Patio version of the band with Neil. John Craig got so caught up in the role that he would come down to the El Patio dressed in a trench coat and get us in the dressing room and turn into Knute Rockne. He'd be pacing back and forth giving us a pep talk, addressing his team saying, 'Go get 'em guys!' John loved it. It was a lovely aside for him, a hobby. We would use his house to rehearse in, his limousine to travel around in, he bought us our equipment. Whenever we were broke we would run up to Eaton's store, up the stairs past all these guys in suits waiting outside his office, no knocking, just walk right into his office and whine, 'John, we need money.' And he'd give it to us."

Neil's decision to abandon his solo career required no second thoughts. "I had to eat," he emphasizes. "I needed a job and it seemed like a good thing to do. I still liked playing and I liked Bruce so I went along. There was no pressure on me. It was the first time that I was in a band where I wasn't calling the shots. It was a good band. It had something going on. It was a folk rock kind of thing at first when I came along but then later it was just rock. They weren't doing any of my songs. It was more of a Rolling Stones kind of R'n'B thing." Given the course of Neil's career before and since, what seems surprising in his decision to become a Mynah Bird is that he was not the leader, merely one of the sidemen. Ricky James Matthews was the focal point and driving force of the group. Equally surprising given his prolific nature is the fact that he contributed very little to their original material. Only one song was ever registered to Neil from that period, *I'll Wait Forever*, co-written with Ricky James Matthews, copyrighted May 2, 1966, though Neil claims to have written another tune, *It's My Time*. The other members of this lineup were John Yachimak on rhythm guitar and Richie Grand on drums.

"Neil started with an acoustic twelve-string guitar with a pick-up. It was the most ridiculous thing ever heard of — it made no sense at all. Inviting somebody into a rock'n'roll band who only played acoustic twelve string and who didn't have much of a voice at that time baffles me. I don't know why we even considered that application but we did and somehow it worked," Bruce recalls. Not long afterwards John Craig Eaton purchased a Rickenbacker electric guitar and Traynor amplifier for Neil and he was on his way. Within a few weeks of his joining, The Mynah Birds signed a recording contract. "I only played a couple of gigs with The Mynah Birds before the recording sessions," recalls Neil. "I played a high school somewhere in Toronto and a couple of clubs like the Mynah Bird club, the El Patio, and Club 888 or something like that." The contract with a major American label was the envy of every Toronto band, most of whom toiled away in relative obscurity. "Morley arranged something with Motown, how he arranged it I'll never know because it wasn't even like a demo. We went straight to Detroit, right into the studio, Smokey Robinson was involved in production and we were making an album. Everything couldn't have been going finer for us. Motown was one of the most happening labels on the planet and we were essentially the first white band they had hired, with the exception of Rick. It was a major turning point for them." Neil adds, "We recorded for five or six nights and they gave us whatever we needed. If one of the guys couldn't play something, they just brought in one of their session players to do it. It was starting to sound hot."

Their optimism was quickly dashed. "We were just getting started when Ricky was busted," laments Neil. "We knew he was an American but we didn't know he was a draft dodger." Matthews was found to be AWOL from the American navy; the authorities arrested him right in the studio and promptly hauled him off to the brig. Motown suspended the sessions, canceled their contract, and the remaining Mynah Birds limped back to Toronto to assess their future. The Mynah Bird tapes remain securely in Motown's vaults to this day.

Though Neil's tenure in The Mynah Birds proved to be brief, a mere six weeks or so from mid-January to early March 1966, it was certainly eventful. Besides the roller coaster ride with Motown, Neil was initiated into the drug culture. "Ricky introduced me to amphetamines and that changed my life," he claims. "When I had arrived in Toronto, there was a whole new culture that I was introduced to. I had done nothing like that up to then. Completely au natural. We used to pop amyl nitrates before going on stage and walk on just killing our-selves laughing and rolling around from these things. We used to do all kinds of weird stuff. It was quite a time. I remember at the high-school gig, I was so high that I jumped off the stage and pulled my guitar jack out in the middle of a song."

Determined to push on with his dream, Neil's next decision, with Bruce in tow, was neither impetuous nor ill-conceived. "Neil and I were sitting at the Cellar club in Yorkville one night in March just after the Motown deal fell flat," Bruce recounts. "It's a wonderful little club that was actually like a cellar with brick walls. We were just sitting there and Neil turns to me and says, 'Let's go to California.' I thought that was a good idea. There was nothing else happening. So we decided then and there to head out to Los Angeles." From his visit to New York the previous November, Neil knew that Stephen Stills was some-where in Los Angeles.

Neil Young and The Squires (left to right: Ken Koblun, Neil Young, Bob Clark) with their hearse 'Mort'.

Live at the Fourth Dimension, Fort William, April 1965, where Neil Young first met Stephen Stills performing with The Company.

63

Jack London and the Sparrows in 1964; left to right:
Bruce Palmer, C. J. Feeney, Jack London, Jerry Edmonton (drums),
Dennis Edmonton.

The Mynah Birds live at Chez Monique in December 1965 with
Ricky James Matthews a.k.a. Rick James on vocals and Bruce
Palmer behind him on bass.

§

THREE

Hot Dusty Roads

I don't tell no tales,
About no hot dusty roads.
I'm a city boy,
And I stay at home.
I make no excuses,
I just don't want to roam,
And I don't like being alone.

Hot Dusty Roads (Stephen Stills)

D uring the summer of 1965, the epicenter of American rock'n'roll shifted coasts, Los Angeles replacing New York as the power base of the music industry. An early sign of the rise of the West Coast to rock'n'roll preeminence came in February 1964 when that bastion of American teen pop culture, *American Bandstand*, relocated from Philadelphia to LA, realizing that the sunnier sounds of the Beach Boys and the then popular surfing/cars/blondes/beaches phase of rock'n' roll had much more of a universal appeal than the already dated Philadelphia teen idol scene. Dick Clark and company were well placed when folk rock erupted out of California a year later. The advent of California folk rock with The Byrds, followed almost immediately by The Turtles, Barry McGuire, The Mamas and The Papas, Sonny and Cher, and Grass Roots, also marked the reclamation of the Top Forty charts from those British Invasion interlopers. By 1966 there were plenty of vacancies in the Brill Building, New York's once holy shrine to popular music, as both the creative and corporate axis of rock'n'roll set up offices among the palm trees of Los Angeles, where it remains to this day.

While folk music was mostly an East Coast phenomenon, centered around the Greenwich Village bohemian coffeehouse college crowd, folk rock emerged from the larger teen nightclubs of the Sunset Strip that throbbed to loud electric guitars, pulsating colored lights, and gyrating nubile bodies. "Folk rock was very much a Los Angeles invention," remarks transplanted easterner Dickie Davis, who had migrated to LA to work at clubs like the Troubadour. "Guys who had been doing acoustic folk two years earlier were now plugging in. The New York Greenwich Village thing was still acoustic folk." New York had a tradition of acoustic instruments; Los Angeles was the fast lane, electric Rickenbacker guitars played through monstrous Fender Showman amplifiers.

"The New York folk music scene was really different from LA," observes The Turtles' Mark Volman, then a recent convert from surfing instrumentals to folk rock. "It was more esoteric in New York and there was more of a downer thing. Tim Hardin, Phil Ochs, Freddy Neil, a lot of guys who were experimenting with pretty heavy drugs. It wasn't that positive an atmosphere, and I think that drew a lot of people out to California. California was more of a good time. It didn't have that downer heavy drug scene yet. Guys like Stephen and Richie soon found that New York was a dead end scene by 1965. The clubs in LA were really booming by then, very dynamic, and radio here was really happening and focused on the music scene. The California music community seemed more honest than anywhere else."

As the surfers, their sun-bleached hairdoes grown out to Brian Jones length, began journeying inland from the beach, their destination was the Sunset Strip and teen clubs like Ciro's, The Trip, and the Whisky-A-Go Go, displacing the former staid adult supper club set. As well, the San Fernando Valley cruising crowd began to venture further afield to the Strip, where the clubs grew exponentially through 1966 to include the Galaxy, Sea Witch, Pandora's Box, Bido Lito's, and the London Fog, among others. Folk rock drew a younger, more hip clientele than straight folk music but it still shared one thing: with the exception of anomalies Arthur Lee and Love, folk rock was almost exclusively white oriented music.

Once The Byrds' *Mr. Tambourine Man* opened the floodgates in June of 1965, other artists dove in headfirst, emulating what would become a stereotypical folk rock sound — poetic, message-laden, Dylanesque lyrics and folk harmonies over chiming electric twelve-string guitars and tambourines. By fall, folk rock was all over the airwaves served up by The Turtles' cover of Dylan's *It Ain't Me Babe*, Sonny and Cher with *I Got You Babe*, followed by Cher alone on Dylan's *All I Really Want To Do* beating out The Byrds' own version, Barry McGuire's doom and gloom *Eve Of Destruction*, the effervescent *Do You Believe In Magic* by the Lovin' Spoonful, the We Five's *You Were On My Mind*, and a surprise entry by session man and ersatz Beach Boy Glen Campbell with *Universal Soldier*. These would be followed in short order by San Francisco's Beau Brummels' *Just A Little*, the Grass Roots' *Where Were You When I Needed You*, and *California Dreamin,'* The Mamas and The Papas' glorious homage to the West Coast, which probably did more for the westward youth migration than any other song in history.

Then there was Simon and Garfunkel with the haunting *Sound Of Silence*, a perfect example of just how desperate record labels had become to milk the folk rock cash cow. Scouring their vaults for anything remotely folk rockish, Columbia Records executives stumbled upon a long forgotten demo by a since defunct duo, an acoustic folk ballad built on superb harmony singing. In other words, by 1965, no commercial potential. Contriving to turn the tune into acceptable folk rock fare, producer Tom Wilson, unbeknownst to either Simon or Garfunkel, the former on an acoustic folk tour of Britain and the latter attending Columbia University, overdubbed electric guitar, bass, drums, and tambourine to create a folk rock masterpiece. With the success of *Sound Of Silence*, Simon and Garfunkel were heralded as folk rock innovators. The progenitor of all this, Mr. Dylan himself, finally weighed in that fall with his own fully electric folk rock album, the stunning HIGHWAY 61 REVISITED, releasing from it in August the groundbreaking single *Like A Rolling Stone*. Folk purists cried treason while rock critics fell over themselves in praise.

It was in this atmosphere that Stephen Stills arrived in California, hungry for his big break. Setting his plans into motion in early August, Stephen journeyed first south to New Orleans, where his sister and mother, estranged from Stephen's father, were now residing. The three then headed west to San Francisco, a destination likely influenced by the fact that the West Coast folk movement was centered there. What he discovered upon arriving, however, was that the folkies were growing their hair, plugging in, turning on, forming groups, and experimenting with a more free-form version of folk rock than the Los Angeles based Byrds and their disciples. The burgeoning San Francisco music scene that would come to define flower power, psychedelic and acid rock, evolved from folk and folk rock roots. Indeed, the debut album by the Jefferson Airplane, the first of the Frisco bands to record for a major label, reveals little of their later psychedelic sound, instead relying on an electrified folk style, not with jingle-jangle guitars or Dylanesque lyrics but thoughtful poetic folk lines and folk-style harmonies over amplified acoustic guitars.

By 1966, San Francisco musicians, greatly affected by mind-expanding hallucinogenics, were straining under folk rock and blues limitations, pushing the boundaries beyond the confines of three-chord acoustic strumming into a more free form exploration. Its roots were folk rock but its boundaries were the sky. Even the topical song tradition of the folk troubadour-as-social conscience found redefinition in San Francisco acid rock, notably by chief practitioners Country Joe and the Fish and later in the Airplane's political rantings on VOLUNTEERS. Stephen was impressed with the Jefferson Airplane's early explorations of folk rock but he was smitten by another folk rock group, The Great Society, whose lead singer, Grace Slick, would shortly join the Airplane, her arrival causing the group to soar to new heights musically and commercially.

Despite the heady atmosphere up in San Francisco, Stephen moved on to LA. Hanging out on the periphery of the LA music scene, he chanced to meet two characters crucial to his future career development: Dickie Davis, stage manager at the popular Troubadour club at 9081 Santa Monica Boulevard in West Hollywood; and Barry Friedman, a kind of music business jack of all trades working for folk music entrepreneur Randy Sparks. Both saw in the novice folk rocker abundant energy, talent and potential.

"Steve stayed with me when he first got to LA," remembers Dickie. "We kept talking about forming a group." Born and raised in New England, Dickie Davis graduated from Deerfield and Eaglebrook private schools before heading west in 1961 at the age of 20, finding employment with Doug Weston at the Troubadour. As lighting and stage manager, Dickie initiated the enormously popular Monday night hoots, where, for a token fee, novice performers could take the stage in an attempt to win the approval of the folk music patrons. Hoot night became a Hollywood institution, one of the Troubadour's most popular attractions over the years, launching the careers of dozens of successful artists. Dickie later handled lights and sound at various clubs around town, including The Trip and the Whisky-A-Go Go on Sunset. Between these duties he worked as road manager for Randy Sparks' Back Porch Majority folk ensemble. Dickie first saw Stephen performing at the Golden Bear in Huntington Beach in a duo with Ron Long entitled Buffalo Fish. For a time, the duo expanded to three with the addition of ex-New York buddy Peter Thorkelson. "I was between gigs, washing dishes and jerkin' beer at the Golden Bear," recalls Peter, "when all of a sudden I hear this voice coming from out in the club. I look and it's Stephen, who I hadn't seen since leaving New York." As Three Shaggy Gorillas Minus One Buffalo Fish, the Stills-Torkelson union proved short lived and before long Stephen was on the lookout for new opportunities when he met Dickie and, soon after, Barry Friedman.

A veteran of the entertainment business, Friedman's resumé was certainly eclectic: circus clown, fire-eater, television producer, and freelance publicist whose clients once included the Ringling Brothers Circus. When Stephen met up with him, Barry was organizing and producing bands for Randy Sparks, founder of the Back Porch Majority, who, once the group became successful, set up a lucrative cottage industry franchising the name and sending out several aggregations under that title.

Friedman's first foray into the music world came via the Troubadour. "I wound up doing publicity for Doug Weston at the Troubadour. We had a rather volatile relationship, but I lived there for awhile. Doug gave people a place to crash. That's where I met Dickie Davis who was doing lights at the Troubadour. I got involved in doing album covers and did one for Hoyt Axton. I was still playing around with the circus stuff but I also got involved with doing publicity for Bob Eubanks who had a chain of teenage nightclubs called the Cinnamon Cinder. I was doing publicity and promotion for that when Bob got a television show on a local LA station. Part of his deal was that he would provide a producer, and being that I had once worked in television, I got the job. So I was the producer of that *Cinnamon Cinder* show, and because I had come from a live music background, we turned out to be one of the first rock shows to have people perform live rather than lip synching. These television guys had no idea how to do live sound, how to mike an amplifier or anything like that, so I became the expert. And because the sound was pretty good for television, some of the artists started inviting me down to the recording studio and that's how I got involved in production."

In early September, Barry and Stephen met. "I thought Stephen was a talented songwriter," recalls Barry. "He knew what he wanted to do; he had a single-sightedness. We were trying to put a group together and Van Dyke Parks was one of the guys we wanted but he turned us down." A former child actor and member of the folk duo the Steeltown Two with brother Carson, Van Dyke Parks was a budding lyricist and LA scenemaker who would go on to garner critical acclaim providing the words to Brian Wilson's tunes for the Beach Boys' *Heroes and Villains* single as well as the semi-legendary never to be released

Smile. At the time he, too, was struggling for recognition much like Stephen. Though their plan failed to materialize, the two did manage to collaborate on a couple of songs with only one ultimately published, *Hello I've Returned*, an early number in the Buffalo Springfield's repertoire.

> *Hello I've returned, I just learned,*
> *You got burned, by another guy.*
> *Come take my hand, let's sit here,*
> *In the sand, while I say what I can.*
> *'Cause you made me blue,*
> *When I trusted you.*
> *You got someone new.*
> *How can you do this to me?*
> *I'm not made of steel,*
> *I can feel what is real.*

Hello I've Returned (Stephen Stills & Van Dyke Parks)

One can barely imagine what the results would have been had Stephen's commercial folk rock sensibilities and ear for a catchy phrase merged with Van Dyke's esoteric lyric style. Nevertheless, Dickie and Barry both agree that Stephen had a tremendous drive to succeed; all he seemed to lack was a direction. To that end, both determined to assist Stephen towards his goal.

One possible path appeared on September 8, 1965 in *Daily Variety*, the entertainment business trade paper. Placed by hip young television producers Bob Rafelson and Bert Schneider, the notice for an open casting call read: "Madness!!! Auditions -— Folk & Roll Musicians — Singers for acting roles in new TV series. Running parts for four insane boys, age 17-21. Want spirited Ben Frank's types. Have courage to work." Ben Franks restaurant had by then emerged as a popular late night eatery on the Strip for hipsters. Barry brought the ad to Stephen's attention. "I took Stephen down to the audition along with some other guys," claims Barry. Among the 436 who responded to the call were diminutive singer/songwriter Paul Williams, Danny Hutton later of Three Dog Night, singer Harry Nilsson, LA deejay and professional partier Rodney Bingenheimer, and, allegedly, future mass murderer Charles Manson.

"You didn't have to be a genius to figure out what happens

to people who go on television," Stephen reflects upon seeing his window of opportunity on the easy road to fame and fortune. "I figured what a great way to get a recording deal, write a bunch of songs, and make a bunch of money. So I went down and answered all their questions. As it turned out, they didn't want me anyway, but I said, 'I have this friend,' and that was Peter Tork. It just wasn't me." Years later, recalling Stephen's failure to make the cut, Bert Schneider noted the young musician "had a little less abandon. In order to do this kind of thing, guys really had to have a lot of abandon. I suspect Stephen was a bit more inhibited." Though Stephen failed to make the cut, Peter Thorkelson, soon to be transformed into cuddly Monkee teen heart throb Peter Tork, earned the producers' nod of approval. Peter would take the fast track to acclaim and an opulent lifestyle but in the end find little personal satisfaction from it, becoming the first of the four Monkees to defect, disgruntled at his lack of input into their music. Though Stephen was initially jealous of his old mate's instant rise to the top, it would be Peter who would come to envy Stephen for eventually making it solely on the strength of talent and musicianship.

In subsequent interviews over the past 30 years, Stephen has consistently pointed out that he was turned down for The Monkees because he had the audacity to demand he write his own songs for the fabricated group, and that because staff writers had already been lined up, he passed on The Monkees. He maintains that he was not the least bit disappointed at his exclusion. Though there is no doubt that his playing and writing contributions could have helped The Monkees avoid the public relations nightmare that befell them soon after hitting the airwaves when it was revealed the group neither played nor wrote their own songs, and that the music world is far the better for having Stephen free to form the Buffalo Springfield and Crosby, Stills, and Nash, those close to him at the time reveal that he was, in fact, gravely disappointed. Dickie and Barry support that reaction as does Richie who would be in contact with Stephen a few months later.

"Steve was really disappointed that he didn't get The Monkees audition," Richie confirms. "The rejection was based on the fact that it was going to cost too much to fix up his teeth or something. He would have made an interesting Monkee alongside Michael Nesmith. They would have had two talented but stubborn guys." Adds Nurit Wilde who, like Stephen and Peter, had made the trek from Greenwich Village to LA in 1965, working lights at the Troubadour and Whisky-A-Go Go and living in a back room at Barry Friedman's place on Fountain Avenue, "Stephen didn't have the right look. He had bad teeth for TV, too pointed and crooked. And he was already starting to lose his hair. Man, was he uptight about that. They could have fixed his teeth but not his thinning hair."

The Monkees' audition proved to be a minor setback as Stephen resumed his quest for the right musicians for his group. Over the next few months he searched in vain, approaching players he met but failing to win converts to his cause. He remained an outsider in the LA music circle, a hungry young player in search of a band. Relying on the benevolence of Dickie and Barry, Stephen eventually moved into Barry's house on Fountain Avenue in Hollywood, where at various times Doug Weston and Nurit Wilde resided, along with a revolving door of friends, acquaintances, and hangers-on looking for a place to crash.

Barry's domicile was in fact the guest house of a larger residence in front. The place consisted of one large room with a loft that served as Barry's bedroom and sported a few unusual features. "It had a bathtub in the middle of the living room," describes Nurit, "and a secret room behind the bathroom where people carried on liaisons." As Barry explains, "This was a very strange house. It had been a part of police raids and all kinds of things. It had been built by Thelma White of Thelma White and her Hollywood All Girl Orchestra. There were four houses on the property. We had one in the back, someone else had one in the front, and Maston and Brewer had one of the houses. Ours was a big square two storey thing with a lot of stained glass and crystal windows with this big brick fireplace with a huge bathtub that held six people right in front of the fireplace, like a swimming pool."

There Stephen holed up through the winter of 1965-66, writing songs, planning, and dreaming. "I told him I'd help him put a band together, so I asked him if he had his choice of who to play with, anyone, his dream group, who would it be? Van Dyke wasn't one of them — that was my idea — but two of the names he wrote down were Neil Young and Richie Furay."

Handing out tools at Pratt and Whitney Aircraft was hardly what Richie Furay envisioned when he set off for Greenwich Village 18 months earlier. Still, the job provided an income, and

73

living at the Gurney's sustained his relationship with Anne Gurney, Jean's younger sister who was still in school. Frequent trips down to New York to attend auditions and hoot nights kept the dream alive, though by early 1966, even those failed to dispel his ennui. But, much like Neil's blue period languishing in Toronto in the fall of 1965, Richie, too, found inspiration to develop his songwriting. Several tunes, some later recorded by the Buffalo Springfield and Poco, emerged from that period, including *A Sad Memory, My Kind Of Love, Loser,* and *Can't Keep Me Down.*

> *Thought a girl was a girl and then,*
> *Found myself in love again.*
> *Yeah, I'd been in love a time or two,*
> *But it never happened like it did with you.*
> *Do you feel it, too?*
> *It's great having you around,*
> *There's nobody can't keep me down.*

Can't Keep Me Down (Richie Furay)

Upon hearing The Byrds, Richie was inspired to revive his pursuit of a career in music. "I was living at the Gurney's and they brought Gram Parsons over once," recalls Richie. "He lived across the street in Greenwich Village, so we knew each other from when I would come down to New York. He had this Byrds album and he played it for me and I thought to myself, 'I gotta get outta this handing out tools in a tool crib and get back into music. I gotta find out where Stephen is and get ahold of him,' cause I knew he was still pursuing it and I wanted to now, too. The Byrds had a massive sound, the harmonies and this Rickenbacker electric twelve string, taking a folk song and making it into an electric song. It was something I had never heard before, it was so different from the stuff even I was writing at the time. I was never a big Bob Dylan fan but I loved the way The Byrds did his songs and The Turtles, too. I thought, 'This is good. I'd like to be a part of something like this.' I figured I had the talent and ability but I didn't have a clue about how to go about it, so I immediately thought of Steve. I went back to New York for about three months and then finally wrote a letter to Stephen." Gram Parsons would, of course, find fame initially as a member of those same Byrds, tilting them in the direction of country rock in 1968.

With the only address for his wayward friend being William Stills' residence in San Salvador, El Salvador, Richie sent off an urgent plea to Stephen to get together again. The letter returned, stamped insufficient postage, one cent short. Richie then sent it back again with the postage corrected, and William Stills responded with his wife Talitha's San Francisco address, where he assumed Stephen could be found. The paper chase continued with Richie writing to Stephen in care of his mother. Miraculously, the letter arrived in Stephen's hands at Barry Friedman's on Fountain Avenue in Los Angeles. In early February, two weeks after mailing his letter to Stephen's mother, Richie's phone rang. It was Stephen calling on Dickie's line. "He said, 'Come on out, I got a group and all I need is you,'" laughs Richie.

Needing no further inducement, Richie promptly packed his suitcase, his Martin acoustic guitar, and tape recorder, purchased a one way airline ticket and headed west. "I don't know what was going through my mind after hearing his attempt at a band in New York," relates Richie, "but it was time to go. It was out of character for me to take that kind of chance, but I knew that Pratt and Whitney Aircraft was not going to be the end of the line for me. If I wanted that I could have gone back to Yellow Springs and made tire molds which I had done before I went to New York. I knew I didn't want to be a factory worker. I wanted to make music. But I also felt that even though I was the leader of the group I took from college, I still felt that to be a part of a band was the way to go. I didn't necessarily have to be the front man and I wanted some other guys to work with and support. Stephen and I worked well together. We had fun and sang well together. We had a unique blending of voices."

For a boy from Yellow Springs, Ohio, LA's fast lane proved quite an eye opener, even coming from New York. Assuming that Stephen and Dickie would be at the airport to pick him up, Richie found himself sitting alone for several hours wondering whether he had made the right decision. "I was told that when I arrived in Los Angeles they would pick me up. I probably did have a suit on and a crewcut. I was a folk singer from New York who had been working at Pratt and Whitney, so I didn't look like everybody else in LA. But I sat there making plenty of phone calls. Here I was in a city that I knew nothing about and no one was there to pick me up. I remember watching these cars go around the loop and I'd never seen these kind of cars before and thinking, 'Man, nice cars!' Turned out they were Porsches. It was a real culture shock for me, from the closeness and congestion of New York to this city so spread out and laid back. Little did I know at the time that Los Angeles was going just as fast as New York. It was warm, there were palm trees, I took off my jacket and loosened my tie. I was wide-eyed and excited because I was ready to be in the band. But I was getting pretty uptight sitting around waiting for someone to pick me up by the time Steve and Dickie Davis finally arrived."

Eventually the two showed up and took Richie to Stephen's tiny apartment on Fountain near Fairfax not far from Barry's house "I took one look at Richie in his Brooks Brothers suit and crewcut," shrugs Dickie, "and I thought right then nothing was going to happen." Stephen broke the news to Richie that there was no band. "The whole band was him and me," Richie remembers.

"I just figured, "'Oh boy! Stephen's done it to me again!' It was frustrating but typical." Counters Stephen, "I told him I had a band and that I needed him. I lied. I didn't have a band at all, but it was only half a lie because I did need him." "My reaction when I learned that was, 'Oh man, I can't believe this," Richie counters. "Here I am in the middle of nowhere. This isn't happening.' So I got on the phone to my Mom. I remember my parents had sort of befriended Rod Serling of *The Twilight Zone* because he went to Antioch College, which is in Yellow Springs. She tried to get me in touch with him. I thought maybe I could find an acting school. I wanted to leave LA but I couldn't get outta town."

It didn't take long for Stephen's charm to win Richie over to his cause, tenuous as it was. "We hung out learning songs and trying to get a band together. Stephen taught me some of his songs that ended up on the first Buffalo Springfield album — he'd written a lot of them by then — and I taught *Clancy* to him since we had a mutual friend in Neil. So we put that in our repertoire. It was just me and him sitting in a room, playing our guitars and singing songs to ourselves. We were very influenced by the Beatles and patterned ourselves after Lennon and McCartney doing a lot of unison singing. We'd learn songs all day with the hope that one day we'd do something with them. It was fun but we weren't doing anything with it. There was no direction."

Since coming out to LA, Stephen's songwriting had progressed by leaps and bounds, a point that did not go unnoticed by Richie. Though still working with acoustic guitars in a folk base, Stephen evolved a style that eschewed folk music themes, instead putting into well-crafted rhyme the same teenage boy-girl angst that was the endless fodder of every Fifties to early Sixties platter, only Stephen did it with a clever lyric and a commercial ear in an electric rock music arrangement with folk harmonies over top. Stephen had not embraced the 'topical song' format, at least not until later in the year with *For What It's Worth*.

Working together day in, day out, Stephen and Richie developed a vocal blend, both in unison and harmony, that would become a hallmark of the early Buffalo Springfield sound as presented on their debut album. "From the time we got together on Fountain Avenue and started singing our songs and putting harmonies together, that became a link to the sound of the band. I can't deny that the vocal blend Steve and I had was a signature part of that band. The way we sang together left its impact from that very first record." As benefactor, Barry gave encouragement for their souls, a dollar a day each for their stomachs, and a place to live and practice. Remarks Barry, "They sounded very good to me." In Stephen and Richie, the nucleus of the Buffalo Springfield was forged. All they needed were other musicians to complete their sound.

At a time when the Sunset Strip scene was blossoming and bands like Love, The Doors, Iron Butterfly, Daily Flash, and The Leaves were starting to catch fire in clubs like Bido Lito's and the Sea Witch, Stephen and Richie missed much of it. "We didn't go anywhere. We just worked on songs. We didn't have any money to do much else, so we didn't get around to see other bands. I remember we did go to a party at Barry McGuire's house, and the kinds of things that were going on there, I had never seen before. It was a bizarre scene. For us, going to Pioneer Chicken for dinner was a big deal." Richie, however, had a secret he kept carefully hidden from Stephen and Barry, a small cache of travelers cheques. "I would get up before Stephen and go down to the corner Thrifty Mart and have breakfast while he was still sleeping. I was ornery, man. It was survival of the fittest," laughs Richie.

As the month wore on Richie began shedding his straight, New York folkie look. "I had been going down to this place for a couple of weeks in a row and my hair had been growing out. One day I was sitting at the counter and they wouldn't serve me. This waitress, an older lady who I had talked to on other mornings, ignored me. So finally I asked her why she wouldn't serve me and she said, 'The boss said your hair's too long.'

Behind Barry's house, ensconced in another residence on the lot, Tom Maston and Mike Brewer were busy rehearsing their folk rock group under Barry's watchful gaze. Jim Fielder was on bass guitar, and Billy Mundi played drums. Though still getting their repertoire together, Richie was, nonetheless, impressed and envious."Maston and Brewer were, as far as I'm concerned, terrific, something I had never heard before. And I thought, 'Boy, this could be great if we could do something like they were doing,' and I'm sure Barry was constantly saying to us, 'You guys just work on your songs, then we'll get the other guys to go out and do it with you.' Meantime, I was thinking, 'How long is this going to last?'"

On March 2nd, with no apparent break forthcoming and no revenue, Richie and Stephen applied to copyright several of their compositions with the idea of selling them to other artists. Barry indicated he had contacts who might be able to pitch their material. Among Stephen's copyrighted tunes were *Sit Down I Think I Love You*; Richie's included *Loser, My Kind Of Love*, and *A Sad Memory*. In late March, Barry's insider, Chuck Kaye at Screen Gems-Columbia, the publishing arm of Columbia Music Inc., purchased *Sit Down I Think Love You* and *Loser*. "I got a hundred bucks for my song, *Loser*," enthuses Richie. "I thought, 'Man, this is great. I sold a song for a hundred bucks!' I could live for another couple of weeks."

Think you're gonna take my girl from me,
I think you're wrong.
You can't even stand a chance,
So you'd best be gone.
You know she's not the kind of girl,
That you would want.
I've seen your kind before,
You're looking for a front.
Don't even try, you cannot win.

She is my girl, not just a friend.
Don't even look again, loser.

Loser (Richie Furay)

Though *Loser* remains unrecorded, Stephen's song became a popular number in the Buffalo Springfield's early repertoire, appearing on their debut album, and in March of 1967, becoming a hit for San Francisco group The Mojo Men. Years later, Stephen would come to regret selling this composition.

Sit down, I think I love you,
Anyway, I'd like to try.
I can't help thinking of you,
If you go I know I'll cry.
Can't you see that I'm a desperate man,
I get high just thinking about you.
You know what they say about the bird in the hand,
And that's why I ain't leavin' without you.

Sit Down I Think I Love You (Stephen Stills)

Attempts at tracking down their Canadian friend Neil Young through the month of March had proved futile. Neil, recording in Detroit then languishing back in Yorkville following the abrupt end of The Mynah Birds, had no permanent phone number. Besides, by mid March, though only known to a select few close friends, he and Bruce had already left Toronto. The search did yield a number for Ken Koblun. Using Randy Sparks' credit card, they managed to locate Ken who was on the road with Three's A Crowd, playing the 4-D in Regina. Stephen dangled the same bait that hooked Richie, and Ken, too, jumped at it, leaving his group high and dry for a shot at the big time, or at least Stephen's appealing portrait of it.

Arriving on March 21st, Ken Koblun was brought to Barry's to rehearse with Stephen and Richie. "I thought Kenny Koblun was an amazing bass player," Barry recalls, "very melodic and lyrical, and I really liked his playing." Ken's tenure, however, was short lived, less than a week. "Kenny didn't stay long," recollects Richie. "We figured Kenny was another piece to our puzzle of putting our band together. Stephen and I thought we had convinced Kenny to stay and be a part of our non-existent band at that time. We were sleeping in Barry's house and we tried to bribe Kenny to stay with a meal from Pioneer Chicken. Kenny had told us he wasn't sure he could make this with us. We went to bed that night assured that he was going to stick around after the meal we bought him. I remember waking up in the morning and finding a note on the coffee table saying, 'Steve, I just can't make it, sorry,' and he was gone. I don't know how he managed to get out without us hearing him because we were all sleeping in the living room. I was on the couch and there was this big coffee table in the living room and that's where the note was. We were devastated."

Confirms Ken, "I spent a week with Stills and Furay and nothing was happening. I had to make a decision. I had 20 dollars left in my pocket. Either spend it on food and stay with them in California, or spend it on taxi fare to LA airport and the manager for Three's A Crowd was going to pay my ticket back to Toronto. So that was what I did." By March 29th, Ken was back with Three's A Crowd at Yorkville's Riverboat club, and Richie and Stephen were again at loose ends. Meanwhile, as Ken flew out of Los Angeles across the United States en route to Toronto, a hearse with six unlikely passengers, including Neil Young and Bruce Palmer, rumbled its way in the opposite direction.

Seeing some potential revenue from his charges via their songwriting, Barry, in cohoots with Screen Gems' Chuck Kaye, offered up a contract for exclusive personal management of Richie and Stephen, for 20 percent of their individual gross revenues (originally 25 but revised down by mutual consent) for a period of one year commencing upon signing, with options for six more years. There were no guarantees set out by the would-be managers; however Barry and Chuck pledged their best efforts to further the careers of the two singers. On April 4th, 1966, Richie signed; Stephen had already put his name to an identical agreement. Two days later, in a line of traffic on Sunset Boulevard, they spotted the hearse bearing Ontario license plates.

Neil Young and Bruce Palmer had been searching for Stephen for several days by then, somehow believing he was a key to their musical destiny. "I knew that I was destined for a little more than the Yorkville scene and I felt this drawing down to Los Angeles," reflects Neil years later. "I had to go down to California because I knew that the music that I was interested in was coming from there. There was no way that the music scene in Toronto could support the kind of ideas that I had at that time. The audience just wasn't big enough. Canada just couldn't support the ideas I had. There wasn't a big enough audience for the music I wanted to do. I just couldn't get anyone to listen. There were some people who liked and supported what I was trying to do, there just weren't enough of them. By 1966 I knew I had to leave Canada, and the sounds I was hearing and the sounds I liked were coming from California. I knew that if I went down there I could take a shot at making it."

Once Neil and Bruce decided to leave Canada, they set about acquiring the means to turn their decision into reality. "We were like on a mission from god and there was nothing going to stop us," Neil emphasizes. "Bruce was there with me, determined to go. He was as committed as I was." But how to finance this expedition? "Bruce and I pawned all the band's equipment. It was the only way we could go. The band had broken up. Bruce and I were the only ones who wanted to be the band. Ricky was in jail; there was no Mynah Birds without him. It was the band's equipment but it was really Eaton's equipment." The money provided a road stake as well as furnishing their mode of transportation, a 1953 Pontiac hearse. Ever since Mort, Neil loved hearses. "We got the hearse and left within a couple of days," continues Neil. "We took one guy with us named Mike who's last name I can't remember, Tannis Neiman, and another girl with long red hair, and Jeanine. Three guys and three girls."

Leaving his wife Dale and infant son behind in Toronto, Bruce set out with Neil on their odyssey to find Stephen Stills, with no address, no telephone number, just a hunch that he was out there somewhere. Neil claimed once in an interview that he knew Ken Koblun was down in LA with Stephen but that seems unlikely as the two friends had lost touch with Ken on the road in Three's A Crowd and Neil in The Mynah Birds. Besides, Neil had already left when Ken received the call from Stephen.

Remembering the annoying hassles he and the other long haired musicians encountered with The Mynah Birds at the Windsor — Detroit border crossing, Neil hatched a plan to sail through customs unfettered. While in Fort William a year earlier, he had heard that the customs post at Sault Ste. Marie, where Lake Superior narrows to join Lake Huron in northern Ontario, was a lax affair. So he steered the hearse more than 400 hundred miles out of their way to the Sault. "You have to visualize this," offers Bruce. "Six hippies in an old hearse with musical instruments, men and women, marijuana stuffed into various pockets and crevices, heading towards an international border. What we found was laughable. There was this old man sitting in a rocking chair in front of a little shack out in the middle of nowhere. So we just breezed through." It was a common practice for travelers heading to or from Winnipeg through northern Ontario to avoid the hills and barren terrain by detouring through the United States. Claiming to be on his way home to Winnipeg and brandishing his mother's address in that city, the customs officer waved them through.

Journeying due south to St. Louis, the hearse then veered westward. "We headed down Route 66," Bruce continues, "but were constantly stopped by highway patrolmen who were curious about what this was." It was past mid-March as the hearse rolled across the country, with Neil undertaking the driving duties. "These girls were driving Bruce and I nuts," grouses Neil. "They were destroying the car when they would drive and I was paranoid the car was going to break down. I didn't want another Blind River." Having abandoned a stricken Mort in that northern Ontario town a year earlier, Neil wanted no one to come between him and his vehicle. The toll this took on him had disastrous consequences. "We got to Albuquerque and I got real sick," continues Neil, "almost a nervous breakdown from exhaustion or nerves. I had to lie down for days, three or four days." Bruce views events slightly different. "At that point Neil had one of his first epileptic episodes and that lasted a couple of days with him on the floor. It was certainly part exhaustion as well because he had been driving for several days straight." At this point, Tannis, Mike, and Jeannine abandoned ship to take employment at a desert folk coffeehouse, the oddly named Igloo. Well enough to carry on, Neil, Bruce, and the red haired girl arrived on April 1, 1966 in Los Angeles. Homesick, the red haired girl was quickly dispatched on the next bus out.

"It was just a hunch, a feeling that Neil had that Stephen Stills was in LA," confirms Bruce. "We went driving around town stopping at all the clubs we thought he might be at but we never found him or found anyone that even knew him." Adds Neil, "We slept in the hearse, parking on the street at night. I knew Stills was down there but I didn't know where. Bruce didn't know him, but I had told him about Stills. I was asking about him in clubs and coffeehouses around LA. To get money for gas, cigarettes, and food we used to rent out the hearse for rides from a place where there was a scene happening to another scene. But we never heard anything about Stephen, so Bruce and I decided to head north to San Francisco." And that's when Richie, Stephen and Barry encountered Neil and Bruce.

Precise details of what transpired next have become somewhat obscured over the years. Though the five participants in that fateful moment agree on the general facts, each differs slightly on the fine points. Who was first to notice the hearse? Did they pass each other or was the white van behind the hearse already when the light of recognition came on?

"We were driving in a white van on our way down Sunset Boulevard," says Richie. "I don't remember what we were doing, but we got stuck in traffic and I saw a black hearse with Canadian plates going the other way. I remembered that Stills had told me that Neil drove a black hearse. Stephen was sure that it was Neil. So somehow we pulled up beside the hearse, and, sure enough, there were Neil and Bruce. So we chased them down."

According to Neil's memory, "Bruce and I were just leaving to go to San Francisco. We were on Sunset Boulevard heading north, stopped at a light. The traffic was heavy. Then Stephen and Richie saw us in traffic. Stephen saw this hearse with Ontario license plates and said, 'I know that guy, it's Neil!'"

Bruce, offers a more detailed account. "They were going south, we were going north towards the freeway, and we just passed. Stephen and Richie and Barry Friedman were in a van. Barry was driving the van. This was after a week of searching for them. They knew Neil liked old cars and they noticed the license plate. We heard all this commotion, screaming and yelling, and there was Stephen at the window. So we pulled into a parking lot. The miraculous thing about it was that they had passed us going the other way. They actually turned around because Richie noticed the hearse and the Ontario license plates and remembered Stephen talking about this weird fellow from Ontario who was into hearses and just out of chance or curiosity wanted to check it out. So they turned around and pulled up alongside us and 'bang' that was that."

Barry, the driver of the van, recalls the encounter this way: "I saw the license plate and joked to Stephen, 'Hey, there are your friends from Canada.' I was kidding and he looked over and it was! So he yelled and screamed in the middle of the street, and we pulled off Sunset Boulevard around the corner a block away from the road you took up Laurel Canyon and stopped in front of a liquor store and talked. Then we all went back to my place."

And Stephen simply says, "Richie and I were driving down the street wondering what we were going to do. We passed this old hearse and turned and said to each other: 'Hey, I know him!'"

Regardless of just how they did meet, it was a joyous reunion and once the handshakes and hugs were done, the five repaired to Barry's house to share stories, music, and a little grass. It has often been told that Neil initially remained cool to the idea of forming a group with Stephen and Richie until hearing them sing. That assertion, however, seems highly unlikely given that he had virtually stolen The Mynah Birds' equipment and sold it for himself, illegally entered the United States, journeyed some 3,000 miles to Los Angeles at great risk to his personal health, all in search of Stephen, not knowing Richie was there, too. He did not undertake all that simply to bring greetings. That he needed convincing to throw in his lot with Stephen and Richie, caving in only when they played him their arrangement of *Clancy* as is oft reported, seems unlikely. "I didn't know what was going on in Neil's mind," suggests Richie, "but I think he was impressed enough that he thought, 'Hey, I might try this for awhile.'"

"They needed a guitar player and bass player and we needed a band so it was perfect," smiles Bruce. "We all went over to Barry's house and Stephen and Richie sat down and sang *Clancy* and Neil and I were aghast. It was so good. Clancy had been one of the first songs Neil ever played for me." Confirms Richie, "When Stephen and I started singing *Clancy*, I think it probably sounded good enough to Neil because he had probably never heard the song sung that way before and it impressed him. We had added harmonies to it, and I remember Bruce sitting there nodding his head in agreement. It just all fell together and the next thing we knew we started playing together, the four of us, and all we needed was a drummer. It just naturally evolved. We had all these people standing around us, Barry Friedman, Tom Maston and Mike Brewer, Jimmy Fielder, and they're all telling us, 'Hey, this sounds pretty good. You guys really do need a drummer.'"

One cannot neglect the role Barry Friedman played in the genesis of the Buffalo Springfield. Though he was personal manager to Stephen and Richie, his contract did not extend to the others, nor to any group the two might form and the personnel within it. Yet from the moment they all met, Barry was the catalyst, providing a place to live and rehearse, giving them each money, providing moral support and encouragement, as well as bringing them to the attention of several key people in the music business early on. He even found them a drummer.

"Everything just fell into place," confirms Bruce. "It couldn't have been easier if you had written a script for it. Barry's house on Fountain Avenue was a large house so we all stayed there and slept on the floor. Maston and Brewer were in the house in front of us. We needed a drummer. Billy Mundi came in for awhile but something didn't work out so Billy had to go." Rehearsing with Maston and Brewer, Billy, a UCLA music major who later worked with Frank Zappa and the Mothers of Invention, had committed himself to that group. Besides, Maston and Brewer were ready for live performances, Richie, Stephen and the others weren't. Confirms Richie: "Barry was managing both groups and realized that they were further along at this point in time than we were and ready to go out and play."

By this time Barry had come to work for Byrds' managers Jim Dickson and Ed Tickner. When he told them he had a promising young group in search of a drummer, Jim and Ed suggested Dewey Martin, a former member of The Dillards, another group they handled. Having given up on electric music to return to what they did best, acoustic bluegrass, The Dillards had no need for a drummer so Dewey became available. Three days after the Sunset Boulevard meeting, they had found their drummer.

By the time he arrived within their midst, Dewey Martin had accumulated more experience in the music business than

Richie, Stephen, Neil, and Bruce combined. Here was a musician with pedigree, capable of regaling his younger band mates with tales from the Grand Ole Opry, touring with Patsy Cline and the Everly Brothers, dropping names like Roy Orbison and Carl Perkins casually into conversations. Added to that, he could charm the pants off just about anyone. "Dewey was perfectly cut out to be on The Dating Game," remarks one associate.

Born in Chesterville, Ontario, Canada to Milton and Helen Midkiff on September 30, 1940, although Buffalo Springfield promotional bio's consistently listed the year as 1942 ("We changed that to make it look like I was younger like the other guys," chuckles Dewey), and raised in Ottawa, Canada's capital city, Walter Milton Dwayne Midkiff became Dewey early on. "I couldn't say Dwayne so it came out Dewey." His initiation into music came in his early teens, first attempting the baritone saxophone before making the switch to drums. "I was about 13 and there was a drummer who played at my high school. He would play in the mornings for school things, big band stuff. I used to go into the music room after school and set up this old funky set of drums — they had the makings of about half a complete set of all unmatched stuff, really just junk. When the Everly Brothers hit it big around 1956, I rented a set of drums, set them up in our kitchen with one of these old fashioned radios, and I'd drive my mother nuts playing along with the Everly Brothers' *Bye Bye Love.*"

Dewey soon graduated to his own kit and began working with local groups. "I conned my parents into helping me get a set by telling them I could make enough money to make the payments. The very first band I was in was during high school. We were called the Jive Rockets. Our lead guitarist was Vern Craig who ended up in the Five Man Electrical Band. Paul Anka used to come over to our rehearsals in the basement and help us with our harmonies. We used to think, 'Who is this guy?' Then one day we heard *Diana* on the radio."

Dewey earned a name for himself around the Ottawa Valley in a variety of dance bands and rockabilly outfits, including Bernie Early and the Early Birds, before heading to the States for a stint in the US army. Following his discharge, Dewey made his way to the country music capital, Nashville, and quickly established himself as an itinerant drummer for touring groups. "I sat in with this guy named Hank Garland at Jimmy Hyde's

Carousel Club in Nashville," recalls Dewey of his initiation into the Nashville music community. "Hank had been in a severe accident and was just getting his chops back. All the players would come there — Chet Atkins, Boots Randolph — all the sessions players and jam. I didn't have any drums with me but I was in awe of these guys so I'd hang out there. One day I was in there before it opened and Hank Garland was playing jazz on electric guitar. I had learned how to swing back when I was 14, so I really wanted to get up on those drums. Then the drummer got up and took his drum sticks with him. There was nobody in the place but Hank, the bartender, and one or two others. So I just got up and asked, 'Has anybody got a comb?' I ended up playing the drums with two combs and I was swinging away. Hank turned around and gave me a big grin, so I could tell he was digging it. We played for awhile then stopped and Hank asked, 'Have you got a job?' I said, 'No, I don't have any drums.' And he replied, 'Well, I know this guy that needs a drummer right now and he's got drums.' And lo and behold he got me a gig with Faron Young with no audition. Faron had a number one record with Willie Nelson's *Hello Walls*. That was my first taste of real success. From then on I became the guy available to do live gigs. I played for Roy Orbison, the Everly Brothers, Patsy Cline, and I never auditioned for any of them. I worked with Charlie Rich and Carl Perkins. What a treat to play with these guys and I was still learning." Along the way Dewey adopted the surname Martin.

With Faron Young's group Dewey traveled to Las Vegas and Los Angeles, where he decided to stay. "I got hung up on the palm trees, the beautiful weather, and the girls," smiles Dewey. "So I went down to the Palomino Club, which was really happening then, and met Mel Taylor of The Ventures and he'd get me gigs, enough to keep me alive." The Ventures originated from the Pacific Northwest and soon Dewey found himself working with musicians from that vicinity, ending up in Seattle with Lucky Lee and the Blue Diamonds. There, with a pickup group of players, he recorded a single for A & M Records in November 1964, released under the title Sir Raleigh and the Coupons. The song, a rocked up version of *White Cliffs Of Dover* featuring Dewey on vocals, was released as the British Invasion swept across America, and Dewey found himself carried along with the tide. With the record gaining attention in that region, Dewey returned to Los Angeles to recruit musicians, from the group the Sons of Adam, for a more permanent outfit. Thus constituted, Sir Raleigh and the Coupons became a minor success in the Washington-Oregon area, sharing engagements with the likes of the Beach Boys and Herman's Hermits, releasing four more singles, the last appearing in February 1966. By then the appeal of British bands was waning, and Dewey soon found himself back in LA.

"I was always a drummer that was working," Dewey points out. "When something fell out I picked up something else. When I returned to Los Angeles I worked with the Modern Folk Quartet before joining The Dillards who were trying to go electric. Rodney and Doug Dillard were at odds at that time. They were searching something new, country rock, but they weren't cutting it, and Rodney was pissed off because they weren't going over like when they did their bluegrass stuff. After the tour we did with The Byrds, I was sitting with Doug Dillard, who was my drinking buddy at the time, and we were out at The Ice House in Pasadena. And he said to me, 'We're going back to bluegrass and we don't need you as a drummer any more. But if you call our manager Jim Dickson, he's got a gig for you.' So I called Dickson and he said, 'There's a band that needs a drummer. I've never heard them but they need somebody that's gonna stay with them 'cause their using somebody else's drummer. Go check it out.' He gave me Stephen Stills' number and I called him right then from Pasadena. Stills said he'd heard of me and asked 'When can you bring your drums over and audition?' I'd never auditioned for anybody! Who'd these guys think they were?'"

Joining a fledgling group, whose only currency came via Barry's wallet, was a shock to Dewey. However, it took little encouragement for him to come on board. "I was used to making good money. When I got there I found out that it didn't pay anything. In fact, Richie and I were the only ones with any money and everybody was like starving. Richie had traveler's cheques and he was hoarding them away like mad trying to make them last. But when I walked into the room the first time and heard Richie and Steve sing *Go And Say Goodbye* I knew I had never ever heard a vocal sound like that. And I just took to it."

Barry was at first skeptical of their choice. "Billy Mundi was the drummer initially, a big round Buddha man, and he was a great drummer. But I think Stephen didn't want him. Dewey was a very straight ahead, solid, commercial drummer, and probably, in the long run the right choice as far as the sound went, but Billy was more melodic and creative. Dewey came in and it was a done deal, he was in immediately." Adds Dickie, "Back then, in the folk thing, everyone played guitars, so drummers were a commodity. There weren't a lot of them around, so they were coming in from country and western bands. That's where Dewey came from before he joined The Dillards. Billy Mundi was a better drummer but Dewey looked the part. He had the looks." Michael Miller, who would come to work for the group as a roadie soon after it formed, contends that Dewey was a good choice. "Dewey was lucky because he was a pickup guy who was in town when the band was being put together. But, in truth, he provided a very interesting contrast in character to them. He was a rhythm and blues guy who liked to think he was Otis Redding and had played with some major country guys. They weren't looking for a Keith Moon, they just wanted someone solid."

In Dewey Martin, the group had the final ingredient needed to complete the picture. "Dewey was a piece to the puzzle even if he wasn't who some people thought they would have liked to have had," defends Richie. "If Billy had been in the band everybody would have been excited about that, but Dewey was in the band, so no matter what, we were glad to have him. His out front personality was likeable. Dewey does not know a stranger. He's very friendly and gregarious. He was always smiling and you could feel that he enjoyed what he was doing. That was something that helped to draw people to the band. He may have made the band more accessible to people than maybe Neil or Bruce."

Dewey did, however, set out one qualifier. According to Richie, "Dewey would play with us if he could sing. He said he could sing like Otis Redding. He had some experience. He had worked with people like Faron Young and been in The Dillards, so he could come in and make some conditions. We agreed and he sang Wilson Pickett's *In The Midnight Hour* until I wrote *Nobody's Fool* and *Good Time Boy* for him to sing. So we did *Midnight Hour* for Dewey and that satisfied him. That's the only cover tune we ever did in the Buffalo Springfield."

With the lineup set, all the young group required was a

name. When Dewey walked into Barry's house to meet the other members, he noticed a metal sign plate hanging on the wall. Inquiring the novice group's name, Neil simply pointed at the sign. "They were resurfacing Fountain Avenue," notes Barry on how the group serendipitously found its identity, "and we pulled up in front of the house behind a steamroller. It had a sign on the back that said 'Buffalo Springfield'. We said, 'That's it.' So we took the sign off the back of the steamroller and took it into the house, stuck it on the wall, and that was that."

The band considered no other name, though they would come to be known affectionately in the media as The Herd. "The Buffalo Springfield Roller Company in Toledo, Ohio endorsed us using it," confirms Richie. "They wrote us back and told us they were excited to see the name being used because the company wasn't doing too much at that time. It was an encouraging start."

Walter Midkiff aka Dewey Martin.

Buffalo Springfield at their first photo session with Dickie Davis upper left.

FOUR

Expecting To Fly

There you stood on the edge of your feather,
Expecting to fly.
While I laughed, I wondered whether,
I could wave goodbye.
Knowing that you'd gone, babe.
By the summer, it was healing,
We had said goodbye.
All the years we spent with feeling,
Ended with a cry, babe.

Expecting To Fly (Neil Young)

From the moment of their first rehearsals as a band, the Buffalo Springfield crafted a "sound" that would not only sharply distinguish their identity from other contemporary acts but also significantly influence the course of popular music. The Buffalo Springfield "sound" shaped the Southern California country-folk-rock "sound" of the 1970s, the sound of America's most successful band of the decade, The Eagles, as well as the "New Country" sound of the late 1980s and 1990s. Members of various other bands at the time and the band members themselves sensed something special, if not monumental, happening during those rehearsals.

"It just meshed musically perfectly," Bruce Palmer comments as he recalls the euphoria of the first week the band rehearsed. "Everybody had their own songs, their own technique, we had instant four part harmony which only The Byrds and the Beatles had. Not only did we have harmony, each singer was a lead singer in his own right. And everybody was a great player, not necessarily in a rock sense, except for me because I had that background. They were coming from folk roots with acoustic instruments. The transition into electric wasn't easy, but it was almost seamless, especially for Stephen who got his first electric guitar then. He was already one of the finest acoustic players and he plugged in and that was it."

This melting pot of influences each individual brought to the table — folk, rock, country, R'n'B — forged a highly distinctive style that immediately set the Springfield apart from their contemporaries. In a period when extended instrumental passages and freakouts were becoming the vogue and the focus was on one individual, the Buffalo Springfield stepped back, drawing on their diverse roots, emphasizing a dynamic group sound through tightly structured, well-crafted songs using a folk rock format rather than self-indulgent soloing. In that respect they were akin to The Byrds, though the Springfield's brand of folk rock relied not on electric twelve strings but three guitars, acoustics and electrics played together, weaving lead, rhythm, and melody around a basic song structure.

As Dickie Davis observes, "The Buffalo Springfield's folk rock wasn't like The Byrds with the jangly twelve-string and Dylan. It had more of an older folk feel with country roots and acoustic alongside electric instruments. Stephen and Richie

94

brought those influences to the sound and Bruce added the rock edge." They had a freshness, a warmth and vivacity, unmatched by other artists, with the exception perhaps of the Lovin' Spoonful. But unlike the Spoonful who depended on revved up traditional jug band and blues numbers plus the creative energy of John Sebastian for their repertoire, the Springfield had one of the most envied sources of material in popular music. Having three solo folk singer-songwriters in one group was quite a coup.

"The Springfield came from the folk thing," The Turtles' Mark Volman points out, "so they had that songwriting experience. They'd been doing it for a few years already when they came out to California. They were already gestating in terms of being songwriters that a lot of other bands didn't have. The Turtles were never groomed to live or die by our songwriting. We came out of that Brill Building philosophy. Our managers had grown up as promotion men and knew the value of a hit song. They wanted immediate hits. It was an old school philosophy. They didn't nurture that in us, but the Springfield were writing their own material right from the start. They were given the room to develop their songwriting. Writing all their own songs was one of the classiest things about the Buffalo Springfield."

The fact that right from those earliest rehearsals the five members determined to record and perform only their own music marked them as unique. Even The Byrds were relying on outside sources, notably Dylan, to flesh out their albums. "From the get-go we were doing our own tunes," boasts Richie. "Steve would be teaching us *Go And Say Goodbye,* and Neil would teach us *Do I Have To Come Right Out And Say It.* These two guys were going back and forth with so many good songs that I just stood there and said, 'Yeah!' Stephen and I had a head start, but Neil, Dewey, and Bruce picked things up very quickly. We had a set together in no time."

"The original five of us," Richie continues, "had the magic. There was a connection that cannot be put into words. It was that special. It's like putting your hand in a glove, and it just fits right. Or like holding your wife, you know that when you hug someone else and you hug her, you fit. That's how it was. We were all so different and yet we were all made to make that music at that particular time." "The people were good from the start," enthused Neil to his father up in Canada. "There was no down time. Everybody was ready. These were people who had come to Los Angeles for the same reason, identical, all finding each other. It didn't take any time before we all knew we had the right combination." Adds Bruce, "the early days were great. We all had such regard for each other, we were all so delighted to be making music together. Everyone was helpful, constructive, creative."

Each member carved out a role for himself. As the rhythm section, Dewey and Bruce found an instant chemistry playing together. Dewey's basic uncluttered drumming allowed Bruce the space to provide counterpoint to the melody. Bruce gave the Springfield their rock context. Notes Mark Volman, "Bruce was kind of overlooked because they had three songwriters in the band. It's easy to see the contribution of the songwriters. But Bruce was really a major part of the Springfield sound. He also focused them away from folk and more on rock and gave them an ability to spread out." Offers Byrds' bass player Chris Hillman, no slouch himself on his instrument, "Bruce was a brilliant bass player, a great musician. I looked at him and went, 'Wow!' He was a real bass player, not just a guitar player playing bass, and interesting to watch in his selection of notes." Adds Barry Friedman, "Bruce was very important to their sound because he kept everything very loose no matter what. He was very melodic and did a lot of neat things that tied in with the songs rather than being a tight player."

Neil staked out the lead guitar slot, content initially to be in the background contributing songs and firing off lead lines. "The real core of the group," he stresses, "was the three Canadians — me, Bruce Palmer, and Dewey Martin. We played in such a way that the three of us were basically huddled together behind, while Stills and Furay were always out front. 'Cause we'd get so into the groove of the thing, that's all we really cared about."

Having already crafted their unique vocal blend, Richie and Stephen took center stage. While Stephen contributed second lead guitar, often providing the melody line or finger picking to offset Richie's strumming, it was Richie who was perceived as the front man and lead voice. "I saw myself as lead singer and first harmony singer to Steve," states Richie, "and as a more visual front person, too. That was what I saw my contribution as being more so than guitar player or songwriter. Steve was pretty much set on singing his own songs, although as the Beatles did, we would sing unison on quite a few songs and then break into harmonies. I sang most of Neil's songs early on. I felt I could sing Neil's songs better than Neil could, and I thought I could complement Stephen's songs with my harmonies and vocals. It was like this: Steve and Neil were looked upon as the main songwriters; Richie's the front guy, one of the lead singers. Confirms Neil, "We saw Richie as the big strength. He had a strong vocal presence for the band. At the start I was more the guitar player and writer in the band but that didn't last very long. I started singing my own songs and getting into it again."

Stephen assumed the role of musical arranger, setting out the parts for the instruments and vocals. More than any other member it was Stephen's musical skill and vision that created the sound of the Buffalo Springfield. Though the sum of its contributory parts, the band had his mark stamped on it from its inception. "I will always say the Buffalo Springfield was Stephen's band," declares Richie. "He was the heart and the soul of the band, I don't care what anyone else says or thinks. He was the leader, always. Without Steve, there was no Buffalo Springfield." Though the five maintained there was no leader per se, each acknowledged Stephen's role in shaping the group and setting its direction. "Steve's the leader, but we all are," the other four would respond when asked. His personality was more focused, self-assured and assertive, his material already more defined with a nod to a more commercially accessible lyric than Neil's when the group began rehearsals. Indeed, Neil and Richie were more content to take a back seat to him in the early days, allowing Stephen to set the course. "I really liked Stephen's writing," Richie continues. "He definitely had a knack at that particular time for writing songs that were soulful and had a lot of feeling and emotion to them. I thought he was the emotional impetus in the band."

Visitors to those early rehearsals were awestruck by the talent and energy the group displayed. Barry Friedman brought several music industry kingpins down to see the group, including Dickson and Tickner who gave some consideration to taking the group under their management wings. The Byrds' Chris Hillman dropped by on the recommendation of Dewey and was immediately impressed. "I loved them. They were living in this really funky, weird motel way down Sunset far away from the Whisky. Their songs were great and there was something magical about them. Here was a band with three strong guys similar to The Byrds when Gene Clark was in it, and their first batch of songs were very catchy. I thought Stephen was pretty special, as was Neil, and Richie, too. I got close to Stephen and to some degree Richie. I didn't know Neil real well, but I knew Dewey because, prior to the Springfield, he had been working with The Dillards. Neil was very shy, quiet, and off on his own, not as approachable as Stephen or the other guys. Dewey was a big goof, a lovable kind of guy. He was the one that told me about the group. I already knew Barry and started hanging out with Stephen. Then the Springfield opened for us around southern California. They were good. We were already spoiled, but the Springfield were hungry and playing great and really gave us a run for our money."

As nurturer, provider, supporter, Barry Friedman was in a unique position to observe the dynamics of the five young musicians. "The thing that made it work," he comments, "was, first of all, the time when it took place. If you were to bring that same group of people together now, I'm not sure it would have jelled in one week. There was a lot less competition. And we also didn't know any better. We believed that all you had to do was put a group together, get some front money, make a record, and become stars. That's how it happened so that's what we thought was all you had to do. We were babies." It was that wide-eyed naivete that characterized the group from the beginning. They saw themselves having virtually no competition other than the Beatles or Rolling Stones and expected nothing less than the very pinnacle of success. "Time meant nothing," attests Neil, "we were ready."

What seems mind boggling is the speed at which everything came together. Within a week, seven days from Dewey's arrival, the Buffalo Springfield had fashioned a wholly unique and individual sound and were ready to make their public debut. No wonder there was so much elation between the five as they made music together. They had dreamed of this group all their lives.

Barry had rented the group two rooms at the Hollywood Center Motel, a dingy low rent dive on Sunset down towards

Highland Avenue, Neil and Stephen in one room, Dewey, Bruce, and Richie in the other. As Dewey recalls, "Bruce was staying in the closet of our room. We had no money and were living on hot dogs." The Hollywood was selected because the rundown complex offered a tiny theater for rehearsals, where the Springfield immediately set about the task of becoming a band. One hurdle to be overcome before they could proceed was equipment. Though Dewey arrived with his own kit and Bruce brought with him from Toronto his old Bill Wyman style Framus hollow body bass and a Traynor bass amp, Richie, Stephen, and Neil only had acoustic guitars. The situation was remedied straightaway when Byrds' managers Jim Dickson and Ed Tickner offered to loan the fledgling group the electric gear no longer needed by The Dillards. Richie acquired a Fender Telecaster solid body guitar while Stephen and Neil used Duane Eddy style Guild hollow body electrics. Bruce played a solid body Gibson SG bass. An assortment of Fender, Traynor, and Standel amplifiers was scrounged up for them.

On April 15th, following that one week of intense rehearsals, the Buffalo Springfield made their first public appearance opening for their mentors The Byrds on a short six-date tour of colleges and medium-sized auditoriums in Southern California. Barry had convinced Dickson and Tickner to add the group to the tour roster alongside The Dillards, who had returned to acoustic instruments. By this time The Byrds, now without Gene Clark, were exploring what would become, if briefly, raga rock, a precursor to psychedelic music with the recently released single, the adventurous and misinterpreted *Eight Miles High*, and thus leaving behind their folk rock roots.

The tour opened at the Swing Auditorium in the Orange Showgrounds, San Bernardino, and one person who witnessed the Springfield's performance that day was deejay John Peel. "The Byrds played, and The Dillards, but Johnny Darin and I agreed that the Buffalo Springfield were the best thing there. We were working for radio station KMEN and were very nervous because this was the first concert we'd compered. Neil Young said afterwards that it was the first concert they'd played, too, but it didn't sound like that. Gloats Dewey, "The Byrds could hardly follow us. We had so much energy and got the people worked up so much because we had a high powered set right through and they were digging it. And then they'd come out and stand there and play their *Turn, Turn, Turn.*"

Despite their impressive debut, the headliners did not consider the upstarts a challenge to their supremacy. "I never felt a sense of rivalry with them," responds Chris Hillman, "more so awe: 'Boy, are they good.' I don't know if anybody else in The Byrds realized that, though. I don't think the other guys were aware of it. I was telling them how good the Springfield was, but I didn't feel they were a threat. Being the age we were we didn't think at that point that anyone could unseat us."

The debut confirmed everything the five had been dreaming of. "I remember playing the Swing Auditorium with The Byrds and thinking we were on our way," enthuses Richie. "It was really exciting. Like, 'Hey man, these kids are really going crazy!' They were crawling through windows to get in. The Byrds were real popular then. It was very exciting, rock'n'roll mania! I remember sitting in the dressing room afterward feeling pretty darn good about the band. We had been together no more than two weeks and we must have made enough of an impression to go on and play five more concerts with the number one band in America. So we must have been pretty good. I mean just a few months before I had been sitting in Massachusetts listening to their album saying, 'Wow' and here I was working with them. It was amazing! After that one, we went up the coast for the next shows, though most of the shows were in the Los Angeles area. But the Swing Auditorium is the one that stands out in my mind. It was like, 'So this is what it's all about.'"

Despite bottom billing and a bargain basement fee of $125 for a half-hour set, the five Springfield members sought all the accoutrements of stardom. Even if they were still sharing rooms at a seedy motel and dining on hot dogs, looking the part meant everything. "I used to pick everybody up in the hearse and we would drive it to The Byrds' managers' office," Neil recalls. "Then we would leave it there parked on the street and get into a limousine for the ride to the concert. One day, we got into the hearse and the back end fell out. It needed a U joint, but we couldn't find one so we just left it there." They were able to transport their meager equipment in The Byrds' old station wagon.

Buoyed by the positive response the group received on The Byrds tour, Barry and Dickie came on board and looked to book them into the premier room on the Sunset Strip, the

Whisky-A-Go Go. Located at the top of San Vicente on the north side corner of Sunset and Clark Street (*Between Clark and Hilldale*, a song by Arthur Lee of LA favorites Love, was titled after the block where the Whisky was situated, along with the Galaxy and London Fog), the Whisky was the crown jewel of the Sunset Strip. The club opened in early 1964 in a renovated bank building, but it was rock'n'roller Johnny Rivers, lured away from another popular club Gazzarri's further up the Strip, who put the Whisky on the map with a series of albums recorded live at the club. Initially the clientele was an older, discotheque dance crowd, and the club catered to that base by alternating live music with a deejay in a suspended cage. This ultimately gave way to mini-skirted go-go dancers boogalooing to the bands. Gradually a younger crowd moved in, and the performers became less Vegas and more hip. By early 1966, with the decline of Ciro's (soon to reopen as It's Boss) the Whisky had become the place to be and be seen on the Strip. Virtually every major rock act of the 1960s played the Whisky at one time or another. Johnny Rivers was still holding court, though, when the Springfield debuted as his opening act.

Barry and Dickie knew that to play the Whisky was acknowledgement that an artist had arrived. Furthermore, the prominence of a Whisky showcase would attract record label interest. However, club manager Elmer Valentine, a tough former Chicago policeman, wouldn't give the two persistent young managers the time of day. Chris Hillman interceded on the group's behalf. "I think I might have opened my mouth at the time about managing them," states Chris. "I was only 21 or so and I really had no idea about how to do that so it was a fleeting idea that lasted five minutes probably. I did go to Elmer Valentine, though, and asked him to book them at the Whisky. He didn't know who they were, they had no track record at all, but he did it on my word. He took them for a night or two, then it extended to a week then six weeks." On Monday, May 4th the Buffalo Springfield auditioned for Elmer and Mario at the Whisky and received a cautious nod of approval. The next week, beginning Monday, May 11th, they opened for Johnny Rivers with their engagement eventually extended five more weeks through to June 20th, during which time they shared billing with Them, the Gentrys, The Leaves, Grass Roots, and Love.

The Whisky-A-Go Go looms large in the Springfield saga for several reasons. It was during that stand that the Buffalo Springfield came of age, forging an identity both collectively and individually that would seal forever the image of the band. "The Whisky was as good as we ever were, as dynamic as we ever were, as close as we ever were, as unified, because we were working every day," suggests Richie. "That's where we worked out everything. The Whisky, that was the Buffalo Springfield. It was a strange club. I can still see those go-go dancers in those cages. We were there six weeks and there was a turn over. When we started there it was the typical Whisky crowd, Vito and all these freaks, but not long after, people started coming to see us and the lineups were snaking around the corner and up the street just to see us. We knew things were happening. People were beginning to appreciate us and we honestly thought we were on our way. We were coming back every night for encore after encore. We were tight, we were good, and we felt we were good. We came together quickly and got good real fast during those six weeks. We enjoyed each other, enjoyed playing together, and we saw that, 'Hey, we're gonna make records, too, just like The Byrds and the Beatles and The Mamas and The Papas. The people we felt were important began coming down to see us: The Byrds, The Mamas And The Papas, Johnny Rivers, Barry McGuire. The Hollies hung out with us when they were in town. They all gave us support, they all felt we had a unique sound, and they all said, 'Go for it!' It was there at the Whisky that we all got the clear view that, yes, we can make it."

Two people who were fortunate to witness the excitement the Springfield generated at the Whisky were Michael Miller and Miles Thomas, both of whom would become friends of the band and roadies for the Springfield. "I met the band when they were first working at the Whisky," recalls Michael. "That was the time when the band was most together. I was a student at Orange Coast College and a surfer, but at night I used to come up to Hollywood to go to all the clubs. The Whisky was the scene, the single center of the universe at that time. The biggest thing in the LA music scene was The Byrds, but the Springfield was that and more. The Byrds didn't have any balls, they had no soul. What Stephen gave the Springfield was that Southern accent and feel, and Neil gave it that screaming edge no one had ever heard in rock'n'roll. When Neil would come out with his fringe and that long black hair hanging in his face and play screaming lead, it was overwhelming. The top came off the place. And when Steve and Richie would shout at each other and yell on *Leave*, it was very impressive. *Neighbor Don't You Worry* was great live with Richie singing. I remember them doing *Hello I've Returned*. When they would do *Clancy*, the mood would shift. There was a dynamic and breadth that this band had that no other band in the country had at that time. There was this original sound and talent that was distinctive from anything else in popular music. The band had a great sense of humor, too. These were very bright, young, articulate musicians with a great ego and joy. That was clear right from the start."

"After one of their first or second nights that they ever played at the Whisky," Michael continues, "I went to Norm's restaurant on Sunset Boulevard and ran into Richie and a few of the other members of the band. We just started talking about the band and their set and became friends with them. Neil was living at the Commodore Arms right behind Graumann's Chinese Theater in a one room studio apartment. We would go back there after the gig and we'd sit around and he'd play and write until three or four in the morning."

Miles Thomas had moved to LA in 1966 from Denver with the Soul Survivors, who changed their name soon after to The Poor. Randy Meisner was their bass player, and Miles worked as road manager for the Colorado group before moving over to the Springfield. "You'd go to the Whisky every night no matter who was playing. It was like your home away from home, the scene at that time, the Whisky and Gazzarri's, and the bands were the Springfield, The Seeds, The Doors, The Byrds. The Springfield were at their peak then. They had so much potential when they were at the Whisky. I think they originally had the potential to beat The Byrds. In their early days they had that mystical thing being the darlings of the local nightclub scene in Hollywood. People loved them. They had a really unique sound and there was a real innocence to them."

Someone who was not impressed with the Springfield at the Whisky but who later become a convert and almost a member of the group was The Byrds' David Crosby. "I took David Crosby to the Whisky-A-Go Go to see the Springfield," Chris Hillman recalls, "and I said to him, 'This group is incredible,' and they were great live even in their infancy. So Crosby hears them and says, 'Ah, they suck. I don't like them.' Then a year later he's hanging out with them and playing with them at Monterey."

On stage, the group was the definition of dynamic, combining energetic presentation with superb original music. Though serving as opening act, the Springfield often upstaged the headliners. "At the Whisky it seemed they'd been together three years, not three weeks," Dickie Davis recalls. "In the early days Richie was the powerhouse of the group on stage. He was all over the stage like Mick Jagger. He'd bounce from one end of the stage to the other on his tiptoes backward, and he'd be playing and screaming. He was a big part of their appeal initially. Stephen and Neil were off to the sides and playing the guitar parts but Richie was front and center. Bruce was a very 'anti-performer' performer. He would turn his back to the audience because he was into the music. Every once in awhile he'd face the audience. I used to have to yell at him from the side of the stage to turn around. He liked to hear himself playing." Responds Bruce, "I just wanted to be next to the drummer. It made sense to me to face the drummer and if that meant turning your back on the audience so what? Let the singers and guitar players do the show up front and you take care of what you gotta do behind it all. And that necessitated turning my back."

In a time of Nehru suits and British velvet-collared jackets, the Springfield brought an American image to pop music, their very name conjuring up echoes of the Old West, wide open skies, wagon trains, cowboys and Indians. Stephen and Neil deliberately cultivated this look, Stephen appearing in smartly tailored suits and a cowboy hat; Neil appearing at times as a self-styled Hollywood Indian, wearing a buckskin jacket with fringes, at other times as a Confederate soldier dressed in uniform. "I had seen what The Byrds were doing with their characterizations and their modeling of individual looks and costumes," Barry Friedman explains, "each one with his own trademark: David with his capes and McGuinn with his glasses. And that's what we wanted to carry through with the Springfield, individual identities." "No one was going around in Comanche war jackets and Indian beads or Confederate uniforms until the Springfield," offers Mark Volman. The other members set out their own presence as well, with Richie the friendly, easy-going Joe College, affable Dewey, the clown in Carnaby suits and pipe, and Bruce the unknown factor, dark and mysterious.

"There I was making a 120 bucks a week at the Whisky as a musician," explains Neil on how his identity unconsciously developed. "I've always liked fringe jackets. I went out and bought one right away with some pants and a turtleneck shirt. Oh yeah, I thought I was heavy. I wore them on some TV shows and whenever we worked. Then I went to this place on Santa Monica Boulevard near La Cienega. I saw this great Comanche war shirt, the best jacket I've ever seen. I had two more made. The group was Western, the name Buffalo Springfield came off a tractor, so it all fit. I was the Indian. That's when it was cool to be an Indian." The shop was Sidereal Time, 8582 Santa Monica Boulevard, and Neil's patronage did much to enhance their business. He also had outfits custom made at Hell Bent For Leather at 6727 Hollywood Boulevard."

Notes Mark Volman, "Richie was put forward as the pretty boy to give him a role. Of the three of them, Richie would be the one because Stephen was already losing his hair and Neil was far from being capable of fitting into that kind of image. Plus he was Canadian and no one knew what the significance of coming from Canada meant back then. It was like coming from another planet. They had an individuality within the band that other groups didn't have." That sense of separate identity within the overall look of the band allowed fans to choose a favorite to idolize, something which began to happen in the teen magazines. Many people believed Neil was, in fact, an Indian because magazines like *Teen Screen* and *TeenSet* constantly referred to him as 'Neil the Indian.'

Publicity bios of the group portrayed Bruce as an enigma. He offered no details of his background, contributing further to the conundrum. "Bruce brought an immediate mystique," comments Richie, "he and Neil, but Bruce more so because he was so introverted. All he ever said was, 'Yeah, man, this is good' and he'd just be playing. As long as he was playing and staying high he was okay." Nurit Wilde offers a less romantic assessment of Bruce's public persona. "I think he was just stoned all the time. People can pass that off as Zen, mysterious and deep. He was a really likable guy, very charming, but he was irresponsible. He had a wife and kids that he didn't look after. He was getting high all the time. He never seemed as committed as Stephen, Neil, or Richie." The air of ambiguity that surrounded Bruce, Barry feels, attracted a certain kind of groupie. "The girls felt sorry for him or something. I think it was the fact that it looked like the wind would blow him away he was so thin and unhealthy looking."

As the focal point of the Hollywood music scene, the Whisky-A-Go Go drew a large contingent of groupies. In short order the Buffalo Springfield became the 'group de jour'. "Back then," notes Miles Thomas, "there were two kinds of groupies, the girls who simply came faithfully to dig the band and their favorite member, the real innocent fans, and the ones who wanted to screw the coolest guy in the band." The Springfield managed to attract both in droves. "None of those guys in the Springfield ever lacked for girls," Miles recalls. "It was like shooting ducks in a barrel. There were always girls around the band. And none of those guys were angels." Notes Nurit Wilde, who by then was working the lights at the Whisky, "Neil had that dark, silent Scorpio way about him. He didn't have a steady relationship but lots of girls were in love with him or had crushes on him. He was all over the place. He never suffered for female adulation."

One girl who fit into the former category was Nancy Jennings. Introduced to Richie at the Whisky by Michael Miller, who first met Nancy when her mother taught him in junior high, Nancy became a frequent visitor to the club that summer. "I had a boyfriend, Bill Reinhart, from The Leaves," remembers Nancy, "who wanted to get back together with me, so he told me to go see this terrific band, Buffalo Springfield, at the Whisky. I knew it was an ulterior motive to get back together because he would be there and I would be there, but I wasn't interested in getting back together with him. I just saw Richie playing and somehow or another there was an attraction." Nancy was the quintessential California girl and frequented the Sunset Strip clubs. "My girlfriend and I used to go to the clubs together, we both looked alike with blond hair, both named Nancy. Richie never wore his glasses on stage so he couldn't tell us apart. He would sing *Sit Down I Think I Love You* and look right over at us and he couldn't tell us apart. But we never met and he would go home with another girl, Anne, so I never pursued it."

Following graduation from school, Anne Gurney, accompanied by her sister Jean, had come out to LA from Massachusetts to be with Richie. But in his rapidly changing world that summer, their relationship would become one of the first casualties. "One night I was standing outside the Whisky on the corner," recalls Nancy, "and Richie came by and asked, 'What's your name?' So I told him and he said, 'See you tomorrow' but I went off to Hawaii for three months. While I was there I got a phone call from my girlfriend who told me she was dating Dickie Davis. And she said, 'You won't believe who wants to take you out? Richie Furay.' So I came back and my mom, my grandmother, and I think my aunt all came to meet me at the airport. Supposedly Richie was meeting me at the Whisky that night, so I drove my mom, grandmother, and aunt to the Whisky with me. Michael Miller, who was a friend of both of ours, interceded on Richie's behalf and we finally got together. I used to go down to the Whisky every night and just stare at Richie. My attraction was him, not the band." Less than a year later, Nancy and Richie were married.

It was at the Whisky that the Springfield became the darlings of the teen fan magazines, notably *TeenSet*, whose female editors took it upon themselves to serve as unofficial publicity agents for the Springfield, dubbing them "the most good looking and talented group to come along since the Beatles." Beginning with the November issue, *TeenSet* never failed to mention the Springfield in each and every issue, frequently featuring multi-page profiles on both the group and its individual members. To its credit, *TeenSet* did much to raise the profile of the group beyond Southern California and expand its fan base once the group began releasing records. "I loved them right away," noted *TeenSet* editor Judith Sims in a 1968 interview. "They just knocked me out. It was obvious they loved playing with each other and respected each other's musicianship. They were a joy to behold."

One of the problems that plagued the Buffalo Springfield throughout their career was how to market such a diverse and creative group. The Springfield did not fit the tried and true starmaker machinery; they were not just another LA pop group. The wisdom of the times was to push the band as your usual cutesy pop group with teen-oriented features in *TeenSet, Teen Screen*, and *Tiger Beat* magazines. The dilemma was that the Springfield's music transcended the teenybopper, pop idol idiom and their individuality proved unsuited to such simplistic presentation. Being marketed as the teenybop flavor of the month ultimately became a hindrance to their progress in being accepted as artists. Each member had a distinct persona and following of his own. The idea of presenting fully defined personalities as opposed to a collective group identity opened a rift between the five band members.

Though acknowledged by all five as the group's defining moment, the gig at the Whisky also marked the beginning of the problems that would eventually cause the break up of the Buffalo Springfield, as Stephen explains. "The first week at the Whisky was absolutely incredible. That's when we peaked, at the Whisky, and after then it was down hill. That was before the ego trips, when we were a band, when we lived together. But then at the Whisky all those strange chicks started chasing me and Neil, and it kind of blew the whole balance. Neil flipped out at the Whisky-A-Go Go and so did I and so did Bruce, because immediately there were all these chicks hanging out and feeding us more and better dope." It was there that the group encountered the under side of the entertainment business, the distractions — the groupies, drugs, and sycophants. "That whole scene is so strange," Neil commented in an interview a few months after the Whisky engagement. "It really doesn't have anything to do with music. That's where you meet people who are supposed to be the connection for you to make it, you know. Johnny Rivers was playing at the Whisky and I really thought that was great. 'Johnny Rivers? Out of sight. I've got to go in.' Then we played second to Johnny Rivers. We were really down to earth then, we were natural. Stephen and I did something that neither one of us would do now. We sat up there in front of Johnny Rivers when he was on stage, and Steve and I were really digging Johnny Rivers, really getting into Johnny Rivers. Yelling and clapping when he took guitar solos. It's not hip to be there, I guess. You can't do that kind of thing and survive, apparently. That's a really funny scene."

"In front of an audience, egos were more important than music," observes Dickie, "and although it drove the group for quite a while, it was also a fatal flaw. Steve and Neil were always involved. Even then you could see it. Steve always wanted to become a lead guitar player and felt a loss of prestige or love or whatever it was from the audience because of Neil's lead guitar playing." No matter what Stephen did as leader, arranger, co-lead singer, and driving force behind the group, Neil's dark, brooding image and staccato lead guitar lines as well as Richie's cute, energetic stage presence drew much of the focus away from him. "Stephen always wanted to be a star," speculates Nurit Wilde, "and I think that was the difference between him and Neil. Neil's more of a serious artist, not that he didn't want to be a well-known musician, but that was primary on Stephen's list, more so than Neil. Neil wanted the same thing as Stephen but was more subtle about it, whereas with Stephen it was hanging on his sleeve. You knew about it. He always wanted to hang with people who were stars and was awed by other rockers who had big names. Stephen's a very talented guy but he was dying to be a rock'n'roll star." As Richie observes, "Neil obviously came to LA with this vision of his own personal success. So when those kinds of influences start to get to you, you start believing your press, believing what people are saying about you. 'Yeah, I am the guy, I am the most important part of the band.' When that happens you get a false impression of your importance. It went to our heads, there's no doubt about it."

In the midst of their six-week Whisky stand, the group made the startling move of ditching Barry Friedman as their manager. Pitched by several high profile handlers, including The Byrds' Dickson and Tickner, the five members were dazzled by two of the greatest hucksters Hollywood had ever seen, Charlie Greene and Brian Stone. As managers of Sonny and Cher, Greene-Stone had shepherded the duo to the top by early 1966 before losing them. With a stable that included rock groups the Daily Flash and The Poor as well as *Elusive Butterfly* singer-songwriter Bob Lind, Charlie and Brian were on the lookout for rising new talent when they ventured into the Whisky in late May.

"The LA music scene at that time was sensational," recalls Charlie, "a lot of good music, and there were some standouts like the Springfield. They weren't The Doors or Iron Butterfly, they were sensational. The Whisky was the place at that time. Everybody hung out at the Whisky, playing for beers or bullshit money. Everybody knew each other and played with each other. There was a real sense of community. The motivation was the music not the dollar. It was a delicious time."

Why would the group turn its back on the man that virtually gave birth to them? It's a point that still bewilders Barry, though Richie puts the decision into perspective. "We had stars in our eyes, and Greene and Stone were the big time. Barry Friedman, who the heck was he? That's how we felt then. I feel badly now about that but we probably didn't know any better. We saw Greene and Stone as our vehicle and probably didn't think twice about Barry. We were looking around trying to get anyone that we could who could take us to the next level. Although Barry was a salesman back then and convinced us he could do it, we were looking for someone with a little more glamor, a little more glitz, a little more influence to move us along quickly. That was always the thing: move along, move along, fast, fast, fast. And it eventually caught up with us." Sympathizes Dewey, "Charlie and Brian aced Barry out of the band. Barry was right in there and he shouldn't have gotten stiffed."

While in New York with The Byrds during the Springfield's Whisky engagement, Barry was pressured by Charlie Greene to accept a buy out of any claims he held to the Buffalo Springfield. As Barry remembers it, "I was on the road schlepping for The Byrds and Charlie came to New York, picked me up at the hotel, got me so drunk and stoned, and drove me around in the back of this limousine. He wouldn't let me out until I signed something giving up the group. I feared for my life. He had me sign off of the band on a mustard stained napkin for $1000. I didn't see the guys after that. I regret signing that. I should have put up a fight. The band was worth it and I was chicken shit by not going ahead and telling the band that these guys were creeps. I didn't say anything and let them do what they wanted to do. I didn't think it was my place to get involved."

Dickie Davis was kept on in the role of road manager with a five percent stake in the group. "Dickie did hustle for them and served them well," offers Michael Miller. "He was smart, aggressive, talented, intelligent but he was inexperienced. Dickie was the guy who ran the lights at the Troubadour and at that point, everybody was telling the band how great they were so they did not consider Dickie to be the guy they wanted to invest their career and future to." Adds Charlie Greene, "Dickie Davis had a good ear but unfortunately didn't have the talent or the chutzpah to do anything with the group." Barry remains magnanimous in his praise for Dickie hanging in with the group after the move to Greene and Stone. "He deserved it because he was there for them. He didn't pose a threat to

Greene and Stone. Dickie was the ultimate back room operator. His degree of politeness, sophistication, and decorum throughout the whole thing was so professional. He really had it together back then. He made it all happen. He was constantly there for everybody and quietly supportive. That was an important factor in their success." No attempt was made to hold Richie and Stephen to the personal management contract they had inked with Barry and Chuck Kaye two months earlier. "Chuck was pissed off at me for selling my piece in the group," notes Barry. For a brief time Herbie Cohen, later to manage Frank Zappa and the Mothers of Invention, was involved with the group financially though his interest related to publishing. Herbie and his brother Matthew — or Mutt as he was known — ran a publishing company in New York during the heyday of the Greenwich Village folk scene, publishing many of the new, young folk artists. With the arrival of folk rock, they shifted their operations to Los Angeles. Stephen knew Herbie from New York.

"The Springfield ended up with Greene and Stone, with whom you counted your fingers after you shook hands with them," Chris Hillman comments. "Charlie and Brian whirled into town and sweet talked them. I had known them before I was even in The Byrds when I was playing bluegrass because they managed a folk-bluegrass group from Seattle. I know that Jim Dickson and Eddie Tickner did not want to manage the band, though I think the band approached them about management early on. They should have, though." Under the more astute tutelage of The Byrds' management, the Springfield story may have turned out differently.

According to Bruce, "We went to Tickner and Dickson's offices and we sat around. They had super plush offices. But for some reason we just didn't click with them. We went out for lunch afterward and said, 'Nah.' Greene and Stone had the longest Lincoln limousine in Los Angeles. But it wasn't just that. Charlie Greene was a really good talker." Stories of Charlie's notorious hustle abound. While Brian served as the business mind in the partnership, Charlie was the mouthpiece. "Charlie's a real schmoozer," smiles Nurit Wilde, who came to work for Greene and Stone at their office in Suite 408, 6725 Sunset Boulevard for a brief period. "He can be very charming but he's a scam artist. He and Brian were hustlers, especially Charlie. Brian was the quiet one, the studious bookkeeper. Charlie did most of the talking and had all the far out schemes, whereas Brian was more the voice of reason. When the pair arrived in Hollywood, they boldly walked onto a movie company lot, found a vacant office, and simply moved in. They were there a couple of months, used the office and phone lines, before being discovered. That's the kind of guys they were. The band was very naive, novices to the whole business thing. Everybody wanted to make it big and were willing to believe stories of overnight success. Charlie and Brian were good at illusions. They could spin fantasies. 'Look what we did for Sonny and Cher and we can do the same for you.' And they had a limousine with a black driver who was very cool. He would drive everybody where they wanted to go and roll joints and throw them in the back. The guys loved driving in the limo because it made them feel like rock stars. Think about it: you're young and living in some shitty pad but you're driving around in a limo."

The impact of that limousine cannot be minimized. As Richie ruefully comments, "They had a big car, that's what did it for us. Somehow Greene and Stone sweet talked somebody and off we went with them." Most hold to the view that it was Stephen who pushed for Greene and Stone. "Stephen Stills saw me driving in a limousine and said, 'I want that guy!' maintains Charlie. Miles Thomas attests, "Charlie and Brian were the best bullshit artists of all time. And the best drug store in town. They had a stretch limo and Joseph the driver who sold us our weed. In those days, the Stones or somebody might ride in a limo when they came to town, but the guys in the Springfield had that limo to use any time. And Stills always wanted to have limos and play the role."

Greene and Stone immediately set about grooming their new charges. For group members, their immediate priority was the need for equipment. The two arranged for each member to acquire whatever he needed. Neil picked up an orange Gretsch Chet Atkins model 6120, hollow body, the exact same model he had with The Squires in Winnipeg. Stephen found a blonde Guild hollow body, while Richie obtained a Gibson electric twelve-string for a fuller rhythm sound. Bruce acquired a Fender Precision bass. They all now plugged into Fender Twin and Showman amplifiers. The five were set up with credit at a variety of hip clothing shops, and cars were rented for each of them, Corvette Stingrays being the vehicle of choice, though Stephen later acquired a Ferrari. Richie, being more practical and frugal, chose a Volkswagen. Greene and Stone advanced the band $5,000, which they "kept for us and gave us," claims Dickie. "They'd rented cars for all of us. We had our rent paid. Whenever we needed money, we'd just ask for it. And we got credit anywhere we wanted it." In this sense, the Buffalo Springfield had become stars even before they had a recording contract.

P rior to signing with Greene and Stone, the Springfield had been wooed by several record companies. A bidding war quickly ensued, though the oft reported 23 offers is overstated. There weren't that many labels operating in LA then. Nevertheless, Dunhill Records, local impresario Lou Adler's own label specializing in LA-based folk rock acts like Barry McGuire, The Mamas and The Papas, and the Grass Roots, offered the group a decent though hardly staggering $5,000 advance to sign. Dickie verbally accepted on behalf of the group until Warner Brothers countered with $10,000. Elektra Records' Jac Holzman expressed serious interest as well, having expanded his stable of folk artists into rock territory with the recent signing of Love and was in the midst of signing The Doors. Once Greene and Stone came on the scene and won the group to their side, Atco, a subsidiary of New York based Atlantic Records, the premier black R'n'B label, came through with a hefty $12,000 tender that sealed the deal.

"Charlie and Brian were a one note wonder," chuckles Miles Thomas on the group's signing with Atco. "They knew Ahmet Ertegun because of Sonny and Cher and that was about it. They'd call Ahmet every other day and play him something over the speakers." So excited was Atlantic president Ahmet Ertegun that he flew his brother and business partner Nesuhi out to LA to hear the Springfield firsthand before inking the contract. "I loved the Buffalo Springfield immediately," noted Ahmet years later. "There was something about how Steve and Neil worked off of each other. And all the members became very dear to my heart." In an unprecedented move, the group did not have to submit demo tapes for consideration before signing. As Bruce recalls, "We got the Atco Records deal solely on the strength of our live performances at the Whisky. They came to us." Adds Bruce, "When I came to Los Angeles, I had 20 cents. In a matter of weeks I had $1,600." The statement was less an expression of greed than astonishment at the group's instant good fortune.

Before stepping aside, Barry Friedman had encouraged the group to give serious consideration to the Elektra offer because of that label's history of supporting its artists, nurturing their talent rather than simply exploiting it for hits. "I brought Jac Holzman in from Elektra, who offered them ten grand or something, but it wasn't enough for them. I said, 'Listen you guys, this is where you should go. You really should be with Elektra.' But they chose the sleaze brothers. Greed took over and it was a shame because had the group not been exploited and pitted against each other the way they were by Greene and Stone and Atlantic, and had gone with a label like Elektra, they would probably have achieved a lot more. But they had stars in their eyes." Dickie disagreed with Barry's recommendation: "Lenny Waronker at Warner Brothers made the best offer in my opinion, but when the band signed for personal management with Greene and Stone, Charlie and Brian turned them away from Warners towards Atco." The offer from Elektra hyped by Barry had been turned down by the group on Dickie's recommendation, which caused bitter feelings between Barry and Dickie. Barry maintains that the group recorded several demos at Capitol Records' studio in Hollywood prior to signing with anyone; however, none of the band members can corroborate that. Capitol has no record of such a session.

In a further bid to extend their control and maximize their return on investment, Charlie and Brian sold themselves to the group not only as personal managers but record producers as well. Claiming credit for Sonny and Cher's meteoric conquest of the pop charts, they convinced the naive members of the Springfield that they were personally responsible for the duo's recorded output. In reality, Sonny Bono, an experienced session man under the guiding light of none other than Phil Spector, had assumed that role in the studio. That fact that Charlie and Brian had limited experience behind the glass booth surprisingly didn't seem to come up.

Near the conclusion of their last week at the Whisky in mid- June, the group had begun recording at Gold Star Studios at Santa Monica and Vine in Hollywood, with Charlie and Brian producing along with help from Stan Ross and Doc Siegel engineering. Stan Ross, with partners David Gold (hence the name GOLD STAn Ross) and Larry Levine, had opened the studio in 1950, and although the facility had been the source of several hit recordings, including the Teddy Bears' *To Know Him Is To Love Him*, it wasn't until ex-Teddy Bear Phil Spector returned in 1960 to turn the studio into his own private gold mine that Gold Star's reputation was secured. Boy wonder Spector devised his distinctive 'wall of sound' recordings at Gold Star on such rock'n'roll classics as *Da Doo Ron Ron, Be My Baby, And Then He Kissed Me*, and the immortal *You've Lost That Lovin' Feelin'*. To create the dense sounds on those recordings, rather than relying on overdubs as is the practice today, Spector instead crammed as many as three drum kits, two bass players, six or seven guitarists, and up to four grand pianos into the moderately sized studio floor, along with a chorus of singers, all pounding away live. It was a distinctive sound that became associated with Gold Star, and soon other artists lined up to book the four track facility, including the Beach Boys who recorded *Good Vibrations* there, Herb Alpert and the Tijuana Brass, and Sonny and Cher. For this reason, Charlie and Brian steered the group to Gold Star.

In a move that reflected their internal politics as well as the rivalry already surfacing between the two principle songwriters, the decision was made by the group to go with Stephen's spritely country rocker *Go And Say Goodbye* as the A side, with Neil's moodier *Nowadays Clancy Can't Even Sing* on the flip. These were two of the first tunes the group had learned back in April. Charlie and Brian concurred. Stephen had composed *Go And Say Goodbye* when he and Richie were scuffling together at Barry's house in March, though the arrangement the group committed to tape drew on a suggestion from Chris Hillman. "That intro lick was from Salt Creek, a bluegrass instrumental," notes Chris. "Stephen and I were screwing around and I played it for him and he liked it and used it." The song had all the hallmarks of the early Buffalo Springfield sound: a clever lyric, bright tempo, and Stephen and Richie's patented unison vocal delivery over a country flavored arrangement featuring both acoustic and electric lead guitar lines. It also introduced what Richie refers to as "the Buffalo Springfield lick," a country-flavored triplet played by Neil that appears in several Springfield numbers. *Go And Say Goodbye* was a catchy number that predated country rock by several years.

Clancy revealed the other side to the Springfield sound, Neil's deeper, introspective lyric and a folk rock presentation. Richie sang *Clancy* in a sensitive, vulnerable voice, the arrangement featuring an innovative mid-song tempo change to three-four time, hypnotic guitar lines weaving around harmonies from Stephen and Neil, along with Neil on harmonica. "They had already learned it," explains Neil on the choice of Richie and Stephen as vocalists, "and they could sing it great. They were really good singers." In the group's hands, the song had been transformed into a mini masterpiece of alienation, one of the most sensitive and evocative songs to ever grace the pop music airwaves.

On July 18th, the Springfield returned to Gold Star to complete and mix their debut single. The session progressed well, despite Charlie and Brian's inexperience, though Gold Star's four tracks frustrated the group. According to Dickie's recollection of the session, "Steve had worked real hard at background harmonies for *Clancy*, but there was no room for them, which was disappointing." Richie recalls an attempt to embellish the country tones of *Go And Say Goodbye*. "We tried to get Doug Dillard to play jug on that song, but we could never get the jug in tune. So he kept drinking it to get the right pitch. He'd blow, 'Whoooo' on it and we'd say, 'No, still not right.' By the time we got the right key he was too drunk to play it."

Having laid down the two tunes, the group left Gold Star eagerly anticipating the hasty release and imminent success of *Go And Say Goodbye* a few weeks later. In the meantime, behind the scenes, Ahmet Ertegun vetoed their choice, instead ordering the record pressed with *Clancy*, not *Go And Say Goodbye*, as the A side. The group was informed that, due to heavy pressure from distributors who favored *Clancy*, their debut release had been switched. "We said fine," offers Dickie. "We were convinced it was going to be a hit, because we figured the distributors wouldn't have bothered to demand anything if they didn't think it was going to be a hit, right? Well, we were lied to a lot in those days. In the end the band was infuriated by that decision." Charlie Greene defends the last minute flip flop. "*Clancy* was a great song, fantastic. *Go And Say Goodbye* was a little too much of a shit-kicker for that time. Too country and western. But *Clancy*, unfortunately, was too sophisticated for

AM radio. It was still a year away from FM."

Charlie next set about raising the group's profile in preparation for a late July release. To do so, he managed to secure a prestigious opening slot on The Rolling Stones' Hollywood Bowl concert July 25th sponsored by KHJ radio. He and Brian had already cultivated a close relationship with the station through Sonny and Cher. Boss Radio KHJ, the top-rated AM Top Forty station in LA, would become major supporters of the Buffalo Springfield over the next two years. The station had come on the air in May of 1965 and immediately caught the Los Angeles folk rock wave, becoming actively involved in promoting the LA music scene. Ron Jacobs was program director at that time. "It was through Sonny and Cher and their management, Greene and Stone, that I got to be involved with the Buffalo Springfield," recalls Ron. "Those two guys had chutzpah. Charlie lived down at the end of our street, and being the cunning guy that he was, started building a social relationship with me which I tried to avoid because of my job at the station. So Charlie wormed his way into my life and began hyping Sonny and Cher to us. He and Brian were around the station all the time. They both had this tremendous energy. They manipulated me into putting this local band of theirs, the Buffalo Springfield, opening for the Stones. That was a favor for Charlie and Brian. We promoted the hell out of it, and I'm sure we hardly mentioned the Buffalo Springfield in the ads. The show was a sell out because the Stones were that big a draw. There was no Ticketron or anything like that, so tickets were only available through a mail-in to the station and we sold 19,000 tickets." For their opening slot, the Springfield were paid the paltry sum of $125, but money was not an issue, for they would have appeared for free in order to boost their name.

One week after the session, the group played The Rolling Stones show at the Hollywood Bowl. Introduced to 19,000 screaming Stones fans by KHJ deejay Frank Terry, the group barely stood a chance but boldly stepped out to perform four numbers for the assemblage, most of whom had no idea who they were. On a bill that included The McCoys, whose *Hang On Sloopy* and *Fever* had been huge hits, The Standells, enjoying a moderate chart run with *Dirty Water*, and the Trade Winds, who had a minor hit the previous year with *New York's A Lonely Town*, the Springfield were the unknown factor. With Neil in his fringe buckskin, Bruce sporting an Indian motif in beaded moccasins and fringed chaps, the others in neatly-trimmed suits, the Springfield nervously ran through *Go And Say Goodbye, Clancy, Sit Down I Think I Love You,* and Richie's *My Kind Of Love.* They went over reasonably well with the teenyboppers, garnering a polite mention in reviews the following day. That next day, Charlie Greene's publicity machine kicked into high gear with a press release proclaiming that television producer Nick Vanoff was so impressed with the Buffalo Springfield that he had signed them up on the spot to make an unprecedented six appearances on his ABC-TV Friday evening extravaganza *The Hollywood Palace.* Prior to the Stones show, the Springfield had their first photo session with Ivan Nagy at a variety of locations, including Laurel Canyon and on the beach under a pier. In one series of shots, the group is positioned with arms linked together in a show of solidarity as Dickie peers around a tree behind them.

On July 28th, Atco issued *Clancy* in Southern California, with national distribution to follow a few weeks later. On August 6th, *Cashbox* reviewed the record, noting that *Nowadays Clancy Can't Even Sing* is a "pulsating, folk-ish item with some inventive, unexpected melody changes." The review went on to describe the B side, *Go And Say Goodbye,* as "a fast-moving, twangy, infectious, romantic jumper." It did not, however, suggest the single had hit potential. After airing it heavily, *Clancy* entered the KHJ charts on August 24th at No. 25, where the record stalled two weeks later before dropping from sight. "Charlie was relentless in pushing the group," recalls Ron Jacobs, "and somehow he got me to put that record on. We managed to force it to No. 25 in all of its two weeks when it never even showed a glimmer on *Billboard.*" Clancy charted at No. 110 on the *Billboard* charts on August 20th before disappearing.

Though artistically innovative, heralding the arrival of a major talent, the Buffalo Springfield's vinyl debut was nonetheless a commercial stiff, perhaps because of the choice of *Clancy* for the A side. "*Clancy* was an odd choice for an AM radio single," suggests Richie, who feels the song was too ambitious for the pop charts. "It was too deep. To me, that wouldn't have been my first choice. I don't know why it was even considered for AM radio. I would have thought that *Do I Have To Come Right Out And Say It* would have been a better choice for a debut single as far as being a commercial type song, or *Sit Down*

I Think I Love You. Those two and *Go And Say Goodbye* were the most accessible songs we had." Dickie's hindsight analysis is similar. "I preferred *Go And Say Goodbye* because it was upbeat. *Clancy* wasn't an AM radio song. It was 25 seconds too long for a single and it had the word 'damn' in it. It was supposed to be the B side. So naturally it didn't get much radio play. It also came out against Los Bravos' *Black Is Black* on KHJ, and that song got all the new airplay."

"When *Clancy* bombed," Richie relates, "we all panicked and started climbing on Charlie and Brian's backs. We really began to have communication problems, and after several months we grew further and further apart. Everything happened too fast." Still, the Buffalo Springfield had managed to establish their sound in the influential LA music scene in just over 6 months time, no mean achievement. "Playing with The Rolling Stones at the Hollywood Bowl in front of twenty thousand people after only a couple of months together, we were just beside ourselves," Richie recalls. "No matter where we were on the bill, as far as we were concerned we were right up there. In the naivete of our youth, we thought we were right up there with the Beatles and Stones. Each one of those things, opening for The Byrds, playing the Whisky with people like Johnny Rivers, the Hollywood Bowl with the Stones, with every one we figured the next step was just around the corner. We truly felt we could do it."

Auditioning for the Whisky-A-Go Go, on borrowed equipment, May 1966.

Live at the Whisky-A-Go Go May 1966 (above) and October 1966 (below) with Jim Fielder on bass.

Backstage with KHJ dj Frank Terry and on stage at the Hollywood Bowl opening for The Rolling Stones, July 25, 1966.

§

FIVE

When The Dream Came

When the dream came,
I held my breath,
With my eyes closed.
I went insane,
Like a smoke-ring day,
When the wind blows.
Now I won't be back,
'Til later on,
If I do come back at all.
But you know me,
And I miss you now.

On The Way Home (Neil Young)

The late 1960s are well-known in American cultural and political history as an era of protest, inspired, on the one hand, by the ideals of a college-educated generation envisioning an "Age of Aquarius," and on the other hand, by the racial inequities of a nation still coping with the "heritage" of slavery. The mass demonstrations at the Democratic Party nomination convention in Chicago, the inner-city race riots in Detroit and Watts, the civil rights marches led by Martin Luther King until he was assassinated, and widespread student protests against the war in Vietnam were all seminal events of the era. With this spirit of protest came a desire for more liberal drug laws, sanctioning the widespread use of hallucinogens during this time among the "Aquarians," as well as widening the so-called "generation gap" between 1950s right leaning parents of the Eisenhower years and their left leaning children coming of age in the Kennedy years. The Buffalo Springfield, perhaps more than any other rock, folk, or pop band, were able to capture the spirit of this era in their music, notably in the song *For What It's Worth*.

If the first single released by the Buffalo Springfield was not a hit, their recording of *For What It's Worth* five months later in December 1966 proved to be not only commercially successful but also culturally resounding. The song eventually rose to No. 7 on the *Billboard* charts, and as the authors of the authoritative *Rock of Ages: A History of Rock'n'Roll* claim, this song was "the first explicit document of an unbridgeable generation chasm, helping to consolidate the youth movement" of the late 1960s. While the political circumstances that prompted Stephen Stills to write this quintessential protest song are specific to Los Angeles and the Sunset Strip, the cultural repercussions have transcended the event, echoing through the anti-war, anti-establishment, and civil rights movements of the past 30 years to become the soundtrack for an entire generation of political activism.

There's something happening here,
What it is ain't exactly clear.
There's a man with a gun over there,
Tellin' me I got to beware.
I think it's time we stop,
Hey, what's that sound,
Everybody look what's goin' down.

There's battle lines being drawn,
Nobody's right if everybody's wrong.
Young people speakin' their minds,
Getting so much resistance from behind. . . .

For What It's Worth (Stephen Stills)

While the band was performing in San Francisco during early November 1966, Stephen heard about a street riot that had taken place the evening of November 12th on LA's Sunset Strip in the Crescent Heights area near Pandora's Box. Tensions between the teen crowd who patronized the rock'n'roll nightclubs and the established business community along the Strip flared up. Worried over the increasing teen and hippie presence along the Strip during the evening hours which scared the adult clientele away, the supper club and otherwise establishment businesses who catered to older patrons panicked. Seeking support from the city to 'clean up the Strip,' the municipal council responded with more frequent police patrols. They further enacted anti-loitering laws and a curfew aimed directly at the young crowds. None of these measures succeeded, and the youth struck back with a boycott of Strip businesses they viewed as the enemy. Attempts by the teens to demonstrate by congregating in front of these anti-youth establishments brought out the police who waded into the assembly with truncheons. Demonstration turned to riot as the police grossly over-reacted to the poorly organized youth resistance. The incident hit all the papers, under the headline "Sunset Strip Riot."

"The first night, the cops tried to sweep the kids off the streets for violating curfew," recounts Dickie Davis, who witnessed the incident firsthand. "It wasn't a riot but the cops had to give way to the kids. So the next night 200 police showed up in a show of force. They were ready on the second night and really wailed on the kids. Then a riot took place. I was watching it all from an apartment above the Strip with David Crosby, Peter Fonda, Brandon DeWilde, and some others. The Springfield were up in San Francisco playing the Fillmore at the time. Steve heard about it on television and called me and I told him about it over the phone."

Once Stephen got wind of the encounter, he phoned Dickie back in LA for some background, then, upon returning a few days later, let his imagination do the rest. Retreating to his rented house in Topanga Canyon, he emerged the next day with *For What It's Worth*. As Stephen explains the genesis and topic of the song, "It was the first time the police acted like goons. It was a bunch of kids hanging out on the street tying up traffic. Then all of a sudden it's like the Gestapo lined up across the street. When I write about something, like the Sunset Strip riots, I'm separating myself from the whole thing. I'm an observer because I'm a songwriter and I'm here to spread the news like the minstrels of the fifteenth century. The news is that the straight world has been getting worse and worse ever since World War II. Those boys that won the world by fire were great, but now they're trying to do it again. Except they're going to lose this time 'cause the fire's too big. There's got to be an answer." Subsequently, Stephen claims he was inspired by the American troops fighting in Vietnam and wrote the song in part for them.

With this one song, Stephen Stills struck a receptive chord in the hearts of American youth, particularly on the West Coast, and created an anthem not only for a decade but an entire generation. In an ironic twist, Papa John Phillips of the Mamas and The Papas, who had become spokesmen of sorts for the LA hippies, composed *Safe In My Garden* as his own reaction to the Sunset Strip Riot, taking a much less reactionary slant to the incident than Stephen.

As with most accounts of such musical and cultural landmarks, there are conflicting opinions on the motives of the artist. Miles Thomas suggests the motivation behind the song may not have been as altruistic as appeared. "Charlie told Stephen to write that song," he asserts. "Charlie said, 'Hey, the riot on Sunset Strip got so much publicity you gotta write a song about it and get into the studio.' That's the way I remember it. I think they had a lot of songs better than that."

Dewey Martin claims to have been an eye-witness to the genesis of *For What It's Worth* and supplier of the chemically-induced medium that brought forth the song. "I was over at some girl's house and somebody had given me a grocery bag of fresh peyote. Stills was with me. So I said, 'Come on, Stephen, this is as earthy as you're gonna get, man. Forget the LSD, this is way better.' He was worried that he'd puke it up, so we went and got a quart of milk each to chase it down. So he takes a handful of it and chases it down with milk and we managed to keep it down. He took off before it came on, it was about four in the afternoon. Now when you're on that stuff you wanna visit people. I went up to see Richie at Mark Volman's. I walk in and all of a sudden, charging in with this combination of Peter Sellers and Groucho Marx walk that he had with his knees bent, comes Stills. And he says, 'Come and listen to this, I just wrote it.' He was with some girl who was the first to hear it. He had written the words out on paper and laid them down and played the song. Afterwards he said, 'What do you think of it?' And we arranged it right there. I thought it was a hit right away. So we sang it for Charlie and Brian the next day. We cut it on a Monday and it was on KHJ by Friday."

Charlie Greene lays claim to the song's title. "I was riding in my limousine, and Stephen was in the back with Brian and me. Stephen said, 'Let me play you this song for what it's worth.' And he played it and I said, 'What's the title?' He said, 'I haven't titled it yet,' and I told him, 'Yes, you have.' And he said, 'No, I haven't.' I replied, 'Yes you have, *For What It's Worth*.' That was it. Stephen was right on the money with that song and probably it's the best he ever sang then or since." Charlie credits Atlantic Records' Ahmet Ertegun with urging the inclusion of "Stop, Hey What's That Sound" in parenthesis on the single's label, a wise move given the catchy hook the chorus possessed.

Session time was hastily booked at Columbia Studios on Monday, December 5 with the group recording and mixing *For What It's Worth*, intended for rush release to capitalize on the aftermath of the riot. Ahmet urged the group to set aside other projects to get this one out. The group insisted Charlie and Brian enlist some help in producing the single. Though Stephen himself directed much of the session, Gold Star owner and engineer Stan Ross was recruited to suggest ways to better capture the Springfield's sound. With Gold Star booked that day, the group had opted for Columbia's eight-track facility but brought Stan over anyway. "I asked Stan Ross to come down," maintains Charlie, "and he suggested putting the mike inside the kick drum but Brian and I produced it."

The introductory 'bump, ba, ba-bump bump' bass drum sound was catchy and innovative and set a drum sound the group would utilize in later recordings. Dewey recalls the creation of that distinctive sound. "We were cutting it at Columbia

where The Byrds cut a lot of their hits. They had all these engineers who were all union guys, so we brought Stan Ross up from
Gold Star to oversee and produce us, but he couldn't touch
anything. Bruce and I just locked into a pattern right away. I
came up with this beat, which was basically the bass drum pattern from *Get Out Of My Life Woman*, but we weren't getting a
good sound on it. The bass drum was booming rather than
thumping. I had this RCA 44 ribbon mike on it, which would
make it boom. Then I remembered seeing Ron Bushy with Iron
Butterfly at Gazzarri's with no bass drum head on. So I said,
'Wait a minute,' and I spun the head off fast — I was on uppers
so it was twice as fast. I folded up a Fender amp cover, threw it
into the bass drum, and we got it in the first few takes once we
got that bass drum sound."

The basic track utilizing acoustic and electric guitars, bass,
and drums was laid down in a couple of takes with the vocals,
Stephen on lead with Richie and Dewey on harmony, overdubbed afterward. Neil contributed the ringing harmonic notes
played on the slowest vibrato speed. The Byrds' Jim Dickson
claims he implored Charlie not to bury the word "heat" from
the line "What a field day for the heat" under a cymbal crash in
describing the police. Charlie feared repercussions from the
law. Not wishing to waste time recording another song, an
existing track, Neil's *Do I Have To Come Right Out And Say It*, was
tagged for the flip side. By week's end radio stations all over
Southern California were airing the song.

"I had a sixth sense that *For What It's Worth* was a hit and to
go with it," asserts Bruce. "It was timely, politically correct,
but on the other hand it wasn't rock'n'roll, it didn't have a
barrage to it, but it had a simple message." Surprisingly, Richie
was less enthused with the song as their next single. "I didn't
think it was a hit, personally. I was pretty surprised. I thought
For What It's Worth was a nice song but I didn't think it was the
greatest thing I'd ever heard, nor did I think it was a Number 7
song. I felt different about it when it started climbing the charts.
'Hey, we've got a hit on our hands.' But to ask me if I thought at
the time that this was going to be the record that we would
become known for or the song that would launch our career, I
didn't hear it at the time."

Released in LA in mid-December and nationally in early
January, the single would almost top the chart on KHJ. "For

What It's Worth, which I thought the opposite of from *Clancy,"* offers KHJ's Ron Jacobs, "sounded like a great record to me right from the first notes and was truly appropriate to LA because this thing had happened two miles from the station. The record debuted on our charts three days after Christmas in 1966 and stayed on our charts for nine weeks making it to Number 2. So now they had a genuine top ten hit. And Charlie and Brian were getting totally out of control." The record peaked on *Billboard's* Hot 100 at No. 7 by March 1967 and hit the same spot in *Cash Box* on April 1, enjoying a lengthy three-month chart run that saw the single grow regionally rather than taking off with a bullet. The record faced some stiff competition that kept it from the top slot: The Beatles' double sided hit *Penny Lane / Strawberry Fields Forever,* The Turtles' *Happy Together, There's A Kind Of Hush* from Herman's Hermits, and The Mamas and The Papas' *Dedicated To The One I Love.* Nonetheless, the Buffalo Springfield had scored a bona fide hit record.

"For What It's Worth gave us recognition," Richie points out. "When we went out on stage and played that song, people knew who we were outside our little cult following in Los Angeles centered around the Whisky-A-Go Go. People knew something about the band. When a record goes Top Ten it's selling, not just being heard on the radio. Somebody's putting out money to buy it. But at the same time, the band was falling apart. Bruce ran into trouble with drugs, and Neil started getting restless."

Such restlessness had begun months earlier in August 1966 following the failure of their first single and during the recording of their first album, simply called BUFFALO SPRING-FIELD. The autumn of 1966 found the five members of the Buffalo Springfield struggling to keep their heads above water. Gigs became few and far between. Despite Charlie and Brian's best efforts to maintain the group's profile, a number of obstacles, both personal and professional, impeded their early momentum. As frustrations mounted, recriminations surfaced and fingers pointed. Yet despite these adversities, the five managed to pull together to create a standout debut album that, although failing to capture the electricity of their live show, nonetheless committed to vinyl all their creative energies to that point.

"That first Buffalo Springfield album is probably one of the classic albums of the folk rock era," suggests The Turtles' Mark Volman. Though the group would release two more albums, their first stands as the best example of the Buffalo Springfield sound and proved to be the only time the five musicians shared a common purpose in the recording studio. "The band *was* that first album, and it was never captured again," stresses Richie. "That album represented the Buffalo Springfield, the five of us together in the studio. This was the group that I remember most fondly."

In a time when hit singles remained the determining factor in a record label requesting an entire album's worth of material from an artist, the wisdom being that the presence of a hit sold the album and recouped the label's initial investment, the Springfield's contract with Atco called for the release of four albums regardless of whether they first scored a hit single. It was recognition that the group offered more than mere pop chart fodder. Despite *Clancy*'s poor showing, Atco had not lost faith in the Springfield's potential and therefore booked a block of session time for the group in mid September to produce an album in anticipation of the pre-Christmas sales rush.

Optimism ran high as the group entered Gold Star's four-track facility to lay down tracks with Charlie and Brian producing. The album largely represented their live set, and this familiarity with the material allowed the sessions to proceed quickly. As arranger, Stephen took control in the studio from the outset, though each member exerted his own input to the tracks. Having honed a distinctive sound, the five knew what they wanted to hear from the tracks and assumed Charlie and Brian could bring that sound out from them. Each of the 12 songs was well-crafted, stressing the group's signature vocals over concise, punchy arrangements that avoided instrumental meanderings. More than most albums of the period, the Springfield's debut reveals a unified group eschewing the soloist-as-focal-point approach. Overall, the album presents a positive, fresh turn in pop music.

Juxtaposing Stephen's polished, accessible, commercial songs with Neil's more cryptic, introspective, moodier numbers, the album is a creative powerhouse. "Back in the Springfield days," concedes Stephen, "Neil's lyrics were far superior to mine. His songs were like poems in a way, while I usually got straight to the point." Despite their individual writing styles, there is a homogeneity to the entire album, a sound derived from folk rock yet rooted more in the latter than the former and built around their distinctive vocal delivery. "The sound we were going for on that first album was the duet singing of Steve and Richie," confirms Dewey. That sound was effectively achieved on tracks like *Go And Say Goodbye, Sit Down I Think I Love You, Everybody's Wrong*, and *Baby Don't Scold Me*, where the two share the lead vocals.

Despite the camaraderie and unity of purpose, rivalry between Stephen and Neil caused friction in the studio. With so much riding on their debut release and knowing that the more songs each placed on the record, the greater the royalty cheque, the two jockeyed for placings on the album. "I'd never seen anything like that before," recalls Dickie on the tug of war between Stephen and Neil, "these two guys vying to get their songs on the album." Stephen's brash assertiveness throughout the sessions at Gold Star and later at Columbia Studios prompted Neil to advance his own cause, pushing to sing more of his own compositions, thus edging Richie out. As well, frustration flared up as the studio limitations of Brian and Charlie were becoming obvious as the sessions proceeded.

Michael Miller attended the sessions and found the unease palpable. "There developed a combativeness in the studio," he claims, "that was about the dominance of one voice over another. When the band started Richie was the voice. That didn't last very long. Stephen had a voice, an incredible voice not just as a harmony partner but as a solo singer. And Neil was starting to develop an audience for his voice and wanted to sing more." The success a year earlier of Bob Dylan's *Like A Rolling Stone* opened the doors for non-singers like Neil Young to be accepted. Observes Richie, "Steve and Neil were more focused in direction than I was, and that's why there was such a clash between those two." Dickie noted a marked contrast in studio demeanor between the two rivals: "Neil was fairly easy-going in the studio, whereas Stephen was in command or trying to be, exerting himself." Dewey's assessment is more blunt. "They were like two brats who had to have everything their way. Richie wasn't pushy at all. He'd just shake his head with a disgusted look and walk away."

Bruce offers a more philosophical spin to the feuding. "In a collage of people, an ensemble, there's always jostling and you've got to react. It's cause and effect. It was inertia, each guy moving ahead. In that band there was a polarity five different ways."

In the end, Stephen placed seven songs on the album to Neil's five, with Richie contributing none. "I didn't think that much about having one of my songs on the first album," he argues. "Sure, it would have been nice to have a song on the album," concedes Richie. "It would be a boast to anybody's ego but I didn't feel pushed to the side or rejected. It wasn't, 'I'm gonna leave the band if I don't get my song on the album.' I kind of saw my place as a singer not as much a songwriter at that time, though I was writing. By the time of the second album I felt, 'Yeah, I'd like to have some songs on the record.' *My Kind Of Love* and *Sad Memory* had already been written back in New York." The former, with a bridge added in LA, was recorded for inclusion on the album, going as far as appearing on an early acetate. However, in the latter days of the sessions, Neil came forward with a new composition, *Flying On The Ground Is Wrong*, and a last minute decision was made to bump Richie's track for Neil's, though Richie got the nod for lead vocals after an initial attempt by Neil proved unsatisfactory.

Granted, the decision was a wise one as *My Kind Of Love* is a rather pedestrian track when held up to the evocative *Flying On The Ground Is Wrong*, one of Neil's finest and most underrated Springfield efforts. Confirms Charlie, "We were looking to maximize the group's sound, and *Flying On The Ground Is Wrong* was just a better song than *My Kind Of Love*." The song never did appear on a Springfield album, though Richie resurrected it three years later in Poco. Acknowledges Richie, "Steve was an innovator and unique and so was Neil. I felt I was unique but I also saw myself in a complementary role, too. Yes, I saw myself as one of the three front men of the band and a leader with them but also in a role where I could complement these two who I saw as being a step in front of me, at least as far as where they wanted to go. But I felt I had talent to contribute that was equal to theirs." There was no question at that point that Stephen and Neil were far more experienced songwriters than Richie, whose star would later shine with Poco, contributing the bulk of that band's material for their first six albums. He openly acknowledges the lessons learned from his time with Stephen and Neil.

Shut out of the writing stakes, Richie assumed he would retain his role as lead singer, only to find himself passed over for two of Neil's tracks. Though he did feature on three others, including the previously recorded *Clancy*, *Burned* was one number he had pinned his hopes on. The decision to go with Neil delivering his own composition hurt. According to Dickie, "Neil wasn't singing anything but background harmonies at the time, but he started pushing more and more for lead positions in vocals, justifying it by saying, 'I wrote the song and nobody else can sing it,' although the whole idea originally had been for Richie to be the lead vocalist. So Richie was going through a hard ego blow. If he wasn't going to be the lead singer, what was his value in the group to be? Stephen had lured him out to California to be a lead singer. He wasn't much of a guitar player, nor did he write that much, so he saw that as his role. It was another blow the group never recovered from." When the time came to lay down *Burned*, Richie assumed he would get the nod as vocalist. "I wanted to sing it," claims Richie, "but obviously the lead singer was always the focal point of a song and what everybody wanted to be so Neil wanted to sing it." Both Dickie and Miles Thomas consider that decision a turning point in the group dynamic. "Things really started to unravel," confirms Miles, "and there wasn't anyone, neither producer nor manager, who they respected enough to keep them together. Nobody could have straightened out the mess." Richie remains circumspect: "I think they had me sing a couple of Neil's songs just to appease me, to keep me quiet."

Though the best of Neil Young's Buffalo Springfield work would come to be characterized by a more obtuse, introspective and less direct lyric, he, too, was skilled at pulling out of his hat the occasional straightforward love song gem such as *Do I Have To Come Right Out And Say It* and *One More Sign*, the latter recorded in demo form only to be rejected for the album. Both reveal the influence of Stephen's commercial sensibilities on Neil's writing, though his songs remained less accessible. "Neil also wrote more of your typical songs, too," Richie suggests. "But then there were some of these songs that were uniquely his, like a *Clancy* kind of song, very personal. What you got from Neil's songs was, 'This is my life.' There always was and always will be that mystique about him. You might think you know the guy but you're not sure you really know him." That Neil achieved more notoriety for his more abstract compositions served to reinforce that direction for him. *Do I Have To Come*

Right Out And Say It, however, stands out as one of his most personal of songs on the album and a track well suited to Richie's smooth vocal delivery. An early take included a lovely double-tracked acoustic guitar break that was replaced on the album by a simple piano figure from Neil.

> *Do I have to come right out and say it,*
> *Tell you that you look so fine.*
> *Do I have to come right out and ask you*
> *To be mine.*
> *If it was a game I could play it,*
> *Try to make it,*
> *But I'm losin' time.*
> *I gotta bring you in,*
> *You're overworking my mind.*

Do I Have To Come Right Out And Say It (Neil Young)

Neil's other track, *Out Of My Mind*, was written and presented to the group during the sessions with the composer as the intended vocalist. In the lyrics, Neil laments the tribulations and frustrations of success, a theme he would later mine to greater success on *Mr. Soul* and *Broken Arrow*. Plagued by personal problems, Neil found the group's lack of recognition that autumn disheartening.

> *Out of my mind,*
> *And I just can't take it anymore.*
> *Left behind,*
> *By myself and what I'm living for.*
> *All I hear are screams,*
> *From outside the limousines,*
> *That are taking me out of my mind.*

Out Of My Mind (Neil Young)

Dickie finds Neil's singing of limousines and screaming crowds perplexing. "That must have been wishful thinking on his part," he chides, "because it wasn't happening to them then. But Neil worried about that kind of thing. He was frightened of making it, scared of that kind of success. The band had the illusion of success but not the reality."

The two rockers on the album, *Leave* and *Baby Don't Scold Me*, stray from the folk rock base revealing the group absorbing current trends. Neil's staccato fuzz guitar lead on *Leave* slashes through the mix, inaugurating a unique guitar style he continues to this day. The song was a powerhouse number in their live set. *Baby Don't Scold Me* initially appeared in a more straight ahead folk rock arrangement on the early acetate with Richie's voice prominently featured on lead and Stephen in support. Apparently still a work in progress, the completed album take rearranges the number, offering the group's sole dabble in psychedelia with Neil's sustained fuzz guitar intro and an extended freak out coda beginning with a cop of the Beatles' *Day Tripper* riff before devolving into dual lead guitar interplay over random shrieking. Of note are the vocals: on the final version, Stephen is now up front with Richie relegated to support. With its manic fade out, *Baby Don't Scold Me* seems out of place among the more commercial folk rock fare.

Stephen's *Pay The Price* receives a faster gait on the album than their stage rendition due in part to a chemically-induced ambience. "Bruce and I dropped acid to go play that session," recalls Dewey. "*Pay The Price* was one of the songs we did, and if you listen to Bruce on that track he's amazing. He's really playing fast all over the frets, and I'm playing eighths — that's fast — but I made it. I looked at him and he was just glowing. Listen to it. I played it for him years later and he couldn't believe what he was doing on it." Although attention is more often focused on the front three, Bruce and Dewey hold their own throughout the album tracks and exerted their own creative input during the recording process. "I put together the bass parts I wanted, what sounded right to me, what felt right," Bruce emphasizes. "Stephen and Neil would come into the studio and lay it down. Sometimes they'd go into the studio apart from the rest of us, to work out their songs. I would then listen, oversee, and baby sit all that had to go on." Adds Dewey, "Nobody ever told me what to play, ever. They gave me complete total freedom for my drum licks. They may have suggested the tempo and that was it. After that, Bruce and I just locked in intuitively." Both provide solid backing with Bruce's adventurous bass playing counterbalancing the melodies throughout the album, adding a further dimension to the group's sound.

Several more songs were recorded during the sessions but ultimately failed to make the cut. *Neighbor Don't You Worry* was a strong live number that would have fit comfortably on the album. "That one was written in the very first batch of songs that the group had, and we recorded it for that first album," Richie confirms. "It sounded like our first record. I liked that song, and I don't know how it missed being released." *Hello I've Returned* was also attempted only to be abandoned. Stephen's acoustic ballad *So You've Got A Lover* was cut in demo form for later consideration, though it, too, remained in the can. Richie attempted a version of the song in 1973 with Poco but chose to leave it unreleased. Two of Neil's plaintiff minor key ballads, *There Goes My Babe* and *One More Sign*, were recorded as demos, though the latter was worked up in a group arrangement before being discarded.

In an effort to broaden their careers as songwriters, several tracks were intended for other artists to record. Neil laid down a take of *The Rent Is Always Due*, a song dating from his brief Toronto folk singer fling. Charlie often took Neil or Stephen into the studio on their own to record songs as demos and recalls one such session. "We did a song with Neil called *The Greatest Song On Earth*. I took Neil into a separate studio while the Buffalo were doing some overdubs with Brian in the other studio, and we cut the song with Neil playing everything. We didn't have a drum set in that studio, so he played it on his guitar case, and we miked it and it sounded like drums. It was sensational." *The Greatest Song On Earth* would later surface as *Sell Out*, one of Neil's most caustic lyrics, never to be released. Some of the above mentioned tracks appeared years later on various bootleg recordings, a fact that does not surprise Charlie. "In those days we had no fear of giving tapes to people. We weren't afraid of plagiarism and there were no bootlegs. It was the love generation."

Once the sessions shifted over to Columbia's eight-track studio in Hollywood, with Tom May engineering, the discontent that had been building at Gold Star erupted as the group realized Charlie and Brian's production deficiencies. "There was a lot of tension in the studio," Dickie recalls. "Stephen was frustrated that they weren't getting the sound he wanted and was furious when there were no tracks left for his guitar solo in one song. The group never managed to capture their powerful live show in the studio. They experimented a lot but the record sounded flat.

Charlie and Brian's production experience was so weak they couldn't take advantage of their live sound." For Bruce, the crisis came when the group listened to a preliminary mix of the album. "We finally realized they were not producers. They wanted something to do at night after the office, so it was, 'Let's be producers.' They didn't know any more about a recording studio than we did. We were terribly disappointed. By the time it was mixed and went to vinyl it was horrendous. The bass is just thud, thud, thud."

Despite impressive songwriting and musical performances, the album suffers from lackluster production resulting in an overall vapid sound. The group was devastated. "The five of us had been pretty optimistic in the studio," recalls Richie. "On our side of the studio glass, we were doing our part and enjoying the recording process. We didn't know what they were doing or not doing on the other side of the glass until we heard the mix. At first we were enamored with Greene and Stone because they had convinced us that they did know what they were doing and that we didn't know what we were doing. What did we know? We all had very limited studio experience. We figured, 'These were the guys who produced Sonny and Cher.' They were managers and probably looking to expand their career in record production at our expense even though they didn't know how to produce a band. It was all down to who could talk the fastest and say the most. That's how it worked back then."

For Stephen, the group's arranger whose musical vision had initially shaped the Springfield's sound, the disappointment was profound. "When we got to our first recording session, we went into the studio and cut this one song, the voice came over the talk-back saying, 'No, that's too long. Play it faster.' Neil and I looked at each other and said, 'We better learn how to work this shit ourselves.' From then on it was a race to see who could learn the most about making records, about electronics and engineering, the whole nine yards, because we wanted to get the records to sound more like us live. We wanted the rhythm section to sound like Motown, but we couldn't discover the tricks to get that sound."

Charlie remembers the tense atmosphere heating up several times yet remains defiantly supportive of his work on the album. "Stephen and I almost came to blows. He all of a sudden became a producer. Everybody in the band hated that album;

meanwhile that's the classic Buffalo Springfield album. It was fresh, clean. Then they started hanging out with different producers and guys who wanted to make them slick. 'You need production value,' they'd claim. Bullshit! You need the music to come out the way you wrote it. The group had a sophisticated sound but a guy in Montana could understand it also."

During these conflicts, pressure mounted from Atco to complete the album for pre-Christmas release. "We had decided Gold Star was not good for a vocal sound," notes Dickie, "so we took our four track over to Columbia and played it back on their eight track and, as a consequence, we lost a generation on nearly everything on the first album, sometimes two generations. We did some vocals there, then we did a final mix-down at Gold Star. And then we went to Columbia again, re-recording as many vocals as we could. By now, Atco was screaming: 'You have to have a November release or we can't get it out for Christmas!' They gave us two weeks. The pressure was on."

The five members were embarrassed by the final stereo mix. Balances were off from track to track, the fidelity was flat, the bass sound lost, and harmonies buried. Overall, the album lacked presence or definition. "We got a two-sided master dub of the album," Dickie continues, "and charged over to Steve Saunders' house, where there was the best sound equipment we knew about. Saunders was working for The Mamas and The Papas then, and John Phillips was there when we arrived. We put the dub on the record player, and I could have hidden for shame. Levels were so far off from one track to the next, it sounded like they were from two different albums. It was terrible."

The group begged Atco to let them redo it, even going as far as to suggest Barry Friedman be recruited to assist in re-recording several tracks. Atco refused both requests but did relent in allowing Stephen and Neil to mix the mono version, though the difference is negligible. "I would have loved to have recorded them," responds Barry, "but they never called me. The songs were there, the music was there, and the guys played well but the production was bad." "Who knows what may have happened had we had someone like George Martin to mix the pot together?" Richie postulates. "Who knows?"

Rushed out by late November, BUFFALO SPRINGFIELD garnered favorable reviews and decent, though hardly staggering, sales for a debut artist. Reviewing it in *Crawdaddy* magazine, Paul

Williams called the album "a lovely, moving experience," going on to caution, "you have to be into it. All the songs seem to sound alike, but what the Springfield seem to do is rise above the sameness, employing beautiful changes and continually fresh approaches within their particular framework." The recording quality of the album did not escape scrutiny. "As for the thinness, the production job on this lp is sadly amateurish. The bass is under-recorded, the drums misunderstood, and the guitars tend to tinkle when they want to ring." One observation of interest: "Bruce is the secret master of the group," an acknowledgement of the key role Bruce played in shaping the Springfield sound.

In the *Los Angeles Times*, Pete Johnson dubbed the Springfield a Renaissance group, noting that "their melodies are simple, almost commonplace but their musicianship is tight, and they write lyrics with more wisdom and poetry than anyone else around." He goes on to praise their sense of roots in country, folk and rock: "The streams ran through all their songs, sometimes coming together equally, other times one dominating the others." The rather partisan *TeenSet* could hardly be expected to criticize their favorites: "Like solid, the Springfield come on like a steam roller and just don't quit. Their material and performance are distinctly original and varied. *Nowadays Clancy Can't Even Sing* is the best known cut, and any further listing of titles would be arbitrary since each track is an 'A' side. Sensational album!"

The album sleeve, in a nod to teen fanzine profiles, offers a variety of adjectives to introduce each member of the group to the record-buying public at large, describing Neil as deep and dark; Bruce as mysterious and inscrutable; Dewey, sincere and generous; Richie, easy going and a true friend; Stephen as energetic, "youthful-sometimes childlike" and more prophetically stating, "Steve's the leader, but we all are."

Pressed for his thoughts on the album in a 1967 *Hit Parader* magazine interview, Neil diplomatically offered his critique: "The first album was an introduction to the fact that the group had actually been in a recording studio. That's about all that it represented. We were there! The material was more commercial than the material on our second album; however, it was recorded by our old managers who have different recording techniques than we would like to use." Nevertheless, the group learned some hard lessons from the experience and vowed to exert greater control over their recorded product in future.

Shortly after recording had begun on the album, the five members of the Springfield, along with de facto member Dickie Davis, formed an equal six-way partnership in Springalo Toones Ltd. for their songs under BMI's corporate publishing umbrella. Not wishing to be left out of the anticipated windfall despite their share as managers and producers of the album through their own York-Pala Productions Company, Charlie and Brian set up their own publishing company, Ten-East. All the songs on the album, with the exception of *Sit Down I Think I Love You* previously assigned to Screen Gems, were jointly published by Ten-East, Springalo, and Cotillion, Atlantic Records publishing arm. Any split in publishing royalties required some fairly intricate mathematics, leaving the individual writer with a fraction of the intended amount. Neil once remarked that a writing cheque due to him for $25,000 was whittled down to a mere $1,000 once all the percentages were parceled out. Springalo Toones still exists today, administered by Warner-Tamerlane Publishing, its principles being Stephen, Neil, and Richie. Brian Stone retains control of Ten East, Charlie having sold out his portion several years ago.

Despite the problems over recording their album, one positive experience for the group that September was The Big Kahuna Luau hosted by KHJ. Throughout the previous summer, the radio station had promoted its Big Kahuna contest, creating a fictitious character whose imminent arrival in LA from Hawaii was to be a cause for celebration. Each week a new wrinkle to the contest was added in which listeners took part in various gimmicks, stunts, or mail-ins, the grand prize being a ticket to the luau where the Big Kahuna would appear. For several months it was Kahuna-mania all over LA, and the Springfield, through Charlie and Brian's connection with KHJ, were enlisted to provide a theme song for the impending big event.

KHJ program director Ron Jacobs takes up the story. "Kahuna in Hawaiian is at the least a religious elder or deity. It's a term I would never have used in Hawaii because Big Kahuna is like saying The Big Archbishop or the Boisterous Bishop. It would make no sense there. But it was a great phrase so we figured we should use it. We laid out a scheme to create this character by making chapters of his life doing old fashioned radio dramas, scripts, sound effects and actors. Abandoned by his parents and raised by dolphins, he was coming to America to search for the magic jewel and on and on. We had the Bobby Fuller Four do a reworking of I Fought The Law as The Ballad Of The Big Kahuna. I found this totally crazed guy hanging around Laurel Canyon who I had known in Honolulu who had worked as a roadie for the Paul Butterfield Blues Band named Chris Varez. He could talk pigeon English so we paid him $300 a week and took him over to Western Costume and got him a cape and saber-tooth tiger teeth, beads, feathers and all this shit. We even gave away coconuts with messages on them. The way you got into the luau was to win a Big Kahuna coconut. That was your admission. We asked the guys in the Buffalo Springfield to come up with a theme song and they recorded an instrumental called *Kahuna Sunset.*"

Written by Stephen and Neil in one of their few collaborations, *Kahuna Sunset* became the background music to the radio spots for the luau. Preceded by authentic sounds of the ocean surf hitting the shores, the song opens with the spoken passage "Softly to welcome the sea . . ." then proceeds into an instrumental passage with a slight Latin motif followed by a key change and ending with another spoken passage, "Hear the peaceful storm . . . It's at the time of the beginning." Cyrus Faryar of the Modern Folk Quartet guests on the track playing wooden shells. "It was fabulous," claims Charlie Greene, who still retains the tape. The song has taken on a semi-mythical status among Neil Young and Buffalo Springfield aficionados who have speculated for years about the origins of this mystery tune. Published by the group in 1967, it has never seen the light of day.

During the fall, the Springfield played various concert venues and clubs in the LA area, and began to live the stereotypical rock musician lifestyle. On September 2nd and 3rd, they appeared at the Melodyland Theater in Anaheim, supporting British Invasion ex-patriots Chad and Jeremy along with Ian Whitcomb. Billed as a "Special Atomic Attraction," eager fans of the group were no doubt surprised at the absence of one of their beloved Buffalo. Earlier that day, Bruce had run afoul of the law, his first of several drug busts, and a temporary replacement was urgently required. Jim Fielder, from Maston and Brewer, got the call and deftly filled in. "I knew all their songs because I had watched them getting together at Barry's," states Jim who would receive a similar call a month later.

The Melodyland gig is also memorable for the fact that Neil succumbed to an epileptic seizure and had to be carried off stage mid set. "We had to stick a spoon in his mouth," relates Charlie Greene of the incident. "I had to put him in UCLA Medical Center. That's where he wrote *Mr. Soul*, in the hospital." Noting the incident in his book *Rock Odyssey*, Ian Whitcomb, unaware of Neil's affliction, assumed that the guitar player's over exuberance had gotten the better of him and had fainted. "They were heavily into the Davy Crockett frontier look," wrote Ian, "and they huffed and puffed onstage to such an extent that one of their members had to be taken off-stage on a stretcher."

Since his collapse in Albuquerque during his journey to Los Angeles, Neil had managed to keep his malady relatively secret until that fall when he experienced his first grand mal seizure that laid him out unconscious. Bruce was with him at that moment. "We were in some kind of convention. I think it was a music convention and there was something going on on stage. We were standing in a crowd of hundreds of people and Neil was beside me. Then, all of a sudden, he wasn't. He was on the ground having a seizure. It was pretty frightening." A further incident following the album sessions may have contributed to Neil's recurring epileptic episodes. One afternoon, Dickie stepped from the Whisky intending to plug the parking meter when two members of the sheriff's department pulled up to speak with him. Words were exchanged, and one of the officers pinned Dickie to his car. At that moment Neil drove up in his rented Corvette with friend Freddy Brechtel, saw Dickie in distress, and came over to check out the situation. Seeing Neil with long hair and sideburns decked out in his fringed jacket, the officers instead turned on him. "If you had long hair in 1966," relates Dickie, "the police didn't like you. There was this antagonism that existed. The police were trying to clean up the Strip because there was a growing majority of long-haired kids hanging out there. I thought they were acting irrationally at the time, but that's the way they treated long hairs." This attitude set the scene for the riot later in November. Ascertaining that Neil had several outstanding parking violations, the officers attempted to escort him in custody to the sheriff's station.

Emerging from the Whisky, Charlie Greene then entered the fray, following Neil and the sheriffs to the station. Aware that the long-haired Canadian was in the US illegally, Charlie attempted unsuccessfully to extricate Neil from the situation. With Neil physically hustled off to a cell, the sheriffs next turned on Charlie, throwing him into another cell on the pretext of traffic tickets before Brian could arrive to pay whatever was required to free both of them. "It took a few hours to get Neil out," remembers Dickie, "but when he did come out to the car I could see that he had been beaten up and had been crying. Apparently, a cop had made a comment about him being an animal, and he responded with 'Who you calling an animal, grasshopper?' The other cops left him alone in the cell with this sheriff, who beat him up pretty badly." As Charlie tells it, "When finally we got the money together and bailed everybody out, Neil came out bruised. No catastrophe but they kicked his ass, no question about it. Neil got beat up by the police. We took him to the hospital. That's when the wars against the police began. That's when they became pigs." Tests were conducted at UCLA Medical center though no serious neurological damage was diagnosed. Nevertheless, the incident left Neil physically and emotionally shaken and his bout of seizures would follow soon after Ironically, Neil's seizures ceased after the Springfield split up.

"We got pretty adroit at handling Neil's seizures," Dickie claims, recalling several instances where Neil passed out on stage during performances. "He was taking medication daily but strobe lights would trigger them and he'd collapse on stage. Richie stood nearest to him and would always grab his guitar before it hit the floor and we'd have to run over and frantically yell at them to turn off the strobe light." According to Richie, "People would accuse Neil of being on drugs when he'd have one of his epileptic seizures during a gig. If it was a part of his life, I think he quickly realized he had to be careful. He did take medication. He had a few seizures on stage. You could tell because he wasn't just getting into his playing, he was going out. So I would grab his guitar and get zapped with a shock because sometimes our grounds weren't the same. I hated when that would happen." Apparently some fans believed the seizures to be a part of the Springfield's stage act. It did attract female attention, though. "We thought he used to stage some of those whenever there was a good looking girl in the audience," snorts

Dewey rather cynically about Neil's onstage episodes. "And he'd end up with his head in her lap and a wet cloth on his head, the girl wiping his brow." Confirms Barry Friedman, "Dickie saved Neil's life when all the epilepsy business happened. Dickie was the one who nursed him back to health along with a number of neighbor ladies. I was amazed at the number of young ladies who would bring him soup. 'Eat my soup.' No, eat my soup.'"

Epilepsy, along with the failure of the group to hit it big, merely compounded Neil's frustration that autumn. Increasingly he felt alienated from the LA music scene with all its hangers-on. In a rambling letter to an old girlfriend back in Winnipeg, he poured forth his anxieties, admitting his dabbling in drugs and worrying over the pressures he felt both from management and the other members of the group. Though Stephen was the one most driven to make it, Neil, too, craved success. Not adulation — he already had that and found it spiritually wanting — but acceptance as an artist.

By November these dreams seemed remote. Their second single pulled from the debut album upon its release, Neil's own *Burned* backed by Stephen's *Everybody's Wrong*, featuring Richie and Stephen's duet vocals, failed to chart even briefly. Though a solid up tempo number, the world wasn't yet ready for Neil's voice. Many close to the group agree that the song would have been better served in Richie's capable hands. "If Richie had sung *Burned* it would have been a much bigger and better record," asserts Miles Thomas.

Bruce's drug use was another source of concern for the group. "Charlie got me out of two busts that were hilarious," smiles Bruce, relating his various run-ins with the law that fall. "They were both buy outs." The first was prior to the Melodyland gig, the second occurred on October 22nd when the Springfield made their triumphant return to the Whisky subbing for LA favorites Love. Once again Jim Fielder covered for the gig. As Dewey recalls, "Bruce was with this young girl who was under age and she had the joints and dropped them on the floorboard of his car." The police found the drugs and took Bruce in. A phone call to Charlie brought a swift response, and Bruce was out on the street. At greatest risk was the possibility of deportation given the fact that he and Neil were illegal aliens, but Charlie had the connections to pay off the right authorities.

Still, Bruce's drug intake was not yet a matter of serious concern.

In the LA music fraternity it was hip to be stoned, and psychedelics such as LSD and mescaline were fast supplanting marijuana and hashish as the drugs of choice in Southern California. "Bruce was just a happy-go-lucky guy who loved his LSD," claims Dewey. "He took it every day when he had it." According to one insider who chooses to remain anonymous, "Owsley used to give Bruce baggies full of acid, a thousand tabs of purple. Somehow he befriended Bruce so we never lacked for LSD." The five members of the Buffalo Springfield were certainly no babes in the woods when it came to the drug subculture. "Stills was getting high a lot once he started hanging out with David Crosby," the insider continues. "The Byrds were the ones who turned a lot of people on to opium, forget hash and pot. Crosby liked to get paralyzed, so I'm pretty sure Stephen did too. A lot of people thought Neil was really stoned all the time but he wasn't. He couldn't because of his epilepsy. Richie was pretty straight, the all-American boy. He smoked a little pot but not ever real seriously. Everybody in the world was smoking pot then. Dewey liked speed and alcohol. Charlie and Brian really floated the speed. 'Pop one of these, we're gonna be up all night.' Everybody was getting all the legal pills from four or five famous doctors in LA. So a lot of us were walking pill cabinets."

"I don't think drugs were a big thing for all of us, though I might have been naive at the time," comments Richie, whose initiation into the world of drugs came after moving out to Los Angeles. "For me, personally, it wasn't that big a thing. Marijuana was around, it was a part of the LA music scene. I always thought that Steve had tried it in New York. I remember when we were in New York, Gram Parsons wanted to give me a cube of acid, and I said, 'Uh oh, no way. I know better than this. I'll smoke some dope and I'll sit with you guys but I'm not taking that.' Those guys were out there for the rest of the night."

Between the completion of the sessions and release of the album, engagements remained sporadic through October and early November 1966. On the weekend of October 7th and 8th, the group shared a bill with The Turtles at the Third Eye club in Redondo Beach. A friendship immediately developed between Richie and Mark Volman, prompting Richie to move out of Dickie's house at 1331 Formosa and in with Mark and his wife on Lookout Mountain Road, where he remained until marrying Nancy in March of 1967. "Richie impressed me as a genuine person, very down to earth, not a part of the whole Hollywood scene," notes Mark. "We did a few gigs with the Springfield, and Richie needed a place to live. I had a house with three bedrooms, so I volunteered my house for him to move into. His band wasn't making any money at that point. My house cost us a hundred bucks a piece, which was nothing. And there was music happening around the house all the time. There was a small community of people, musicians we all knew like the guys from The Leaves, Jim Pons, John Beck, Billy Reinhart, a very small group of musicians who were all friends at the time." The following weekend, the group returned to the Third Eye this time alongside two new groups, The Knack and The New Generation.

As the Springfield struggled through the late summer and autumn of 1966, a plot was hatched by several members to oust drummer Dewey Martin. At times abrasive to the point of obnoxious, Dewey was wearing out his welcome in the eyes of one member, who, unbeknownst to some of the others, made overtures to recruit a replacement. The Jefferson Airplane's original drummer, Canadian Alexander 'Skip' Spence, had left the San Francisco group, replaced by Spencer Dryden, a more seasoned player. For Skip, the move was no surprise as he had never been completely content behind the skins. He was a guitar player, who, in the same manner The Byrds enlisted Michael Clarke, was assigned the role in the embryonic folk rock group on the basis of his appearance. To leader Marty Balin, Skip "looked" like a drummer. After leaving the group high and dry on an unannounced vacation to Mexico, Skip was informed on his return that his services were no longer required. It was soon after that clandestine discussions were held with Skip to join the Springfield.

Skip was brought down to LA, where he stayed with Bruce, but, fortunately for everyone involved in the affair, declined to join, instead opting to take up a rhythm guitar post in a newly forming San Francisco group, Moby Grape. Michael Miller confirms the Skip Spence story, but expresses relief that it fell through. "Skip wasn't a drummer, he was a guitar player. Skip was whacked out. He invented whacked. He just looked better than Dewey." Skip ultimately spent much of the 1980s either institutionalized or homeless. Charlie Greene remains in Dewey's corner. "Dewey was not the greatest drummer of all time; however, he was the Springfield's drummer and he did absolutely add to their sound and their personality." "Dewey was a crazy son of a gun," chuckles guitarist Jerry Miller soon to form the group Moby Grape with Skip, "but they made a wise choice because Dewey was more versatile than Skip."

"Dewey, in my mind, was always expendable," states Richie who was not a party to the Skip Spence gambit but does not deny that such a move took place. "He may not like to hear that but that's the way it was. It certainly wasn't that way with Steve, Neil, Bruce, or myself, but that was the cold, hard fact. If we could find somebody better, he'd have become the Pete Best of the band. He was always riding on whether he was going to be there or not be there. I always had a good relation-ship with Dewey while we were working, but if Steve would have come along and said, 'Okay, we're going to replace Dewey,' I'd have probably said 'Okay'. I don't know that I would have stood up and argued for him or against him." From the group's inception, Dewey was the odd man out. The last to join, the only member not a part of that infamous traffic jam meeting, older and more experienced in the music business than the others and well-connected, he never quite fit in. "The four of us hung out together in the early days," points out Richie. "Dewey wasn't always a part of it. He was definitely more social and cruising than we were."

On the weekend of November 11th to 13th, the Buffalo Springfield made their debut at San Francisco's premier venue, the Fillmore ballroom, opening for Berkeley favorites Country Joe And The Fish and Brazilian guitarist Bola Sete. Operated by the often gruff, no-nonsense promoter Bill Graham, the Fillmore had grown to become the central venue for the bur-geoning San Francisco psychedelic-acid rock scene with the Jefferson Airplane and Grateful Dead the popular local attrac-tions frequently featured. As a Los Angeles-based group with an image targeted more to the pop charts and teen magazines, the Buffalo Springfield were initially looked on by the spaced-out Frisco freaks with suspicion about their artistic integrity. San Francisco groups flaunted their defiance of the LA music machine, maintaining an aura of artistic purity. They viewed the Sunset Strip club scene as plastic. The Springfield seemed to embody all that they despised. For the group, winning approval from the discerning Bay area audiences would be no easy task.

"The first time we played the Fillmore," recalls Dickie, "we were not warmly received by the management because we were viewed as an LA song-oriented dance band. But the crowd liked them so we were asked back. That was the difference between Los Angeles and San Francisco. LA bands played to the teeny-boppers because that was the business there. People used to talk about the California sound, but there was a big difference between the two scenes." The San Francisco bands did have an impact on the Springfield's presentation. "After playing the Fillmore and Avalon in San Francisco," offers Dickie, "the group began to stretch out more on some songs."

By early 1967, San Francisco would eclipse LA for a brief time as media hype focused attention on Haight-Ashbury and the whole flower-power hippie phenomenon. Despite signing up most of the better San Francisco groups, the LA music scene never relocated northward to the Bay area and once San Francisco had been mined for whatever money could be made from its music scene, the LA-based record executives simply carried on with business as usual. Nevertheless, for some members of the Springfield, notably Stephen and Neil, cracking the San Francisco scene became an important goal, and the relationships they cultivated there would have a lasting impact on their careers, though not so for Richie.

"I never embraced the San Francisco sound, the Grateful Dead, Jefferson Airplane, Quicksilver and those bands," counters Richie, "and I don't think we were ever embraced by San Francisco. We played there, but I'm not sure we were a major attraction. I don't have a lot of fond memories of San Francisco. I didn't like the music or the town, even though the Fillmore was the happening place on the West Coast. But I was impressed with Janis Joplin. Her singing was honest and I appreciated that."

For their San Francisco stay the group rented rooms in an older Victorian style house adjacent to several members of the Jefferson Airplane in the Haight district, as Dickie recalls, "Neil and Jorma became good friends."

Following their Fillmore sets, in an effort to get their name about, the group undertook a couple of showcase spots at the Ark in Sausalito, sharing the stage with recently formed Moby Grape. They also appeared at the Gay 90's and the Fillmore's main competition, the Avalon Ballroom, run on a more authentic hippie ethic by Chet Helms, where Big Brother And The

Holding Company found a home. Moby Grape guitarist Jerry Miller recounts his time with the Springfield at the Ark: "It was this ferry boat permanently dry docked there and it was kind of halfway sideways so the dance floor was cockeyed. Some nights we'd start about ten o'clock and some nights at two o'clock. But the music would go on all night, then we'd all have a sausages and eggs breakfast. There was one night we had us, the Buffalo Springfield, Big Brother And The Holding Company, Lee Michaels, and Ramblin' Jack Elliot all there and musicians from other bands were wandering in after their gigs. So the place would be full of musicians."

During their engagement at the Ark, the Springfield and Moby Grape struck up a strange rapport. With Skip Spence already known to the group and a close friend of Bruce's, the two bands found much in common, perhaps too much in common, with the Grape even copping the same three guitar line-up to lesser success and mimicking the Springfield sound on songs like *Omaha*. "The first time I heard the Buffalo Springfield," recalls Jerry Miller, "I was sitting upstairs at the Ark and my ears perked up. I said, 'Who are these guys?' Cause we were doing the same thing. We were putting together a three guitar band with vocal harmonies and interweaving parts and that's exactly what they were doing without ever seeing them. We didn't know anybody else was doing it that way. So I went down stairs to check this band out. I thought they were a mighty fine band. We just all chummed around together and exchanged ideas. We did gigs with them at the Avalon and Fillmore." With Jerry Miller's fluid lead guitar lines, Peter Lewis's finger-picking style and Skip Spence's chunky rhythm guitar overlayed with three and four part harmonies and short, snappy three and four minute songs, the similarities were more than coincidental.

Dickie feels that Stephen resented the Grape lifting his band's format and sound. "He believed they had stolen the idea," maintains Dickie. "When he wrote *For What It's Worth*, he based part of the arrangement on Moby Grape's *Murder In My Heart For The Judge* as a kind of revenge." According to Jerry Miller, there was an affinity between Stephen's song and a number the Grape performed in their live set. "We had this song called, *Stop*," confirms Jerry, "and it kind of went 'Stop, children, can't you hear the music . . .'" Adds the Grape's Peter Lewis, "later when they came back to the Avalon, Stephen told me,

'Hey, man, we just cut this song and when we were done we realized it was two of your songs stuck together.' And it was cool. The Springfield were just really good at juggling things around. I just told him, 'Who cares?' It wasn't a case, like now, of 'I'm gonna sue your ass.' Some of my happiest memories of those days were of sitting around Bob Mosley's apartment in Mill Valley with Stephen and Neil and Richie, smokin' dope and playing each other our songs."

Critics often labeled Moby Grape more of an LA band than a stereotypical San Francisco acid group. "We were looked on as an LA type band," notes Jerry, "because we were tight and had our arrangements together and were slick, kind of opposed to the free space San Francisco regulars. We were polished and professional and would pop from one song to another. The Springfield were like that, too. The harmonies were polished. You'd see a lot of other bands and they were pretty loose but that wasn't us or the Springfield. But we were kicking ass."

Charlie and Brian expressed more than a passing interest in managing Moby Grape, who, unfortunately, were tied up with ex-Airplane svengali Matthew Katz. "Moby Grape tried to rip them off becoming the Springfield," suggests Charlie, "but it didn't work. We changed the line-up of rock'n'roll. There were no three guitars and three singers before the Springfield." When Moby Grape were officially launched in early 1967 to much hoopla and media hype, Richie claims there was some indignation on their part. "There may have been some resentment over the attention Moby Grape was getting and that we should be getting that attention. They were definitely influenced by us. *Omaha* had a Springfield sound."

One witness to their San Francisco adventure was influential music critic Ralph J. Gleason of the *San Francisco Chronicle*, who was taken with the Springfield's immense talent and exuberance. In a review of one of their performances he praised the group in general, and Stephen in particular, an event that served to buoy their flagging spirits and bestow upon the group a stamp of approval from the Bay area cognoscenti.

Charlie and Brian made the trip northward in their chauffeured limousine escorting influential LA booking agents Skip Taylor and John Hartmann, who, impressed with the group's response, actively promoted the Springfield's cause to the powerful William Morris Agency. "Skip and I were promoting

Buffalo Springfield for William Morris," recalls John Hartmann. "We went up to San Francisco just when it all was starting up there. We were stunned. We just gaped, totally in awe." Despite sending postcards of buffalo and a variety of hype, the Morris agency did not bite.

Prior to breaking for Christmas, the group returned to the Whisky for two dates preceding The Turtles' well-publicized Christmas stand at the club. Richie and Neil then flew home to be with their mothers for the holidays, though for Neil crossing back and forth over the border was risky. Still as yet unreleased in Canada, Neil brought an acetate of their debut album to play for friends in Winnipeg. The group reconvened in LA after Christmas to tape two television performances for Dick Clark, one at the Hullabaloo club on Sunset for the afternoon pop music showcase *Where The Action Is* with an air date of January 9th, and the other a performance for the prestigious *American Bandstand* airing January 21st, where host Dick Clark found the group as a whole, and Neil in particular, pleasant and engaging. Both shows featured the group miming to *For What It's Worth*. Following these the group, with Dickie Davis and Michael Miller in tow, headed off to the Big Apple to make their eastern debut, a ten-day stand at Ondine's nightclub from the end of December into early January, a high profile if rather run down venue chosen by Charlie and Brian to showcase the Springfield. They, along with Nurit Wilde, would join the group a few days later to lay down tracks for a follow-up single at New York's Atlantic Studios. The trip quickly turn into a nightmare of epic proportions that would leave the group demoralized and fractured.

Meeting with Charlie Greene (centre) and Brian Stone (bottom right) at their office.

Loading their gear on to The Ark, Sausalito, November 1966.

SIX

Hung Upside Down

Look what's happening to me,
I'm going blind, please help.
There I sat until three,
Getting further behind myself,
By myself.
And I'm hung upside down.
And I know that I'm bound to be found,
Hangin' 'round.

Hung Upside Down (Stephen Stills)

The Turtles' Mark Volman possesses an astute understanding of the machinations of the music business. His
years with The Turtles, who both suffered and succeeded
at the hands of myopic record companies and self-serving
managers, as well as his closeness to the Springfield, make him
eminently qualified to offer the benefit of his wisdom in assessing the dilemma facing the Springfield in the spring of 1967.
"Stephen was a songwriter who was capable of tapping into
what radio would play," Mark suggests. "He had a commercial
ear. He was capable of writing a song that the record company
would want to release, and he had a very strong voice in terms
of radio. The sound of the Buffalo Springfield was really Stephen
Stills' voice. Neil was kind of like Frankenstein's monster. Neil's
Mr. Soul was the first time we actually heard a voice ever on the
radio quite like that. It was really not a radio voice from what
radio had conditioned us as listeners to hear. Stephen fit more of
that pattern. He had a more soulful, bluesy, pop quality that
Neil didn't have.

"Charlie Greene and Brian Stone were picking the music,
and more often were choosing Stephen's music over Neil's in an
effort to attain what *For What It's Worth* had brought them.
Who can argue with that? After that first hit happened, the
record company was looking for the next hit and was immediately drawn to Stephen Stills because he had that radio-friend-
ly voice. And you can't fault that. If it worked once, why won't
it work again? That, I'm sure, laid the foundation for the problems between Neil and Stephen. Everybody kind of looked at
Stephen as the Buffalo Springfield, and I don't think Neil was
comfortable with that. But that's the way the Sixties was: find
the one guy to focus on. That was the blueprint that everyone
followed and the Springfield didn't fit into that. And that still
goes on today. Name me the guys in Pearl Jam other than
Eddie Vedder? If another guy sings a song, the record company
would say, 'So what!' I don't think the Springfield were able to
comprehend the record company's power and influence. Record
companies weren't really in it for the long haul. They were
made up of shoe salesmen, not visionaries who knew how to
develop talent artistically."

"All through 1967, the group was scattering, fragmenting,
breaking up, coming and going," laments Richie on the problems
that plagued the Buffalo Springfield on the heels of the success

of *For What It's Worth.* "There was never a straight line; there were so many sidebars, so many diversions, so many hurdles. For other bands that stayed together and kept on track, there was at least a straight line of momentum. It was always so frustrating. It was, 'Who are we going to get to replace Bruce, then Neil? How are we going to fix this up? How are we going to get ahead?'"

The slow fall of the Buffalo Springfield during 1967 can be attributed, perhaps, to poor management, perhaps to the bulging egos of key band members, perhaps to a peculiar form of stage fright, perhaps to the temptations of the rock'n'roll lifestyle, drugs, booze, sex. Despite these nagging and eventually debilitating problems, the Buffalo Springfield recorded their second album in 1967, BUFFALO SPRINGFIELD AGAIN, further establishing them as one of America's most creative and influential bands. During this period the peculiar genius of each of the three lead members — Stephen Stills, Neil Young, and Richie Furay — emerged, perhaps to the detriment of the band per se, but to the benefit of the history of rock'n'roll, for each singer-songwriter wrote at least one song in 1967 that could be called a masterpiece.

Following the taping for *American Bandstand* at the end of 1966, the Buffalo Springfield headed east to New York. "*For What It's Worth* opened up doors for us to play outside Los Angeles and make a little bit of money," states Richie. "Before that, we couldn't get out of Los Angeles. Now we were going out of town and out of state. But I don't have a lot of fond memories of some of those trips." As Stephen recalls, "We went to New York as a band with a reputation, and we ended up in this pretty small club for a rock'n'roll band to play in. We were all playing little bitty amplifiers to try to make it tolerable." Comments Neil, "That was when we were supposed to be making it and we bombed out in New York. We all cracked."

A combination of illness brought on by an unseasonably cold spell, frustration at the size of the venue compared to the larger rock clubs of LA, drugs, and ever increasing ego clashes, all conspired to torpedo the trip. Following a showcase gig at the legendary Night Owl Café, home of the Lovin' Spoonful, the Springfield began their ten-day stand at Ondine's. "Ondine's was a disaster from my standpoint," confirms Richie. "New York was cold and dismal, a typical winter. We were cooped up with our colds and sore throats in a suite at the Wellington Hotel. There were three rooms and seven or eight of us on beds, cots, and the floor. We were doing three long shows a night, and because of our sicknesses, it was quite hard to get it together." One night matters came to a head. "The stage at Ondine's was so tiny, we didn't have a lot of room at all," Richie continues. "Steve and I were up front, and Bruce was on the second tier. Bruce kept hitting Steve in the head with his bass. I don't think he meant to, but Bruce was just into the music and 'wham' he'd hit Steve's head. I could see Steve turn and look at him the first time. The second time, he glared at him. The third time, Steve swung around and punched him, 'Boom,' he hit him." Steve subsequently played bass for the final set that evening.

On another night, Neil succumbed to one of his seizures. "I was standing near the door to a hallway in the back where the bands could change," notes Nurit, "and I could see that Neil was having an epileptic attack coming on while he was on stage. But somehow he hung on and managed to finish the song. The minute the song was over he rushed to the back and collapsed on the cement. We put a jacket under his head and a pencil in his mouth."

One of the few bright spots came the night Dewey's hero Otis Redding stopped by to check out the group. Accompanied by Atlantic Records' president Ahmet Ertegun, Otis was just beginning to crack the white rock market after years on the chitlin circuit as the premier soul man on the R'n'B charts. Dewey managed to coax Otis on stage to join the group for *In The Midnight Hour,* singing in duet with the drummer. Other luminaries to drop by during the engagement included Mitch Ryder and members of the Rolling Stones. Michael Miller recalls that during their stay the group hung out with Jesse Colin Young and the other members of the Youngbloods who were performing at Arthur, a posh Manhattan nightclub frequented by New York's jet set. The Youngbloods lived in Greenwich Village, where Stephen and Richie managed to renew a few old acquaintances. "I came down to see them at Ondine's," recalls Jean Gurney, "and I'd never heard anything so loud in my life. I came out of this little club and my ears were ringing. But they were good."

Once Charlie and Brian arrived, the group entered the studio during the day to record. The group intended to lay down a recent composition from Neil, a rather jaded barb at the Hollywood music scene and its affect on his own psyche entitled *Hello, Mr. Soul*, penned following his hospital stay and inspired by the women who hung out at of the Whisky-A-Go Go. A rocking uptempo number and popular concert favorite derived from a standard blues guitar figure that had been the basis of The Rolling Stones' hit *Satisfaction*, the lyrics found Neil at once perplexed and cynical, musing over the changes he was experiencing with the adulation the group had accrued. Like *Out Of My Mind*, Neil directs his pen to the shallowness of stardom and his sense of alienation.

Oh hello Mr. Soul I dropped by,
To pick up a reason,
For the thought that I caught,
That my head is the event of the season.
Why in crowds, just a trace of my face,
Could seem so pleasin'.
I'll cop out to the change,
But a stranger is putting the tease on.

Mr. Soul (Neil Young)

"There were a lot of problems happening with the Springfield," Neil told Nick Kent years later on the genesis of *Mr. Soul*. "There were a lot of distractions, too. Groupies, drugs. Then there were all these other people. They were always around, giving you grass, trying to sell you hippy clothes. . . . I never knew what these people really wanted. And there were so many of 'em! Not to mention all the women . . . all the clubs, places to go, things to do. I remember being haunted by this whole obsession of, 'How do I fit in here? Do I like this?'"

"Unfortunately," remarks Richie concerning this recording session, "we were constantly having run-ins with Charlie and Brian." As Bruce concurs, "we were recording in New York for the *Mr. Soul* sessions, and halfway through the sessions we couldn't abide by Charlie and Brian's way of doing things, even though we knew nothing about production. We knew what it was supposed to sound like and what we wanted to hear. So we evicted them from the studio. It was quite a scene." Adds Dewey, "We had to give Charlie one of Neil's valiums to calm him down and get him out of there. I never saw such a heart-broken guy when he walked out." The group continued record-ing for the better part of a week while Charlie and Brian returned to LA. "That was the start of the break up of our rela-tionship with them," suggests Richie. "It seemed the best thing but it wasn't. Certainly having them around wasn't a help, but then we were left on our own with no one to help us. We lost either way."

Though Greene and Stone carried on in their capacity as the group's managers, from that point on the group members, notably Stephen and Neil, undertook production duties with the support of Ahmet Ertegun and a variety of sympathetic record-ing engineers. Subsequent recordings throughout that year, however, would continue to bear the York-Pala Productions credit and share publishing with Ten-East.

Early in the session doubts arose over Neil's decision to take the lead vocals on *Mr. Soul*. Both Stephen and Richie took a turn at recording the song. "Initially, Neil didn't consider him-self a singer compared to Stephen and Richie," Bruce explains. "Neil's voice is a voice and it isn't a voice. It's a mystery but it must hit some cerebral point in our subconscious. You can't define it." Charlie recalls Ahmet Ertegun expressing some reser-vations over the lack of commercial appeal Neil's voice pos-sessed. "Everybody fought me on Neil singing that song," he argues. "Ahmet called me aside and said, 'Hey man, Neil can't sing.' I said, 'He has something.' And Ahmet says, 'What's he got? He doesn't sing good?' And I said, 'Every girl would love to nurse him to their breast, that's what he's got. He needs love and he needs mothering.' Nobody wanted Neil to sing lead."

Even the intervention of an interested third party failed to sway Neil. "Otis Redding wanted to record it to follow-up *Satisfaction*, but Neil wouldn't let him," claims Dewey. "I had brought him to the *Mr. Soul* session in New York, and after the second take he had all the words. He took me aside and said, 'I gotta have that song, Dewey.' So I went in and talked to Neil, who was doing his whining vocal. I went up to him, he took off his earphones, and I said, 'Otis Redding is outside just chomp-ing at the bit. He wants to do *Mr. Soul*.' And Neil said, 'Tell him I'm gonna do it.' Otis was disappointed." Confirms Charlie,

"Otis Redding was standing there going, 'Man, if you guys let me, I'll record that song and do it my way.' It would have been sensational by Otis."

Through Ahmet's mediation, the track was finally completed, and although the eventual single included the York-Pala Productions credit, when the song appeared later in the year on the group's second album, the credit read, "Produced by Charlie and Brian with a little help from their friends." Mutters Charlie, "I think that was because it was the session of the fight between me and Stephen and everybody helped out after that. Now everybody wanted to be a producer."

Several other songs were attempted during the sessions, including another stab at Richie's *My Kind Of Love* and Stephen's *We'll See*, a leftover from their live set as yet unreleased and one of the last recordings to utilize Richie and Stephen's unison singing approach. From that point on, Buffalo Springfield tracks would feature solo voices.

On the last day of sessions in New York, Bruce was again arrested on drug charges, busted at the Wellington Hotel in what he maintains was a sting. This time, however, Charlie wasn't present to grease the appropriate palms, leaving Bruce to face immigration alone. The rest of the group reluctantly left Bruce behind, returning to Los Angeles to fulfill commitments.

"We were staying at the Wellington Hotel," says Bruce, recounting the details of the sordid affair that capped a disastrous New York stay. "It was so odd. I was sitting at a table at Ondine's and I met a young lady and we were talking. This fellow comes out of nowhere and sits down and starts talking. He wondered if, in fact, were we going back to the hotel because he had some marijuana. My ears perked up immediately, so I invited him back to the hotel. The young lady and I went back to the room, and this guy showed up with a brown paper bag full of marijuana. It must have been more than a pound. I thought the guy was crazy, there were only three of us. But then again it was marijuana and a lot of it so, 'Whoopee,' come on in. We proceeded to roll it up and smoke these cigar-size joints. We're in wonderland, then for some reason he has to leave. So he goes and he leaves the marijuana. Again I go, 'Wow.' But I still haven't clicked on this. The girl then goes to the restaurant to get some food, and I'm sitting in the room alone. The phone rings and it's the young lady calling from the restaurant. 'They won't let me up to the room.' Boing! I'm at the door, out of that room, because I realize I've just been set up. And there they are coming up the hall the other way, six of them, cops. So in my wisdom, I run back to the room and try to flush the stuff down the toilet. But the door didn't close, and they stick their hand in, grab the door, pull a gun and say, 'Don't do it.' So I figure, 'Okay, you got me.' At that moment, that guy shows up and the cops say, 'Whose is this?' And I say, 'It's his.' 'No, it isn't. It's his.' 'Whose room is it? 'It's mine.' The cop then goes, 'Okay, then it's your stuff.' So they take us away to the precinct. I don't see the guy again. Obviously it was a set up to get the rock guys. So I called the William Morris Agency. In comes the William Morris agent and he takes this cop into a corner and they're talking back and forth for ten to fifteen seconds. Then the arresting detective takes me into his office and lays it on the line. 'It wasn't yours but I'm sorry I can't let you walk out of here right now. You'll go before a judge in the morning, it'll be fine, don't worry about a thing.' He changed the whole circumstance. This was my first confrontation with New York City graft, the way the system works. So I figured, 'Oh, this is how it works. You pay them and they let you go.'

"I spent the night in jail and the next morning there's nobody from the band there. Not even Dickie Davis. They didn't even tell me they had left. I felt I was left high and dry. They probably figured the fix was in and I'd walk out of there. And I did, but as I did there's a tap on my shoulder and its immigration. That was a whole other payoff that hadn't been considered. 'You're here illegally blah, blah, blah. Here's the badge. You're busted. Deportation. Let's go.' So I received a voluntary deportation back to Canada, but not before spending some time in the New York house of detention."

Despite efforts by Charlie and Brian to extricate Bruce from his legal entanglements, including an attempt to smuggle him across the border, Bruce cooled his heels in Canada for the next four months while the Springfield floundered through a series of personnel shuffles, abandoned recording sessions, and missed opportunities. The band never fully recovered from the loss of an integral member at such a critical juncture. "When we started having the problems with Bruce and his immigration papers," offers Richie, "that's when the whole thing fell apart."

In the first few days following the bust, the group still

believed Bruce would soon be back in the fold. However, by the time they prepared to tape their appearance on ABC-TV's Friday night star-studded variety hour *The Hollywood Palace* on January 20th, they realized a replacement was required. Dickie Davis hastily subbed for Bruce at the taping before a live audience at the Hollywood Palace Theater on North Vine, silhouetted, his back to the audience, seated on a stool facing the other four, vamping the bass parts to a pre-recorded tape. The group edited together portions of their single of *For What It's Worth* with a tape of *Mr. Soul* from the recently completed New York sessions.

Hosted by nightclub entertainer Tony Martin, the Buffalo Springfield were introduced with the wise-crack, "In the past year, they've sold enough records and made enough money to buy all of Buffalo and half of Springfield." To a smattering of teenybopper squeals the group launched into *For What It's Worth*, Stephen front and center attired in neatly trimmed suit topped by a cowboy hat, flanked by Richie and Neil seated on Fender amps. Following a verse and chorus, the number segued into Neil's *Mr. Soul*, with Stephen duckwalking off to his left yielding center stage to Neil in a bid to introduce what they believed would be their next single. Dressed in one of his Comanche war jackets and beads, Neil proceeded to pick up the pace as the others danced about behind, Richie doing his tip-toeing routine. When the guitar solo arrived, Neil ventured over to where Dickie sat, gesturing towards him before returning to finish the song which abruptly ended with the stop of the tape. Tony Martin then rushed out to shake Dickie's hand, ignoring the other members of the group.

With a run of engagements pending, including a tour with The Seeds, an urgent call was placed to Ken Koblun, at that moment performing with folk rockers Three's A Crowd in Halifax, Nova Scotia, with a pitch to join the Springfield. Abandoning his group at the completion of their week-long run at the Brass Rail, Ken promptly flew out to Los Angeles to begin rehearsals. In the meantime, Love's bass player Ken Forssi stood in for a gig on January 22nd at Gazzarri's, newly christened the Hollywood-A-Go-Go. In a 1996 interview in *Discoveries* magazine, Forssi recalls his relationship with the Springfield. "I was kinda close to Neil Young, and singer Richie Furay. And their bass player, Bruce Palmer, was kind of a quiet guy, he'd stand in the corner and face the corner and play bass. I think he had stage fright a lot but he was a really good bass player. I used to look up to him because he really impressed me. The Springfield asked me to stand in for Bruce one night. They were playing at Gazzarri's and Bruce was out on a trip somewhere! They gave me their first album and the *For What It's Worth* single to learn in one day. I said 'Okay, I'll do it.' It went off pretty well, we all laughed about it, you know, 'What's he doin' in there?' That started a bunch of rumors, like I'd quit Love. Everybody had fun and I made a hundred bucks that night."

Why the group chose Ken Koblun over Jim Fielder, who had so ably covered for Bruce previously, remains speculative. Ken was given preference in part due to his connections with the group in its embryonic stages and the high esteem in which he was held by Neil, Stephen, and Richie. "It seemed like we didn't have any other avenues to turn to," Richie suggests, "so we went back to what was familiar. We'd tried Kenny once before back in 1966 and we knew him." The fact that Ken was unfamiliar with their repertoire, in contrast to Jim, proved not to be an obstacle. But what Ken failed to realize when the offer came through was that his services were, in fact, not considered permanent. "I thought I was joining the group," he offers, "but they thought I was just filling in." The others were not yet ready to abandon hope of Bruce's return. After furtive rehearsals, Ken debuted with the Springfield in San Francisco on January 25th at the Tempo. Two nights later he was introduced to the group's adoring Sunset Strip following at the Hullabaloo.

On January 28th, before their second of two nights at the Hullabaloo, the group played an early evening set at Rolling Hills High School in suburban Los Angeles to rapturous response. As Dickie remembers, "The group went on stage and the place came apart; the kids never stopped screaming. Everything they'd dreamed about was happening." An article on the Springfield in an LA newspaper column entitled "El Gaucho" on February 1st introduced Ken as the newest member, going on to state that *For What It's Worth* "will be very shortly followed up by an even stronger, hard-rock sound entitled *Mr. Soul.*" The announcement seemed rather premature given that *For What It's Worth* had only entered the *Billboard* and *Cash Box* charts on January 28. The same day the article appeared, the group was on a ranch in the Santa Inez Mountains north of Los Angeles taping another episode of *Where The Action Is*, where they performed minus Neil whose ongoing problems with epilepsy kept him from the taping. Miming to *Sit Down I Think I Love You*, currently riding the charts in a note for note cover version by San Francisco group The Mojo Men, Stephen and Richie duetted Everly Brothers' style, kibitzing about on acoustic guitars, with Richie vamping Neil's guitar solo, while six-foot-seven-inch Ken looked on smiling and nodding. Decked out in cowboy hats, all four were positioned around a hay wagon. The episode aired February 22nd.

Following a further engagement at the Hullabaloo and gigs in Santa Barbara and San Bernardino, the group embarked on the deceptively titled "Hollywood Cavalcade of Stars" tour, a hastily arranged package with LA garage band The Seeds, whose punkish *Pushing Too Hard* and *Mr. Farmer* had been moderate hits. Opening on February 5th at the Hollywood Palladium, the tour next stopped at the Cinnamon Cinder in Long Beach before heading out of town. Organized by aspiring impresario Tony Ferra, owner of the Red Velvet Supper Club, a noted Hollywood discotheque, the tour bill included BJ Thomas and The Triumphs, plus several lesser known artists. "The first part of the show featured one of Tony Ferra's acts," laughs Dickie, "his twelve-year-old daughter Tina who sang songs like '*You're a Dum Dum*' dressed up in cute little mod boots. He also had someone named Jimmy Velvet who'd had a cover hit on *Teen Angel*. Rudy Dee and the Skyliners who played 1956 rock'n'roll songs. And three girls called The Carousels. Rudy Dee and the Skyliners backed up everybody, and The Carousels vocally backed everybody. The second half was The Seeds and the Buffalo. Whoever turned up first going on first."

With its mismatched acts, the tour was a fiasco from the start. Piled into a decrepit bus, the package headed east to New Mexico and Texas. The Springfield had been guaranteed $2,500 a week for the three weeks out but poor turnouts at the initial stops, fewer than one third to one half full halls, threatened the viability of the whole affair. "We weren't getting paid and were driving around on a bus," recalls Richie. "We had taken off from Long Beach in the middle of the night. The shows were awful. We'd go and play these roller rinks and bowling alleys, where at some stops there'd be more people on stage than in the audience. When we reached Lubbock we weren't even sure we were going to be able to get back to Los Angeles. It was a nightmare."

"In Albuquerque, we played to about 50 percent of a large house," recalls Dickie. "And the next show, in Santa Fe, there was nobody there. A week of this and we decided to hell with it. We could be in town working for $750 to a $1,000 a night and doing television — we'd lost *The Smothers Brothers Show* because of this tour — and starting to record again. So we jumped ship in Texas. They were twelve hours late in paying us, and I said, We're not going on." Nevertheless, that final show in Lubbock proved memorable. "Lubbock, Texas loved them," continues Dickie. "People lined up 20 deep outside the club to see them. They had to put loudspeakers outside for them. When they played *For What It's Worth*, the kids went crazy and it wasn't a national hit yet. As far as I was concerned, the band was never tighter than that night in Lubbock. I still meet people who rave about that night."

When they returned to LA, the Springfield once again shuffled the deck, dealing Ken Koblun out. The group had come to the conclusion that he was not the player they once believed him to be, a surprising assessment given the stellar playing he would exhibit later in the year back with Three's A Crowd on their one and only album, CHRISTOPHER'S MOVIE MATINEE, produced by Mama Cass. Nevertheless, Ken was, as one insider points out, having a bit too much fun in the fast lane. "It must have been a real let down for him," concedes Richie. "He didn't leave much of an impression. I thought he was a really nice guy and the tallest guy I ever saw. I wondered why he was playing bass and not basketball." Dickie is more blunt. "He never fit in with the guys. He wasn't a hippie at all and he smoked cigars which offended the other guys in the group. Neil had championed him as a good bass player, but he wasn't as good as we believed. I think this bothered Neil."

The group then turned to a more familiar face, Jim Fielder. As Richie recalls, "Steve flipped out saying, 'We've gotta get Bruce back,' and yelling at Greene and Stone, 'You've gotta get him back.' So there was more confrontation with Greene and Stone because Steve was insistent that we had to have Bruce. Eventually we got Jim Fielder in. I'm sure Steve was the one who went out and got him." But not in time for a crucial television appearance. Their guest spot was rescheduled on *The Smothers Brothers Show*, with taping set for February 17th. Jim was still a member of the Mothers of Invention and had yet to serve out his notice. His unavailability necessitated another substitution. Miles Thomas received the nod this time, perched on a Fender amplifier, the neck of the bass turned sideways to obscure the fact that he had no idea what he was doing. The group mimed through *For What It's Worth*, Stephen once again in his cowboy hat, with Neil looking decidedly disinterested off to one side. On the line, "There's a man with a gun over there," the scene quickly cut to Tommy Smothers in ten gallon Stetson, gun aimed at the camera, before returning to the group obviously bemused. The Springfield also performed *Go And Say Goodbye*, in which, for a brief moment, the camera focuses directly on Miles. The show aired nine days later.

Jim Fielder made his debut with the group on February 22nd at the Valley Music Theater, where the Springfield were second billed to Peter, Paul and Mary but above The Byrds, Doors, and African trumpet player Hugh Masekela on a benefit organized by Charlie, Brian, Jim Dickson, Ed Tickner, Derek Taylor, Elmer Valentine and several prominent Sunset Strip businessmen to raise money for Sunset Strip businesses damaged during the riot crisis. Titled CAFF, Community Action for Facts and Freedom, by all accounts the next day in the papers, the Springfield provided the high point of the concert. "The most animated portion of the evening," wrote Digby Diehl in the *Los Angeles Times*, "was created by the Buffalo Springfield group which roared through tunes to the cheering delight of their fans." The timing of the engagement was not lost on Charlie, always open to any opportunity for some hype. "It just so happened that we put *For What It's Worth* out at that time," he notes ruefully. "It was coincidental but a perfect coincidence. Actually I knew what I was doing." During their set, the Springfield were joined on stage by Doug Dillard who added banjo to a new song debuted by Stephen entitled *Bluebird*. It was an impressive return to the group for Jim.

Born in Denton, Texas on October 4th, 1947 but raised in Anaheim, California from age seven, Jim Fielder was only 19 when he joined the Springfield. His stint with the Mothers had not proved satisfying, so when the Springfield came calling, Jim jumped ship. "I wasn't playing bass, which was the reason I left," states Jim. "They had me playing electric twelve string guitar. It was a great musical experience but not much business-wise. It wasn't what I wanted to do. When the offer came through from the Springfield, I took it because I wanted to play bass. I had always been very close to them through the Maston and Brewer and Barry Friedman connections. Also that's kind of the way it was in LA in those days. All the musicians knew one another and hung out together. Dewey approached me because I was the logical choice. I was in town, available, I knew the guys and their material. All I needed was a haircut, going from being a Mother to a Springfield. I just had a feeling I was out with a bunch of winners. I felt that from the first time I saw them that something was going to happen for them. I just thought, 'Here's a band with great music, great vocals, and the most lovable looking group since the Beatles.' I figured there was no way they weren't going to make it big. As far as I was concerned it was just great fun. We were being the Beatles.''

From his vantage point both outside and inside the group, Jim Fielder offers his assessment of each member and the dynamics of their relationships that spring. "Dewey was Mr. Wildman, balls to the wall, pedal to the metal, the kind that typically become drummers. Richie was a good, honest great-hearted person. What a wonderful voice! He was always up and laughing about things. Probably in the long run he was the glue that held that group together. Stills and Young were always at each other's throats. That was the main play for power. Richie just kind of sat back and watched things go down and Dewey played the clown. Neil was the dark one, the brooding genius, but I found him pretty accessible. He and I got along fairly well and hung out because he was just across the hollow from me in Laurel Canyon in a little shack. Stephen, on the other hand, scared me, still does in a way. You never knew what that guy was thinking. He's strictly in life for himself and if it benefits you coincidently, that's great, but if what benefits him is going to hurt you, he's not going to think twice about it.''

On the financial stakes, Jim was given equal status in the split of gig money though he did not share in Springalo Toones or recording royalties. "All the funds from the gigs went into a common account," he notes, "and expenses were paid from that. What was left was split up between the five of us. At the time it was pretty good money. I was young, single, no obligations. The others had houses on the strength of what they were making." Those homes — Richie and Neil living in hip Laurel Canyon, with Stephen and Dewey sharing a comfortable

Malibu beach house — were merely rented and the group was still living week to week and carrying a debt load to Atco and Greene and Stone. "The band was making shit for money," asserts Miles Thomas, "small time stuff. They never made any money. They were playing clubs or opening act for someone else. Even the Malibu house, Stills was living beyond his means but he always had to. Neil had a Corvette, Bruce had a Stingray and a Triumph Bonneville motorcycle, Steve had a Ferrari. But it was all rented. Richie and I both drove Volkswagens." With writing royalties providing him with a larger slice of the pie especially after *For What It's Worth*, Stephen's wallet was considerably heavier than the others.

Meanwhile, Atco decided to add *For What It's Worth* to the next pressing of the Springfield's first album, deleting *Baby Don't Scold Me*, and adding a sticker to the front cover proclaiming the inclusion of their hit. (The first pressing has since become a valued collector's item.) Besides boosting album sales significantly, upwards of 150,000 more over the next few months, the addition of *For What It's Worth* further served to illustrate the growing sophistication of the group when held up to the existing album tracks, revealing the band fast outgrowing its folk rock roots. Adding *For What It's Worth* also pointed out the weaknesses in the album's production when juxtaposed with a quality recorded track. The band's sound and approach had matured significantly by early 1967.

By now Atco was waffling on releasing *Mr. Soul* on the heels of *For What It's Worth*. Recorded with the specific intent of becoming the follow-up release and touted several times in the media as such, with the group performing it on the Hollywood Palace knowing the show would air in the spring coinciding with its release, *Mr. Soul* never appeared as an A side single. When it did finally come out on vinyl, it was as a B side to Stephen's *Bluebird*, a full six months after the *Mr. Soul* sessions.

The song appeared to be well-suited as a follow-up for a number of reasons. "I thought *Mr. Soul* was a good choice," suggests Richie, "because it had a little Rolling Stones type riff to it. It had a good audience response live." As a hard rock song, it offered a significant change of pace and it featured Neil's distinctive lead vocals. In an interview in *Hit Parader* later that year, Stephen addressed the delay in following their hit. "After *For What It's Worth*, there was a six-month gap of nothing until

Bluebird came out at the beginning of the summer of 1967. We were hassling amongst ourselves as to what to do next because what to do next had suddenly become very important. We became scared; we didn't want to blow it. We didn't want to do another song like *For What It's Worth*. We didn't want to be a protest group. That's really a cop out and I hate that. To sit there and say, 'I don't like this and I don't like that' is just stupid." Clearly, the group had much to lose in their choice of follow up. As well, Atco's money was on Stephen, not Neil.

Richie had more pressing matters than hit singles on his mind that spring. On March 4th, he and Nancy Jennings were married in a ceremony covered by the pop music magazines and attended by the group members and other celebrities. Though they had planned a June wedding, an uncertain tour schedule and time on their hands after bailing out of The Seeds fiasco forced Richie to move up the date to March. Nancy's mother managed to pull it all together on a mere two weeks notice. Richie's mom flew out and met Nancy for the first time. Barely two weeks into the group, Jim Fielder's first official publicity photo with the Springfield came posing together in the wedding party. For the occasion, Charlie and Brian lent the couple their limousine, only to send them a bill a month later. Dewey served as best man and Neil left his war jackets at home. "I told Neil, 'Don't wear your fringe to the wedding.' He always wore fringes, but he said, 'Okay.' So he came in a Confederate army uniform. What a guy! Peter Noone was at our wedding, too. Everything was falling apart with the band but for me it was, 'Man, I've got my girl,'" laughs Richie. "We got married and the next day we played the *Go* show, and Neil wore his Confederate outfit again." The newlyweds postponed their honeymoon to allow Richie to fulfill commitments with the group. After continuing on at Mark Volman's for a few more weeks, the Furay's rented a cozy stone cottage on the corner of Laurel Canyon Boulevard.

Hosted by actor Ryan O'Neal and including Herman's Hermits, Noel Harrison, Brian Hyland and the Jokers, The Swingin' Six, crooner Rudy Vallee, along with advice columnist Abigail Van Buren, *Go* was ABC-TV's bid for the teen market. On the show, the Springfield played *Go And Say Goodbye*, each member elevated on individual risers with Jim sporting a short hair cut and playing his Hofner Beatle bass while Neil staked out the background behind Stephen, decked out in his Confederate outfit. The show aired April 23rd. "We did a lot of TV stuff during my time with the group," recalls Jim. "They were still working on the strength of their one hit." Indeed the group made appearances on the *Della Reese Show, Shebang,* a local LA pop music vehicle hosted by Casey Kasem, and even performed for Dean Martin. Confirms Richie, "We went out and played at Dean Martin's house and Steve McQueen's house for private functions. We played anywhere, even high schools. I met the guys in the Nitty Gritty Dirt Band playing a high school together. Jimmy Ibbotson and I became pretty good friends." At Steve McQueen's, Dewey beat Paul Newman, fresh from his starring role in *The Hustler,* in a game of pool.

Throughout March and April, the Springfield remained active up and down the West Coast, starting off on March 10th playing Rollarena in San Leandro, followed by the Longshoreman's Hall in San Francisco, then a week in the Pacific Northwest based out of Seattle, performing there with Paul Revere and the Raiders and The Seeds on March 21st, venturing as far afield as Corvallis, Oregon to play the Second City club two nights later. "We worked the Seattle area for a week playing skating rinks and auditoriums," recalls Jim. "It was kind of Dewey's big homecoming because he had been up there with Sir Raleigh and the Coupons. The significant thing about those gigs was that the Springfield were headlining, they were our own gigs and they were outside Southern California." The Springfield played the Bay area several times throughout April, including a benefit for St. Ignatius High at the University of San Francisco with the Jefferson Airplane, the Rock Garden, the University of California campus in Davis alongside Moby Grape, and the Fillmore the weekend of April 28th to 30th with the Steve Miller Band.

In the midst of that three night stand, the group returned to LA for a late afternoon set at the Hollywood Bowl in a concert sponsored by KHJ to benefit the United Negro College Fund. Included on the bill were The Supremes, Johnny Rivers, Brenda Holloway, the Fifth Dimension, and The Seeds. Following a brief set, the Springfield boarded a private plane to rush back up to the Fillmore. Jim Fielder recalls that flight vividly. "We did about a 20 or 30 minute set, grabbed our instruments, ran off stage into a limousine, and drove out to Van Nuys Airport to Frank Sinatra's private Lear Jet 23. It was a maximum performance takeoff, straight up. It was so straight up that when you get to the top of the climb they can't just push the nose level because you'd go weightless. They have to go into a 90 degree bank in a race track circle. It was amazing. So we landed at San Francisco where a limo was waiting on the tarmac to meet us, then race to the Fillmore where a second set of gear was set up for us. We came in with just our guitars. We get to the Fillmore just as the act before us was going off stage. Bill Graham was blown away that we pulled this off and actually made the gig. So he went up onstage and introduced us with, 'Ladies and gentleman, the charter members of the hippy jet set, the Buffalo Springfield.' We came on and the place just went nuts. That was a day to remember." Dewey is less enthused about the double booking citing the fact that after paying for the Lear Jet and limousines both ways, each member cleared a mere $13.50 apiece.

In early May, the Springfield undertook a Midwestern tour through Illinois, Iowa, and Indiana in the company of friends The Turtles. Commencing at the Western Illinois University at Macomb, the tour played such locales as Des Moines, Algonquin, Fort Wayne, Decatur, Evansville, and Gary, concluding in Moline, Illinois three weeks later. The two groups remained based out of Chicago during the week, traveling from there to perform on the weekends. "We toured together," recalls Mark Volman, "because we were lumped together as a California sound. Both groups fit that California angst, which represented to the public a kind of teenage rebellion with no idea what they were rebelling against in songs like *It Ain't Me Babe, Let Me Be*, and *For What It's Worth*." Boredom soon set in with the result that Stephen and Neil took to flying back and forth to LA to record during the off time, Neil working with Jack Nitzsche and Stephen beginning work on a new song with The Byrds' David Crosby entitled *Rock And Roll Woman*. The others couldn't afford such extravagance and remained cooped up in their hotels. "I don't ever remember seeing the guys in the Buffalo Springfield really having fun as a group," observes Mark. "They never seemed happy. In The Turtles we were still teenagers and they were already in their twenties. We were just excited about being there and they were already becoming disillusioned. I'm not sure that Stephen and Neil really ever had fun in that group. A lot of that was borne on them with the songwriting weight, everyone counting on them to come up with songs."

Comments Miles Thomas, "I don't remember them as guys who would hang together. The Turtles were a family but by the time I came to work with the Springfield they didn't hang out together. After the show it was every man for himself."

The Springfield remained the darlings of the California teen magazines, even if they were no hits in the MidWest. In several issues of *Teenset*, the group was featured in the gossip columns, participating in the magazine's celebrity kite flying party, croquet match, and scavenger hunt, along with Chad and Jeremy, various Beach Boys and Raiders, even gracing advertisements for TeenSet, a brand of pants, and Yardley toiletry products. *Tiger Beat* and *Teen Screen* championed the Springfield in several features. Though Richie remained the favorite in the cute category and Dewey was "the one the girls can count on for a hearty hello and a big hug," it is perhaps odd to imagine Neil as a pinup favorite, though he rated considerable teen attention and fanzine ink. In one feature, wherein our heroes identify their likes and dislikes, Neil revealed he would like to have dinner with Johnny Mathis, then went on to describe his dream girl as a combination of "summer, Winnipeg, short blonde hair, November 11th, Toronto, Falcon Lake, holidays, trees, wind and rain," qualities that fit an old flame back in his home town.

Still, the Springfield continued to suffer from a lack of recognition outside Southern California. "They had pockets of support around the country," Dickie suggests, "but they never broke out nation-wide. They did not get a great response when they played in Chicago but went over extremely well in the suburbs and surrounding areas where people lined up to see them." Charlie and Brian continued to strike out in their efforts to place the group on a major tour. Returning to Los Angeles near the end of May, the group was heartened with a knock on the door at Stephen's Malibu beach house. Bruce was back. Sporting short hair and a briefcase, he had conned his way across the border and made it to LA to resume his post in the group.

Jim Fielder was then informed that his services were no longer required, as he recalls. "Stephen had kind of led me to believe I was joining on a permanent basis. I think they never expected Bruce to come back into the country, but when he did illegally, Stephen welcomed him back with open arms. That was it for me. I kind of knew he wasn't happy with me. But I found out in the coldest possible way. We had a booking to go to on the road and we were in LA with a few days off before going to the gig. I didn't hear from anyone, didn't hear from the office, didn't hear from the guys in the group. The night before we were supposed to leave I phoned Stephen and asked what's the flight information, who's picking me up, and all that. And Stephen said, 'Well, a funny thing happened. Bruce came back so we gave the job back to him. Thanks very much. Bye.' That was it. There I was in my big house up in Laurel Canyon. Fortunately I hadn't been able to buy any furniture. I was lease optioning it so that was the end of that."

Michael Miller feels Jim never had a chance with Stephen. "Jimmy Fielder was a good player and had all the chops in the world, but Stephen never liked Jimmy's sense of time. Stephen was looking for feel, something punchy, he wanted to hear it and feel it, somebody to play accents off of." One associate suggests a spiritual bond existed between Stephen and Bruce that transcended mere musicianship. "It was as if those two had known each other in a previous life, an intuitiveness or connection, like they were made to play together." With Bruce's return, the five were once again reunited and ready to move ahead. The lengthy period of instability seemed behind them now. "All the bass players we had were all fine players," offers Dewey, reflecting on their four months of limbo with a variety of players, "but none of them had what Bruce had. It would probably take a hundred players to maybe find what Bruce had, maybe. Jim Fielder could play every lick; musically he was a fine musician and a very nice man. But nobody had the fluidity of Bruce and knew when and what to play." For Richie, the family was back together. "Jimmy never fit in. Once you have a family, no matter how funky that family is, it's still the family. And when somebody else comes in, they're not family. No matter what they do or how nice or good they are, it is very hard to get someone to replace one of the family. No matter how dysfunctional we were, that was our family — Dewey, Bruce, Neil, Steve, and I."

On the eve of an important trip east near the end of May for a series of engagements topped off with a prestigious guest spot on Johnny Carson's *Tonight Show* in New York, where the group would be seen by tens of millions, the reunited family was rocked once again. Neil called a meeting to announce he was leaving the group. Suggests Richie, "Something transpired during those dates in Illinois that set the whole thing up for Neil to disappear. He was back in LA working with Jack Nitzsche. That was Neil always having that mindset of 'Neil Young, the solo artist, I'm bigger than the whole.'"

P laying San Francisco that spring made an impact on the group's style and presentation. Noted for their tight, concise arrangements, the influence of Bay area groups like the Grateful Dead, Quicksilver Messenger Service, and Jefferson Airplane resulted in the Springfield stretching out more on stage during several numbers in an attempt to appeal to that particular audience. "After San Francisco," observes Miles, "some songs became longer with extended solos and dueling screaming guitars." With jamming and lengthy meandering guitar trips de rigeur for Frisco groups, Stephen took that as his cue to challenge Neil for the lead guitar slot. Always learning, a keen student of guitar, Stephen had developed into a more than capable lead player by mid 1967 and elbowed Neil for space. The emergence simultaneously in Britain and San Francisco of the lead guitarist as focal point in a rock group had a profound affect on the Springfield. No longer was that role simply a complementary adjunct to the lead vocalist, such as the case with the Beatles, Rolling Stones, and other British Invasion groups.

The role of lead guitarist had now become coveted, having in many instances supplanted the lead singer as the object of attention and adulation by adoring young fans. With this increased prominence came the featured guitar solo, the vehicle by which the guitar hero stepped front and center to shower the audience with lengthy riffs, notes, phrases, and orgasmic crescendos. Eric Clapton's ascendancy with Cream's 20-minute plus guitar excursions heralded the arrival of the lead guitar soloist as demi-god. By the summer of 1967 following his dazzling American debut at the Monterey Pop Festival, Jimi Hendrix accepted the mantle and took the role to dizzying heights. It's no surprise, then, that Stephen came to idolize these two musicians that summer. For Neil and Stephen, there was a lot to be gained in terms of ego and admiration from staking claim to the lead guitar slot. Neil had assumed that position early on, taking a back seat to Stephen's upfront role in the group as arranger and co-lead singer with Richie. Now that the lead guitar had emerged as a driving force in a band's success, Stephen, too, sought to bask in that light.

"That's where things like the extended jamming came out of because that wasn't part of our natural style or original sound," suggests Richie, who found the lengthy soloing less appealing. "Steve and Neil would be screaming guitars back and forth dueling away and I'd be standing there going 'chinka chinka chink' on my guitar for 20 minutes." Dewey recalls a memorable guitar duel between Stephen and Neil. "Things got pretty hot on stage and when Neil and Stephen got into the dressing room they started swinging at each other with their guitars. It was like two old ladies going at each other with their purses." Nancy Furay witnessed the two protaganists throwing chairs at one another backstage following a particularly fierce performance.

Earlier that spring, in an effort to accumulate tracks for a second album Ahmet Ertegun came out to Los Angeles to supervise a number of recording sessions sandwiched between engagements. Shuttling between Gold Star, Columbia, and Sunset Sound Recorders studios, the band managed to record a variety of tracks, but most ended up as either discards, fragments, or demos. Their unresolved bass position often prevented the group from recording as a unit. Ken Koblun's tenure was far too brief to allow for any recording time, but Jim Fielder did manage a couple of sessions, though only one completed track ultimately surfaced months later. Studio musician Bobby West, whose previous credits included The United States of America and The Mothers Of Invention, guested on bass on several sessions, as did New Orleans piano wiz Mac Rebennack, later to become more notorious as Dr. John The Night Tripper. While recording his debut GRIS GRIS album for Atlantic Records at Gold Star, Mac was recruited to lend an authentic New Orleans piano feel to Neil's *Down To The Wire*, though the good doctor later commented that he found his Springfield experience less than satisfying. Even Dewey discovered he was expendable as Jesse Hill assumed the drum stool for at least one session.

Between February and early May of 1967, under Amnet Ertegun's aegis, tracks recorded in one form or another included Richie's *Who's The Next Fool* (later recorded by Poco in 1970 as *I Guess You Made It*) and *No Sun Today; Sell Out* and *Down To The Wire* from Neil; and Stephen's *Come On Lover, Everydays, Pretty Girl Why,* and *Bluebird*. In an unusual move, the Springfield attempted a song by Greenwich Village performer Eric Eisner entitled *No Sun Today* as well as backing an unidentified singer for a demo session. A further attempt at *Mr. Soul* on April 8th yielded a different lead guitar track over the original New York recording. This would become the version released on the AGAIN album later in the year.

Many of these songs are often cited by Springfield aficionados as proposed tracks for an album supposedly to be called "Stampede," which was rumored for release that spring. The "Stampede" story, much like the Beach Boys' legendary "Smile" album, has grown to near mythical proportions over the decades with amateur musicologists poring over song lists and speculating on possible tracks. Though Atco had a follow-up album in mind and assigned a catalog number to the anticipated album, going as far as to print up a sleeve, there was, in fact, no "Stampede" album ever planned by the group themselves. True, they were recording that spring, albeit sporadically with or without several members, but not with the specific goal in mind of a definite album. "At that time, recording was a way of killing time while we figured out what to do," offers Richie. "*For What It's Worth* was still climbing, but we didn't have Bruce, so we had to do something. We had a lot of songs and there was a lot of experimenting with other musicians that all started then. It was, 'Let's not tell Dewey' or 'Let's use Bobby West.' It was probably a way of biding our time until the lineup sorted out. We had some gigs to fill but we didn't have a major tour booked." Confirms Richie, "There wasn't a "Stampede" album but a cover photo was shot for a follow-up album. The cuts that are attributed to a "Stampede" album were just tracks we had cut or going to be cut over several months." In the 1970s, a well-circulated "Stampede" bootleg purporting to be the real thing was, in reality, merely composed of several outtakes from the debut album and New York sessions, two tracks entitled "Raga #1" and "Raga #2" comprised of aimless studio noodlings by Dewey, Neil, Stephen, Richie, and the Nitty Gritty Dirt Band's Bruce Kunkel, plus an obscure live recording dating from the summer of 1967 that does not include Neil.

Nonetheless, Atco went ahead and printed up a sleeve using an existing photo shoot of the group up in the Hollywood Hills posed around a western corral. The less than flattering photo, minus Bruce with Dickie seated out front, a large hat obscuring his face, first appeared in a January 1967 *TeenSet* magazine feature on the group. Given the western motif and the group's name, Atco chose "Stampede" as the title, lettering it in stars and stripes. Close to one hundred thousand of these sleeves were printed in anticipation of the album, only to be given away as promotional items later that fall after the official release of their second album, BUFFALO SPRINGFIELD AGAIN, which was assigned the catalog number originally intended for "Stampede," 33-226.

Of those various tracks, *Down To The Wire* has drawn the most attention. Ultimately released on Neil's triple album compilation DECADE in 1977, the song was cut with Stephen, Bobby West, Jesse Hill, and Mac Rebennack. "It has multi guitar overdubs by Stills and I," writes Neil in the DECADE liner notes. "Steve and I put our hearts into this one." A bootleg version featuring Stephen has surfaced. Richie claims he, too, recorded a take of it with the intention of selecting a suitable vocalist. But like *Mr. Soul*, Neil chose to stick with his own version. "*Down To The Wire* was originally recorded with Stephen singing," maintains Charlie Greene. "We cut that at Columbia Studios in the spring of 1967 with Tom May as engineer. Neil recorded *Sell Out* by himself," continues Charlie. "Brian and I recorded it." Charlie claims possession of the tape.

Sell Out was recorded as a demo and offers one of Neil's most vitriolic lyrics.

> *Overfed, pre-med, outfront gas pump,*
> *Will you fix my car?*
> *Dig yourself when I smile at you,*
> *Maybe I'm a star.*
> *Turned on, tuned in, drop out, sell out,*
> *Do you know who you are?*
> *I took the time to try to fit you in,*
> *Was I off too far?*
> *Drop out, sell out,*
> *Do you know who you are?*
>
> *Sell Out* (Neil Young)

During this same period, Neil was introduced to noted arranger and producer Jack Nitzsche, a longtime veteran of the LA music scene who had learned his craft at the feet of none other than Phil Spector. Jack had impressive credentials, having worked with Gary Lewis and the Playboys, Jackie DeShannon, The Righteous Brothers, Tim Buckley, and The Rolling Stones, among others. As a devoted Spector disciple, he was an adherent to the "wall of sound" technique of recording, and taught the technique to Neil. Neil was a willing pupil, eager to expand his studio expertise in order to translate more effectively the ideas he heard in his head to record. Neil decided to allow Jack to assist him in the production of his own tracks for the Buffalo Springfield. That this arrangement should take place is hardly surprising given the fact that the group was rarely recording as a unit any more, and Stephen and Neil now exercised complete control over their own individual recorded product. To enlist the help of a luminary such as Jack seemed satisfactory to the others who likely had no say anyway given Neil's headstrong attitude and growing streak of independence.

"I was aware that Neil was recording with Jack Nitzsche," confirms Jim Fielder. "As a matter of fact, I was there at one of the initial meetings between Neil and Jack. I was hanging out with Neil that day and he said, 'I've got to go up and see Jack Nitzsche, do you wanna come along?' So I tagged along. They spent several hours at a piano just going over ideas. That was their first meeting. The intention at that point was that they were going to do recordings for the Springfield." Beginning on May 6 and carrying on in fits and starts throughout the summer, Neil and Jack would cut pieces of several tracks, including *Whiskey Boot Hill, Slowly Burning, Ashes On The Floor*, and *Expecting To Fly* with the intention, at least initially, of bringing these to the next Springfield album.

Of his mentor, Neil would say later that year, "He turned me on to a lot of things that I'd forgotten had happened. He taught me a lot about how to record drums and make them sound airy rather than biting. In some of my songs it's better to have the drums sound less like a percussion instrument and more like a sound effect." The two set about recording a body of music at Gold Star Studios light years away from the Springfield's brand of rock. Notes musicologist Pete Doggett, "Nitzsche's forte was orchestral arrangements and his collaborations with Young were lush and ambitious." Regrettably, most of it would never see the light of day, though *Whiskey Boot Hill* appeared as part of the *Country Girl* medley on Crosby,

Stills, Nash and Young's DEJA VU album three years later.

Stephen, too, was busy that spring on his own meisterwerk, *Ballad Of The Bluebird*, that would embody, in his own words, "an Appalachian ballad feeling in the lyrics. I wanted it to start as a rock'n'roll song and slowly develop into what it really is, which it does in the third verse when the banjo comes in. That's the kind of music I started out doing in the Village in little bitty coffeehouses, passing the hat."

Incorporating marvelously crystal clear country-style acoustic guitar flat picking and bluegrass banjo wedded to a rock'n'roll arrangement, *Bluebird*, as it became more simply titled, ranks as Stephen's highest achievement with the Springfield. Constructed in the studio by Stephen with Ahmet Ertegun in support, the multi-tracked recording was the product of Stephen's all-encompassing musical vision drawing on his roots in acoustic music and his growing sophistication as an arranger and producer. With Bobby West on bass and Dewey on drums, Stephen and Neil overdubbed the various guitar tracks, "all 11,386 of 'em," as the liner notes to their second album suggest. Richie's role was minimal other than harmony vocals, but he nonethless was in awe of the final product. "I was sure that we had *the* follow-up with *Bluebird*. I thought *Bluebird* was the song that was going to make our mark and take us to the top."

> *Listen to my bluebird laugh,*
> *She can't tell you why.*
> *Deep within her heart you see,*
> *She knows only cryin',*
> *Just crying.*
> *There she sits, a lofty perch,*
> *Strangest color blue.*
> *Flying is forgotten now,*
> *Thinks only of you,*
> *Just you.*

> *Bluebird* (Stephen Stills)

Affecting his Southern accent in lines like "she can't tell you why," Stephen laments the loss of a loved one, but unlike Neil's songs, it is not the lyric content that is most compelling, though Stephen maintains his high standard of accessibility. What is most striking is the music, juxtaposing acoustic and electric guitar, propeled along by a strident bass line and topped off with false ending and bluegrass-flavored banjo reprise, overdubbed in New York by Stephen's former Greenwich Village contemporary Charlie Chin. "Stephen's roots music came out in *Bluebird*, that Appalachian thing," notes Chris Hillman who was awestruck on first hearing the song. "That song was so derivative of an old mountain song with the banjo and that melody. It was something you didn't hear. I loved it. Stephen has a sense of roots music about him, delta blues, traditional music."

Three distinct versions of *Bluebird* ultimately appeared on vinyl: an edited version for single release at 1:58 that omits the guitar break and banjo reprise; the album track in its completed form running just over four minutes; and an extended version cut but not intended for release featuring an eastern flavored raga middle electric guitar passage with Stephen and Neil at their most ferocious. The latter remained in the can until a local FM disc jockey stumbled upon the tape while housesitting for Stephen at his Malibu digs later that summer. "*Bluebird* was like this cult radio hit here in LA when they had the long form radio format and B. Mitchell Reed would play the 12 minute cut," recalls Miles Thomas. The extended version, with slight editing, was eventually included on the 1973 BUFFALO SPRINGFIELD double compilation album. This tour de force rendition of *Bluebird* became the vehicle for the elongated on stage guitar wars between Stephen and Neil, as Dickie Davis recalls. "They would have guitar duels in *Bluebird* that would last 20 minutes in a kind of raga at the end. They'd be trying to outdo the other."

Edited and mixed for single release on June 6, *Bluebird*, coupled with the months old *Mr. Soul*, became the long awaited follow-up to *For What It's Worth* when released nine days later. Expectations were high and rewarded early when the single raced to No. 2 on KHJ's Boss 30, only to stall at No. 58 in *Billboard*, a disappointing showing for a stunning single obviously too adroit for AM radio even during the "Summer of Love." The failure of *Bluebird* became a turning point for the Springfield. "Each one of them had his heart broken one by one," bemoans Dickie on the group's declining fortunes.

Live at Ondine's, New York, January 1967.

Album cover for "Stampede" with Dickie Davis (front) impersonating Bruce Palmer.

Taping the *Go* show, March 5, 1967, one day after Richie's wedding.

Neil backstage with close friend Peter Noone of Herman's Hermits.

181

Posing in Chicago while on tour, May 1967, with Jim Fielder
(far left).

{

SEVEN

Too Much Fame

Well, make believe is all you know,
And to make believe is a game,
A child's rein, you changed your name.
So sadly I watch the show,
Just to see what you became,
Truth is a shame,
Too much fame.

A Child's Claim To Fame (Richie Furay)

"Well, I sort of dropped out of the group," Neil comments on his decision to leave the Buffalo Springfield in June of 1967. "I couldn't handle it. I don't know why, but something inside of me felt like I wasn't quite on track. I think it was when we booked the Johnny Carson show. Right around the time of the Monterey Pop Festival."

Following their return from the Illinois tour in late May, Neil disappeared, holed up at various locations working on tracks with Jack Nitzsche. Efforts to contact him went unanswered. Finally, he emerged to convene a meeting at Charlie and Brian's office. As Dickie Davis described that meeting to Jerry Hopkins in his 1970 book *The Rock Story*, "We walked into Greene and Stone's office and Neil said, 'I'm leaving the group.' Most were surprised. Steve was angry. I thought it was a drag. We were making a thousand a night and we were looking forward to some good bookings — the Monterey Pop Festival, the Newport Folk Festival. We tried to talk him out of it. We had another single out, *Bluebird*, and in that we'd not been able to promote our earlier singles because of Neil's illness and Bruce's bust, I thought it unfair to hang the group up now. I told Neil his attitude was temporary. He finally said he'd play through the pop festival. Then Steve said that was a lousy idea, because why should Neil get all that recognition from the festival because of the group if he was going to leave anyway. We were about to go on the road again, to Boston, and I thought that was good because the group always got tighter on the road together, and so I thought he'd get over it. I made the mistake of saying that to Greene and Stone, who told Neil that's what I felt. So Neil disappeared and we had to leave without him." Dickie concludes, "Neil felt Nitzsche and he could produce and make a lot more money and be happier than he was with the Buffalo." According to Jack, Neil wanted "lots of money and star fame."

Stephen confirms his disappointment with Neil's defection. "The Carson show was like *The Ed Sullivan Show* at the time. It was an important show to be on in 1967, and we were the first rock'n'roll band to be on the Carson show. We were playing our best ever. But Neil quit the night before we were to leave for New York. It was sheer self-destruct."

Self-destructive, perhaps, and not the first time a rock'n'roll performer balked at the point of becoming a star. Paranoia, perhaps, given Neil's doubts about the life of a "star" in *Mr. Soul*. Frustration, perhaps, after the struggles with Stephen for control of the band. Maybe even an astute career decision. Or a question of taste, as Neil himself suggests. Over the years, he has maintained that the catalyst for his bolting was *The Tonight Show*, citing his belief that Carson's late night shmooze-fest was hardly the place for a quality group like the Springfield.

Stephen offers another, more likely explanation. "He's a genius, an enigma," comments Stephen on his on again, off again partner for some 30 years. "Never played a team sport in his life, so he can't make that kind of commitment because he has too many things to do." With very few exceptions, Neil has always been in control of his career from the earliest days, calling the shots, taking a backseat to no one, including Stephen Stills. His collaboration with Jack Nitzsche may have given his vision of a solo career substance.

"My perspective of Stephen and Neil," muses Richie on the odd relationship between the two, "was that on the surface, sure they had their arms around each other and loved each other, but underneath they were just waiting for the opportunity to show the other one up. They were so concerned with themselves, but they were preoccupied with the other guy, too, to outdo, be better than. I've seen that break up so many things, when one person starts to think they're bigger than the whole thing. Maybe Neil was, because that's how it's turned out, but he had to take his stepping stone from the Springfield first." Most insiders hold to the belief that this strained relationship affected Neil much more than Stephen.

"I was trying to be Boss cat and trying to keep the thing in order," Stephen admits. "You gotta dig that part of my upbringing in the South was very militaristic. Anyway, a lot of the ways I relate to situations like that is to simply take command. Someone has to, because that is the only thing that will work and of course somebody like Neil or Bruce is instantly going to rebel. So there was chaos. Neil was trying to arrange some stuff, which was my trip, and I was getting more into lead guitar, which he thought was his trip. So things got intense for a while. My temper was starting to get in the way 'cause I would watch the shit go down, and I sensed that Neil was resenting the fact that I was starting to play lead guitar. I was the arranger, and all of a sudden I was treading on his territory, so he started getting into mine and so forth, and we just got into this ridiculous twenty-one year old 'boys in the band' gig. Then we were finding fault with everything. Everything started to lose proportion and it got stupid, y'know. It was just dumb, a kid's trip."

According to Miles Thomas, the dynamics within the band had altered irrevocably, causing friction. The initial lines of demarcation had become obscured. "Originally you had this cute little folk rock band doing Richie's and Stephen's songs, then all of a sudden Neil goes off into left field. Neil was obviously the rocker element anyway, guitar-wise. There is always politics in a band about whose songs are going to be recorded because that's who would make the most royalties. The studios became battle grounds between the two of them. Stephen was a great writer, and Neil was starting to get out there, deeper stuff. Stills is a genius, a brilliant writer and guitarist. He can be an asshole all day long, but, in the end, he has tremendous talent. There was no doubt that he and Neil were the strong, talented guys in the band, but though they worked well together in the early days, they were 180 degrees from each other. And Neil resented Stephen's increasing demands to play lead."

Bruce Palmer pulls no punches in assessing the personalities behind these two strong-willed individuals. "Stephen was always hard to get along with; Neil was hard to get along with. Stephen's brash, egotistical and pushy. Neil is the complete opposite. But the end result is still the same: two spoiled little brats. But instead of screaming and yelling, Neil just disappears. He'd constantly be disappearing and we'd have to go find him hiding at Jack Nitzsche's in the closet. He's that self-centered. I remember one day there was a recording session. Steve and I drove up to Neil's place. Neil had called Charlie and whined, 'I don't feel well today.' Meanwhile the studio time had been booked, people waiting around. So we went up there. I stayed outside and Stephen went in like General Sherman and called Neil a gold bricking son of a bitch. That was the level it was on, a lot of tantrums between two dividing powers. I was constantly in between those two, the buffer. It was a civil war. It was frenetic, explosive. That's what I hate about what the business does to people."

"I just think that Neil realized that he wasn't going to be

able to overcome the other voices in the band," speculates Michael Miller. "There was a battle for influence or dominance. These are two of the most influential voices in popular music and they didn't get that way by not being advocates for their own point of view. There was an aggressive streak in both of them. Richie was just as talented but less aggressive — or not as driven as they were — and was hurt by it in the end." Rather than fight, Neil simply walked away.

Suggests Dickie Davis, "Right from the start, Stephen Stills was the leader. The Buffalo Springfield was his group. That's why he hung on until the end even after *For What It's Worth* when he could have gone on his own more than Neil could. Why would he leave his group? He was always the leader. He made the band decisions or played a big part in those decisions." Confirms Richie, "The minute Steve left the band, there was no Buffalo Springfield. He was committed and wanted to keep the band together, Neil wasn't." Although a popular member who contributed to the band's musicality and mystique, Neil was not the leader, nor, claims Michael, could he have been. "Neil is a great writer and he's become a great artist, but he was not in any way, shape or form, a guy who you built a band around back then. He just had a really intriguing look with the fringes, sideburns, and black hair who played some eclectic electric guitar."

"Out of all of them," observes Mark Volman, "Richie was probably the least affected by the problems going on within the group. He was the most level headed. But I don't think Richie understood his influence on Stephen and Neil. He complemented both of them and he loved them. But it hurt Richie a lot to see that they couldn't make it work, yet he didn't know how to save it. He wasn't assertive. The only one who was assertive, Dewey Martin, nobody cared to listen to. He wasn't afraid to speak out and say things that would piss everybody off, but nobody listened because when you got right down to it he was expendable. He wasn't one of the front three."

In retrospect, blame for Neil's defection has been placed at the feet of the Springfield's managers, Charlie Greene and Brian Stone. Suggests Nurit Wilde, "I think they thought that if they kept Stephen and Neil fighting it would spur them on creatively. They promoted the rivalry for their own gain, to have more control." Richie agrees. "Greene and Stone had the attitude that they had to get close to one guy to present their agenda.

That never works. It didn't work for us. Rather than somebody trying to bring us together it split us apart more. I don't think maybe anybody knew how to bring us together. Charlie and Brian certainly didn't know how to do it. It was sad that it couldn't have matured into what it could have been with some kind of help and support. George Martin didn't put a dividing line between John Lennon and Paul McCartney. He used every single bit of whatever talent they had to offer to bring it together to make it work, bringing in what George Harrison and Ringo Starr had to offer to the whole thing. He didn't try to play one off the other. All Greene and Stone had was greed. They were in it for themselves."

Surprisingly, Neil re-joined the Springfield within a few months, only to defect again, and not surprisingly, the second time, returned to the band once again. And so the pattern of Neil Young's career was set.

On June 2nd, the group assembled at LA airport in preparation for a flight to Salem, New Hampshire for a gig that evening at Canobie Lake Park, followed by two nights in Boston at the Where It's At club, appearing as a quartet. Soon after they were scheduled for the *Tonight Show* and then a featured appearance at the Monterey Pop Festival. The summer of 1967, the so-called "Summer of Love," was full of high expectations for the Buffalo Springfield.

Though Neil Young had departed and Bruce Palmer was still rusty from his four month absence, the others remained confident they could pull off the New England gigs. "We thought we'd get it all together in New Hampshire," remembers Richie, "and then go down to Boston. That was the big city, even though it was a pretty funky club. We felt pretty humiliated, though, when they told us not to come back." Forced to accept a reduced fee, the band was subsequently fired after the first night. "Neil wasn't there and the kids knew it; they were waiting for that fringed jacket," bemoans Dickie.

The Carson show remained another matter. Dewey suggested a last minute substitution. "I said, 'Wait a minute. Let's not back out on this if we can get Otis Redding to come on and sing *Mr. Soul*," Dewey recalls with enthusiasm. "So I called up Otis Redding and he took my call. Otis and I were buddies. He invited me to his ranch in Macon. So I proposed this to Otis. I said, 'Man, we're stuck. You know the guy who wouldn't let you do *Mr. Soul*? Well, we're at the airport and he didn't show up and we're just about to cancel the Carson show. I'm calling to see if you'll do *Mr. Soul* and we'll do *For What It's Worth*.' And he said, 'What time?' When I told him it was 7:30 he said, 'Ah, man, I gots'ta do five shows at the Apollo.' He was ready to do it. Neil would have had a shit fit because Otis would have stolen the show. It would have been an incredible moment." The Carson appearance was canceled.

Although the Springfield fleetingly considered going on as a quartet, at Stephen's urging, they recruited a replacement for Neil. Turning to another Greene-Stone managed group, The Daily Flash ("Give Us This Day Our Daily Flash" was their slogan), the Springfield drafted lead guitarist Doug Hastings, an unabashed fan of the group.

Born in Seattle on June 21, 1946, Doug was two weeks shy of his 21st birthday when he became a Buffalo. In early 1966 The Daily Flash had migrated southward from the Pacific Northwest area to try their luck in the clubs along Sunset Strip, earning a solid reputation playing folk and jazz-tinged psychedelic rock. Under Charlie and Brian's tutelage, the group recorded a single for UNI in 1966 entitled *French Girl*, backed by *Green Rocky Road*, that failed to capture their dynamic live sound or garner much attention, a familiar refrain. "We were pretty legendary in Seattle," notes Doug on The Daily Flash's early years. "We went down to LA but the only success we had or money we made was back in Seattle. The problem was that nobody in the band wrote original material so there wasn't a lot we could do. So Greene and Stone didn't have a lot to work with. I began to grow weary of returning to Seattle for another victory tour when I knew we weren't succeeding in LA." An appearance on *The Girl From Uncle* television show and a regular slot on the local LA teen show *Boss City* covering the hits of the day failed to translate into wider success.

In late May, Doug abruptly abandoned the group. His timing was fortuitous. "I was at a loose end when I got the call to join the Springfield," he recalls. "One night I sat in with Iron Butterfly after Danny Weiss had left, but I wasn't looking around very hard when the phone rang. It was just good timing; I was available and that's probably why they approached me. I already knew them and had hung out with them when their first album came out. I remember seeing Neil several times in the waiting room at Charlie Greene's office playing his guitar. I used to listen to him play and think, 'Poor Neil, he'll never get anywhere. He's a nice enough guy, but he really can't play guitar.' What I didn't see at the time was the drive, determination, and persona he had. He was really focused and I didn't understand it at the time. Now we think of Neil Young in capital letters, Neil Young The Star, but at the time he was just the guitar player in the band."

With little time to waste, the Springfield convened rehearsals at Stephen and Dewey's beach house in preparation for a June 8th engagement at Hal Baby's Teen Club in Aurora near Denver, Colorado. "I knew the tunes because I had their album," notes Doug. "Crosby was around helping out at those first rehearsals. He didn't go out and do the gigs but he was helping out. There were some tunes I pretty much felt at ease with and some where I had to play Neil's parts because it was an integral part of the song." Doug proved a willing pupil, learning the group's set, copping Neil's licks, and offering no challenge to Stephen's authority. "Doug Hastings worked well with Stephen as Stephen's boy," notes Miles.

"Stephen looked at Doug's joining as more of an opportunity for him to play lead and stand out," suggests Richie. "But Doug, for as nice a guy and as good a musician as he was, definitely didn't fit in." A more than competent lead guitarist, technically more proficient than Neil incorporating jazz phrasings and a more fluid touch into his soloing, Doug was nevertheless not a songwriter, and as a substitute for the enigmatic Neil, he was a questionable choice. Confirms Charlie Greene, "Doug Hastings was a good guitar player but he could not replace Neil. It was Stephen's idea but it didn't work." The expectations placed on Doug were daunting. "Doug wasn't someone I would have chosen to be in the Buffalo Springfield," Richie states. "He wasn't a writer like Neil or had a following like Neil. It was the wrong choice and he wasn't a part of the family. We were asking him to play like Neil, play Neil's licks, and teaching him the old songs, and it didn't work. The music just didn't have that presence. Neil was an innovator, and Doug, even though he may have been a better guitar player than Neil, was an imitator. I don't think he ever became a part of the band, he was just hired."

Too Much Fame

Offers Doug, "I think Stephen saw me as someone who wasn't going to challenge him. And I wasn't. Most of my inter-action was with Stephen coaxing me to be whoever it was he wanted me to be. He was calling the shots for the band." Doug also had to deal with the emotional residue of Neil's depar-ture. "They were mad at Neil for having left," he recalls. "They were glad he'd left because he was being an asshole but they were also mad because he'd abandoned them."

Within 24 hours of joining the Springfield, Doug was whisked into Columbia Studios to contribute to their next single, Stephen's *Bluebird*. As he remembers, "I probably sealed my fate on one of my first days in the band when I was in the studio with them to finish up *Bluebird*. They had already recorded it, it was pretty well all done, and I was presented with a fait accom-pli. 'Here, play a solo on it.' Stephen had it set up for me to solo over the driving part of the song. It wasn't an easy spot to put in a solo. I worked hard to find a place in there, but I wasn't satis-fied with what I did. Stephen had the more relaxed part to solo in, and I had the attack part. I thought it was a great song, but I listened to the trailer, the long ending, and I made the mistake of saying to Stephen, 'Well, the Beatles had one of these long end-ings and Simon and Garfunkel and that's pretty cool to do right now, but I don't think it's the right long ending. It's a great song but it doesn't need that ending.' Stephen didn't take too kindly to that."

Doug's contributions were excised from the tape, and Stephen completed and mixed the track that night. With dead-lines and several high profile engagements looming, the group chose to proceed as planned with Neil's five-month old *Mr. Soul* as the B side, despite his recent exit.

The new look Buffalo Springfield made its debut at Hal Baby's before an enthusiastic crowd who took little notice of Neil's absence. Opening the show was a popular local aggregation named Boenzee Cryque, featuring two unique attractions, a drummer who sang amazing lead named George Grantham, and an innov-ative rock'n'roll steel guitar player and high-school friend of Miles Thomas, Rusty Young. Grantham and Young would join Richie Furay in Poco after the break up of the Springfield.

"They were my favorite band," Rusty Young comments while remembering this gig and his first encounter with the Buffalo Springfield. "It was the Beatles and the Springfield for me.

Boenzee Cryque's music was pretty similar to Poco, actually. We had the steel guitar and were playing Buffalo Springfield, Moby Grape, basic rock songs and some originals. We were not a bad local band, one of the two big local bands. We had had a record out that had been number one in Colorado for week after week. Hal Baby's was a former supermarket that had been converted into a rock club. It held about two thousand people. Hal was a hot local deejay on KIMN. That night is like one of those moments that remain vivid in your memory like a Polaroid that you hold onto. The backstage was a bunch of little rooms lit with lamps on tables — it wasn't that well lit. I remember really well Richie sitting in a corner in a chair wearing his little round John Lennon wire-framed glasses strumming his twelve-string guitar and singing. I thought that he was a real interesting character because he was so anti-rock star. He looked more like a school kid than a rock star. But the only one I met that evening was Stephen. He wanted to borrow a thumb pick, so I went backstage to give him one. There seemed to be a lot of tension in the room. Doug Hastings was with them. You could feel the tension in the room and everyone seemed to be keeping to themselves. There wasn't a lot of camaraderie. My impression of the Springfield that night wasn't real good. We had played with The Byrds, The Mamas and The Papas, and all the hot shots that came through. But the Springfield were not one of the more impressive bands that night. It was tough because Neil wasn't there and it just didn't seem like their heart was in it."

Rusty did note one feature that set the Buffalo Springfield apart from their contemporaries. "Henley had built them a PA system. This was back when bands didn't carry PA systems with them. You were lucky to have any kind of sound reinforcement. It was basically two small cabinets and two horns on each side of the stage that they put the vocals through. Miles did road managing and mixing."

Following a gig the next night in Colorado Springs, the reconstituted group returned to LA to ready themselves for a crucial appearance one week later at the Monterey Pop Festival, scheduled for the weekend of June 16th through 18th. The group canceled engagements and holed up at the beach house to prepare their six-song set. Inspired by the success months earlier of the CAFF concert in LA, the Monterey Pop Festival was a watershed moment in pop music, a coming together for the first time of the various streams of popular music in one forum. The wide variety of acts presented over three days at the Monterey Fairgrounds ran the gamut of contemporary music from Ravi Shankar's hypnotic eastern raga's (Shankar was the only artist to receive a fee for the event), Lou Rawls' Vegas lounge lizard act, Dionne Warwick's pop stylings, Simon and Garfunkel's polished folk harmonies, to Eric Burdon and the Animals' searing electric blues and The Who's auto-destruction.

Besides being a showcase for existing talent, the festival introduced to the world a couple of artists who would go on to change the very face of rock music including a young Texan with a voice as large as the fairgrounds, Janis Joplin, and an ex-patriot American guitarist who all but reinvented the instrument before setting it ablaze, Jimi Hendrix. The event also served as the formal introduction of soul man Otis Redding to a large white audience who instantly took him to heart as he laid claim to his night of the event. The Festival marked the debut of several new acts, including ex-Butterfield Blues Band guitarist extraordinaire Mike Bloomfield's latest aggregation, the multi-instrumental Electric Flag. Among its motley crew of seasoned players was a behemoth of a drummer in a fright wig fresh from the chitlin circuit backing Wilson Pickett by the name of Buddy Miles.

The first ever rock festival, Monterey also inaugurated the summer of love in all its flower-power, LSD-soaked, love-beaded glory. "If you're going to San Francisco, be sure to wear some flowers in your hair." Sung by Scott Mackenzie, John Phillips' lyrics were, in fact, conceived as a kind of anthem for the Monterey Pop Festival. "I had bought into the San Francisco/ flower child thing to some degree," recalls Richie, who, with Nancy and the other band members, spent the weekend taking in the sights and sounds of the festival. "I wore my Nehru jacket like Steve. I had Nancy make me two or three and I wore beads and thought I was pretty cool making the scene and being hip. But my recollections of Monterey are pretty spacey at that time. I don't remember a whole lot because I was sick with the flu. I remember walking around the complex and visiting all the booths people had with beads and tie dye shirts or whatever. And I remember Jimi Hendrix was quite a mind blower, so was Janis Joplin. Otis Redding was great. I couldn't believe that The Who could do that to their instruments, smashing them up."

With Augustus Stanley Owsley III whipping up a special batch of LSD, appropriately named Monterey Purple, most people's recollections are euphoric at best. "Almost everybody at Monterey was awful," laughs Miles, "but everybody was on LSD so everybody thought it was great. Probably the two best performances at Monterey without a doubt were Hendrix and Otis Redding. Janis was good too, but you listen to the Springfield on the Monterey CD and you think, 'Jeez, that's terrible.'"

Monterey also marked a kind of north-south detente with the San Francisco scene, heavily represented by groups like the Airplane, Grateful Dead, Steve Miller Band, and Country Joe and the Fish, ever suspicious of the LA hipsters who organized the event. Among those music luminaries, including Dunhill Records' Lou Adler and Papa John Phillips, the Springfield was held in high regard and an early choice for the roster of performers, being rewarded with a prime slot on the closing evening. A band with a reputation, the Springfield had much at stake in a solid performance, and much to lose as well. Fearful of critical scrutiny and possibly coming up short, the Beach Boys bowed out at the last minute, earning the scorn of the media and setting back their cause several years. The Byrds succeeded in destroying their eminence with a tepid, fractious, desultory performance. Still reeling from the defection of Neil and gradually integrating Doug Hastings, the Springfield set about hedging their bet with a bit of extra insurance in the form of The Byrds' David Crosby.

Having overcome his initial ambivalence toward the group by the fall of 1966, David and Stephen had cultivated a close friendship in the ensuing months. As mentor to Stephen, David would introduce him to many of the pleasures of the LA scene as well as stimulate his creativity with the occasional suggestion. Stephen's latest project, the ambitious *Rock And Roll Woman*, was instigated by a guitar tuning suggested by David and helped along through its gestation with his suggestions here and there. Stephen would ultimately acknowledge David as the inspiration, falling short of sharing a writing credit.

"Stephen was a little more hip to the LA scene and that's probably what gravitated him to Crosby," suggests Chris Hillman on the relationship between the Byrd and the Buffalo. "They had an affinity for that scene, something they could relate to." Miles Thomas feels the two shared similar traits. "I know the side of Crosby that was hard to get along with but he and Stephen were very similar. They were both very up front, 'This is how it is, don't mess with me, don't argue with me.' They were both like, 'Put the gloves on, pal.' I don't know how they hit it off but they did. The two of them became really close." He recalls the time Stephen and David tuned in to The Beatles' groundbreaking Sgt. Pepper album. "I remember sitting at David's house in Beverly Glen when Stephen and I had gotten hold of Sgt. Pepper as an important moment. David put it on his mega stereo, a recording studio quality system, and we started smoking shit until we couldn't move. But David was able to keep turning the record over. And like everybody, we were just destroyed by that album the first time we heard it."

David had reasons of his own, not altogether altruistic, in joining the Buffalo Springfield on stage at Monterey. By the spring of 1967 his welcome was wearing thin with his fellow Byrds as the group foundered hitless over the past year. In a bid to exert a power play of his own, David had been pushing for greater creative input in the group much to the chagrin of leader Roger (Jim) McGuinn. In some respects it was a re-run of the Stills-Young feud. David's persistence had resulted in the group relenting and releasing one of his own compositions, the multi-textured yet doomed *Lady Friend*, which promptly sank like a stone. David viewed his appearance with the Springfield as leverage in the ongoing battles with his fellow Byrds. No other artist of such stature, while still a member of his own group, had ever sat in with another group at a major public performance. David liked to shake things up.

"Crosby wanted to see what the audience reaction would be if a member of one group played with another group," notes Richie, "so we started rehearsing." Newcomer Doug Hastings was not consulted on the decision to bring in a ringer. "I never thought of myself as a singer, so I think they thought they needed that other voice," he speculates. "It was Stephen's band so I just rolled with the punches. Crosby was his friend and they had a relationship, so what could I say? But I felt crowded with Crosby there."

Though David has consistently denied it, Chris Hillman feels he would have abandoned The Byrds for the Springfield had Stephen offered. "Of course. David wanted to be in the Springfield so bad when he was having problems in The Byrds," he attests. "He would have joined them in a minute if he had been asked. He wasn't happy in The Byrds, and at the time we were working in the studio, he'd take our tapes and run off and play them for the Springfield. So he took the opportunity to jump on stage with them. McGuinn and I were ready to strangle him at that point after he made some stupid comment about Kennedy and the Warren Commission that was totally inappropriate. I don't think we were officially notified that he was going to join them onstage but we heard rumors." Miles Thomas disagrees with Chris's assertion: "Crosby wouldn't have left The Byrds for the Springfield because The Byrds were making money and Crosby was living a very nice lifestyle. The Byrds had their own problems but they were making money. The Springfield weren't." David has always maintained that his presence was purely supportive for a friend. "Neil left about a week before Monterey, so I rehearsed with them for a few days and I said that I'd sit in with them to cover. I was just trying to help. I wasn't in the Springfield and I had no intention of being in the Springfield."

On the evening in question, the Springfield were slated to follow a non-descript jam band assembled on the encouragement of Papa John Phillips known as Group With No Name. Led by ex-Modern Folk Quartet guiding light Cyrus Faryar and comprised mostly of session players, this loose aggregation posed no threat to the Springfield following them. However, at the last minute Big Brother and the Holding Company, featuring Janis Joplin, was parachuted in before Group With No Name to perform an abbreviated encore set, given their tumultuous response at the less well-attended Saturday afternoon concert. Janis proceeded to tear the place apart, making Cyrus and his friends look pretty flacid afterwards. This did not auger well for the Springfield. As well, England's notorious bad boys The Who, making their California debut after a year of rumors of a must-see stage show, were up after the Springfield. Once the equipment, a brace of Fender Showman amplifiers, was in place, Monkee Peter Tork appeared to muted response, being viewed as a pseudo hippie by the real things in the crowd, and introduced the group with the simple, "I'd like you to welcome now with a great big, fat round of applause, my favorite group, the Buffalo Springfield."

The group launched into *For What It's Worth*, Stephen

modifying the lyric to sing, "There's a man with a gun no where," in deference to the peace and love ambience of the event. The Springfield followed that with a set wisely mixing the familiar with several new numbers. *Clancy* was up next, receiving its usual warm welcome, though Richie's usually clear tenor voice was obviously suffering the effects of his ill health. Then came two new numbers, Richie's country music flavored *A Child's Claim To Fame* and Stephen's jazzy *Pretty Girl Why*. Of *Child's Claim*, Richie states, "It was a song we hadn't recorded but everybody latched onto for some reason." *Pretty Girl Why* had been recorded that spring. "*Pretty Girl Why* was one of my favorites," offers Doug. "I saw it as an opportunity for me to do some really interesting solos. I had been infatuated with jazz earlier from people like Gabor Szabo, Django Reinhardt, Miles Davis. On the road one night I stayed up half the night working out solo lines to that song and I think I kept Richie from sleeping."

The Springfield then closed with what unintentionally came off sounding like a medley: the newly rehearsed *Rock And Roll Woman* seguing into the just released *Bluebird*. The band appeared to lose direction near the end of *Rock And Roll Woman* with the guitars noodling around the main riff aimlessly until Dewey saved the day with a whistle, a hasty introduction of their latest single, and count in of *Bluebird*. By that point the group was traveling on a full head of steam and the number was transformed into something of a boogie.

To say that David Crosby's presence on stage caused a stir would be overstating it. His profile was so low key many took no notice of him there save for his ever-present black cowboy hat, and his musical contributions, both instrumentally and vocally, were barely audible. Bruce recalls it rather differently. "Crosby stunk to high heaven," he snarls. "He didn't know what he was doing. He didn't rehearse, thought he knew what he was doing, didn't and embarrassed us to the max, and that's why you won't see our segment in Pennebaker's film *Monterey Pop*. It was so bad I blushed into crimson. 'What's going on here?!' He said he knew what he was doing and didn't; he was all ego. He came on for forty minutes and embarrassed us. That led to some severe repercussions between Crosby and me, a complete disdain for each other." Doug concurs with Bruce's verdict. "David had a gorgeous voice but his problem was that he couldn't play rhythm guitar very well, though he thought he could. In his enthusiasm he would rush the tunes. He would get up there and wham away, sometimes it would be the right time and other times it would be way too fast. He believed he was doing fine, but in fact he screwed things up. He would rush. That was one of the reasons why we sounded so bad at Monterey. I thought we were out of control in *Bluebird*. No one was sure where we were going. We got off too fast and kept getting faster. We couldn't hear anything on stage. There were no monitors. Acoustics were neanderthal. We just plugged in and played and hoped for the best." Offers Dewey brusquely: "We didn't have it together at all. No wonder they didn't put us in the movie."

Richie remains more diplomatic regarding David's role in their less than stellar performance. "I think we were just trying to make something work, make the best of the situation. David was willing to come in and help us along. He sat in just to give us some moral support more than anything else. There's probably a couple of different ways to look at it. I mean, David was just a rhythm guitar player; it wasn't like he had an out front focused part in the group where it would have made a difference. We were trying to put something together with the pieces we had, and if it didn't come together, I think David's contribution as to why it didn't was very minimal. We weren't nearly as ready for Monterey as it was for us, and our set was a disappointment to us. Our excuse was a lack of time to rehearse from the time Neil left until the festival." Richie reserves his frustration over their lackluster performance for Neil. "Personally, I wasn't as excited to perform at Monterey because it wasn't the family. We were struggling because we didn't have the whole band, the family. It was there more than any time that I felt betrayed by Neil's absence. It was a disappointment but I don't feel now, 'Hey Neil, because you didn't stick around we didn't become the Beatles revisited.' It was just the way it was but there were some hurt feelings. When we got fired in Boston it really hurt. 'What? What do you mean we're not good enough?' That was a real slap. We were obviously looking forward to the *Tonight Show* and it was a let down."

Dickie, on the other hand, felt the Springfield held up reasonably well at Monterey. "They really cooked, musically. Vocally, they weren't together and something was lacking — the friendship, something. We got a nice review from an important reviewer. We got a lot of applause. But we weren't as good as we should have been or could have been, and the people knew it." Critics were generally kind, with one apologizing, "The Buffalo Springfield, minus one Neil Young, plus one Doug Hastings, plus one David Crosby did not live up to the expectant crowd's hopes, as they were unused to the new lineup and new material. However, the new material is great. Some is by Neil, some by Stevie, some with David, and several by Richie. Bruce is back, looking none the worse for hair. (Hope he grows it back, though!)" Glowing or otherwise, Monterey did bring the group considerable attention, raising their profile, a fact that did not go unnoticed by Neil Young.

During the weekend stay, several members of the group camped out at Stephen's mother's house in Monterey. For Miles, this resulted in some friction between him and Stephen. "I quit not long after Monterey because I got into a fight with Steve at Monterey. Steve's mother had some personal problems, and the way I remember it he wanted me to take her to the hospital. Here we had The Who, Hendrix, acid, girls balling our brains out, all these things going on and I'm going to take Mom to the hospital? I told him, 'That's not my job, pal.' I didn't even know his mother. Not long after that I was history. I knew I couldn't deal with Stills. The next thing I remember was phoning The Turtles and asking, 'Hey, can you use me?'"

Following Monterey, the group took time off to tend to medical matters, Stephen to have torn ligaments in his leg looked after, while throat problems continued to plague Richie. "I had a really bad attack of tonsillitis while we were in San Francisco staying at Marty Balin's house," he recalls. "I could barely swallow." A prestigious appearance closing the show at the Newport Folk Festival in Rhode Island slated for July 16th, the only rock group invited to perform, was reluctantly canceled as Richie entered hospital to have his tonsils removed.

A week after Monterey, the Springfield were booked to play two nights at the Hullabaloo on Sunset. With Richie still out convalescing, David Crosby agreed to sub for him for the two-night stand, playing a larger role than he had at Monterey by covering Richie's harmonies. During the second set that first evening, to everyone's utter astonishment, who should stroll in but Neil Young. Recognized and invited to join the group on stage, David and Doug Hastings relinquished their spots to allow Neil up for a rendition of *Mr. Soul*. "I left the stage and went out and watched them," confirms Doug. "Hell, where's my position when Neil shows up? That was the spot he had occupied." By all accounts the guest shot went down well, though Dewey found his former mate's visage rather ominous. "Neil came and sat in with us and he looked like he had been living in a dungeon. He was hunched over and very secretive." The next day in a review of this performance, the *LA Times* declared, "It was like old home week." On the second night Richie made an appearance with David. The night concluded with an all-star jam session involving the Electric Flag's Buddy Miles and The Byrds' Michael Clarke joining the group on stage for a percussive battle that the *LA Times* dubbed "the Electric Buffalo Byrd Springfield Flag jam."

That summer, Stephen and Dewey's Malibu beach house, 24058 West Malibu Road, became the focal point not only for Springfield rehearsals but various impromptu jam sessions and get-togethers involving several members of the music world elite. Bruce also moved in, with his wife Dale and children. With a panoramic view of the ocean, the house was spartanly furnished but not lacking for instruments and equipment, Stephen having become a collector of guitars by then.

"They had the house all summer in Malibu," notes Michael Miller, "and I lived nearby and spent a lot of time there including some very late nights. That place ripped. The living room was set up for playing, and there were times when Crosby would be over and Buddy Miles would be on drums, David on guitar, Stephen on bass, Jimi Hendrix on guitar. The lid came off the place — probably the most exciting musical moments in my life. When Hendrix was in town, Jimi would call me and I'd pick him up. For Stephen, it wasn't about the Springfield anymore. Instead it was, 'Here's Buddy Miles, Noel Redding, Jimi Hendrix, and Stephen Stills at the house.' Nice session. This was a whole other level of music. Serious heavy duty blues and rhythm and blues. These guys were on the cutting edge taking popular music to a whole different level. That's where Stephen saw himself but I don't think that's where he saw the band."

Stephen was drawn to Buddy Miles' solid drumming at Monterey where he appeared before his first largely white audience. "Stephen really liked Buddy's foot," confirms Michael.

Dewey was less impressed. "Stephen liked the way Buddy Miles played, but Buddy was not a Buffalo Springfield drummer. He was a hammerer. When we were all living at the beach house my drum set was set up and had plenty of big dents in the heads. He didn't even ask if he could use them. I came home and had to rehead them."

Doug Hastings felt fortunate to participate in one of those impromptu sessions. "I did a jam one afternoon at the Malibu house with Jimi Hendrix, Buddy Miles, David Crosby, Stephen Stills, and myself. I think Stephen played bass. It was the four of us playing in one part of the room, and Jimi playing about 15 feet away from us off in a corner with his back to us. We probably played for a couple of hours. Buddy sang, and Jimi sat off in the corner playing his wah-wah pedal. I was never quite sure that he was ever playing with us or just playing while we were playing. He was popping acid like it was aspirin. He was way out there and taking more because he wasn't far enough out. Later on we went upstairs and there he was with a couple of girls and he was asking for more acid. I watched as he took two more. He had enough to kill a horse."

Like so many others, Doug had been awestruck at Jimi's performance on the closing night of the Monterey Pop Festival. "One of my fondest memories was standing at the side of the stage watching Jimi Hendrix at Monterey. I had never seen anyone like him. He was a pretty amazing guitar player, but that was overshadowed by the visceral, animal approach to rock'n'roll he had. I knew it was R'n'B and I knew it was Northwest R'n'B, so I knew where he was coming from and recognized some of the things he was doing that were things only Northwest guitar players did. But I didn't know where he was going with it. It was so absolutely overwhelming that it frightened me."

Given Stephen's constant need to expand his musical horizons and absorb the styles of other players, it's no surprise that he should strike up a friendship with Jimi. Following their stunning Monterey debut, the Jimi Hendrix Experience appeared on July 2nd as a surprise guest at the Whisky and literally tore the place apart. At Peter Tork's insistence, Jimi moved into his mansion, hanging out with Peter, Stephen, and their coterie of friends. It was during his stay that Jimi and Stephen were involved in a minor car accident while Stephen was driving

Peter's new Pontiac GTO, Jimi aggravating an old army injury to his back. The Jimi Hendrix Experience joined The Monkees summer tour as support act in mid-July, only to be dropped from the bill after a handful of concerts into the tour following complaints from parents over what they deemed the lewd stage behavior of Hendrix humping his amp and simulating oral sex on his guitar, hardly appropriate for the Monkees' prepubescent fans. Though an unlikely alliance from the outset, Jimi managed to reap massive publicity from the affair.

In the ensuing years, Stephen has often acknowledged Jimi as a personal mentor with the two jamming whenever their paths crossed. A somewhat legendary session took place in New York that summer between Stephen and Jimi, with The Monkees' Micky Dolenz beating out a rhythm for the two on the back of an acoustic guitar. The Springfield and The Monkees shared a cordial social relationship based on the bond between Stephen and Peter Tork. Peter joined the Springfield on stage at the Whisky in late 1966 for a rousing version of *Alvin the Alligator*, and in early 1968 several members of the Springfield sat in on Monkees' recording sessions. The two groups partied together in Chicago in July 1967 with The Monkees transporting the Springfield to their next gig in their private plane. "Steve hung with Peter Tork a lot," recalls Miles, "because they were friends from before. Stephen was very frustrated that he didn't get to be a Monkee. It's true. Peter was a real sweet guy. He was the only Monkee that hung out with us. The party went back and forth between Peter's house and Steve's in Malibu. The clique was Buddy Miles, Peter Tork, Crosby, Steve, and right after Monterey Pop they hooked up with Hendrix. We all lived at Peter Tork's at one time or another. Peter had the most incredible stereo system, Altec A7s, Voice of the Theater speakers, and a Macintosh power amp."

The extracurricular activity of the LA music set drifted from Stephen's Malibu digs through David Crosby's Beverly Glen home to Peter Tork's Beechwood Canyon hacienda on Shady Oaks in the Hollywood Hills. Bruce confirms the incestuous nature of the LA music fraternity. "In LA, the family got together. Day in, day out, we would jam together, be at each other's houses, just using society to make a rock'n'roll family. You got to know everybody — Janis, Jimi Hendrix, hell, we even got together with the Beatles, sans McCartney, at Stephen's house. All those people in music had a common bond."

Though generally associated with Stephen, most insiders at the time recall the Malibu house as the band's house. "It was the Buffalo's place as far as I knew," offers Nurit. "Stephen and Dewey lived there, and Bruce with his wife Dale and kids. Neil lived there for awhile before he quit, along with assorted hangers on." A photo session at the house in early September included a widely-circulated promotional shot of the group decked out in various hippie garb in the living room, Bruce still sporting his short hair and Dewey inexplicably holding a hockey stick. Dewey claims the house had a history, formerly owned by movie ghoul Vincent Price, and steadfastly maintains the place was haunted. Dewey added to the legendary character of the house. "Stills and I flipped for the best bedroom and he lost so I got it," laughs Dewey. "No wonder he didn't like me. I'd be bringing these babes home two at a time and he'd be sitting there alone. He came over and asked, 'Can I have one?' And I said, 'No, go get your own.'" LA deejay B. Mitchell Reed would stay at the house when the group was out on the road. Dewey also remembers Neil's brief stay. "Neil built a place on the lower level looking out over the ocean. One of our road guys was a carpenter and he did it for him."

Neil had the lower level renovated to his specifications at a hefty cost before packing up soon after for his own little retreat at 8451 Utica Drive in Laurel Canyon. Located on top of a hill, Neil lived alone in the tiny home, except for his two cats, Black Cat Plain and Orange Julius. "When Neil had his little cabin up in the canyon," smiles Michael Miller, "boy, there were some good looking girls that he got up there, cute little teenybopper girls caught in his snare."

Over the summer, the members of Moby Grape relocated to LA to lay down tracks for their second album. "We got a place down at Malibu Colony," recalls the Grape's Jerry Miller on rekindling the relationship the two groups had enjoyed earlier in San Francisco, "and the Springfield had their place up the beach a ways. So we ended up hanging out down there, too. We'd ride around with Stephen in his Rolls Royce and go shopping for cowboy boots. We'd all hang out at Greene and Stone's and at Ahmet's place, too." Indeed, the partying become so intense that Columbia Records' patience eventually wore thin, and the Grape were packed off to New York to complete the album in a less convivial atmosphere.

In mid-July, with *Bluebird* still on the charts and Richie sufficiently recovered, the Springfield returned to the Midwest, shuttling between gigs in Texas, Illinois, Minnesota, and Wisconsin. It was one of the busiest periods the group had enjoyed and gradually they began to pull themselves together. "Slowly, it started coming back," notes Dickie Davis, who by then was acting in a greater capacity for the group as they sought to distance themselves from Charlie and Brian. "Doug began to fit in. Bruce's playing was coming back. We did gigs all over for about a month." The group briefly returned to LA to tape an episode of the summer replacement show *Malibu U*, another in a succession of teen-oriented television fare, and to fill in for The Byrds at the Whisky when Roger McGuinn took sick. Back out on the road on the weekend of July 19th to 21st, the group joined headliners Jefferson Airplane along with psychedelic one hit wonders The Electric Prunes and garage punk favorites The Shadows of Knight at the Minneapolis Convention Hall for "Happening 67." Reviewers raved over the Springfield's performance, declaring the group had stolen the show from the laconic Airplane.

Back stage on one of the nights, Bruce became involved in an altercation that almost scuttled their appearance. "Bruce got a little testy with somebody," Richie remembers, "and started going through his 'I know karate' routine. Bruce prided himself in his Buddhist meditation and he would do all the movements they did, but the guy he was messing with knew karate, too. I don't think it went to a physical confrontation. It was a stand off but I think Bruce realized he was in deeper than he thought." Confirms Bruce, "I wore a blue belt in karate. I was backstage and somebody pissed me off. The bouncers thought I was an overly boisterous person, so they kicked me out. They didn't know I was the bass player for the band. And I had to bang on the doors of the Convention Center trying to get back in. Dickie Davis realized at that point that I wasn't there and somehow it was related to him what happened to me, so he came out and got me."

While in Chicago, various members of the Springfield and The Monkees took part in what had recently come to be a rock group ritual: having ones private parts immortalized in clay by the notorious Plaster Casters, two full time groupies whose speciality was preservation, not merely pleasure. As Dickie told the tale to Jerry Hopkins in *The Rock Story*, "we were supposed to leave for Hayward, Wisconsin, all the way at the top of the United States. The night before we were to leave, there was a party at The Monkees' hotel. Peter Tork called and said, 'Hey, there's a group of girls here called the Plaster Casters that you've got to meet.' So everybody went, and they didn't get back to the hotel until five the next morning and we were supposed to leave at six or seven to drive to Hayward." Dickie and Richie both declined the invitation.

With a debt load topping $20,000, Dickie had hoped to return from the tour with some money in their pockets and was therefore conscious of keeping expenses down. To that end, the group was relegated to traveling between gigs by car. However, that morning the others refused to head out, instead claiming The Monkees would fly them to their intended destination, an Indian reservation outside Hayward in rural Wisconsin. In their reverie, no one bothered to consider the fact that Hayward lacked a proper air strip. Richie and Dickie then took off on a ten-hour car ride, leaving the others to sleep it off in Chicago. The two stopped in Eau Clair to book hotel rooms for the group, given that no accommodations were available on the reservation. When they arrived at Hayward, they discovered that the rest of the band had not yet arrived.

"There was this big pavilion with a tent," Dickie recounts, "and a light show, the first light show we'd seen outside California. And right next to the stage was a train on a siding, with old 1940's type club cars, dining cars and Pullman cars. That was where we were to eat, and our dressing rooms were in the Pullmans. Well, the plane didn't show up, and we couldn't find it. We called every airport within a hundred miles. Nothing. Then we heard something about a plane having trouble and landing in Duluth, that they were on the way by bus. They finally arrived, three hours late. The promoter didn't care because The Monkees were with them. But it was so late when we finished the gig, we couldn't drive back to the hotel in Eau Clair. And where do you stay on an Indian reservation? There was nowhere to stay. So I rented the train."

Despite their illustrious companions, the Springfield turned in a rather desultory set. "Micky Dolenz got up with us and played but we didn't have much of an audience," recalls Doug. "Stephen got his hands on my Les Paul and was in heaven. I played his Gretsch and we played a few Buffalo Springfield tunes and some other things, but I think the audience was pretty underwhelmed. They came to hear Buffalo Springfield tunes and we did a few, then went off into a bunch of other things. It was one of those evenings where the band indulged itself at the expense of the audience. You could tell Stephen was intoxicated by being with The Monkees and all that fame. I think he imagined he was on one of those television shows where they bring stars up out of the audience. At that point the kids who came said, 'Hey, that ain't the Buffalo. We're outta here.' And they left. By the time we were done there weren't many kids left." The next day, Richie and Dickie drove to Eau Clair to retrieve their belongings and pay for the unused rooms before heading off to their next engagement in Waupaca, Wisconsin, arriving about the same time the others pulled up in The Monkees' bus. "Richie and Dickie were pretty bitter that they had done all that driving while we traveled with the Monkees," chuckles Doug.

On August 1st, the Springfield appeared for an unprecedented six-night stand at San Francisco's Fillmore ballroom, supporting Muddy Waters, with Richie Havens opening the shows. A few days later back in LA, the group played Whittier College in suburban Whittier, where, after performing *Rock And Roll Woman*, Dewey announced to the crowd that the song was possibly their next single. "We're working on it right now." Sessions had convened earlier that afternoon to lay down the bed track for the song. "That was a song I liked a lot," claims Doug, "and I played what I thought was a good embellishing part. I played a lead over the shots in the bridge. But it didn't survive the mixing. The basic track was us, though, the five of us."

Four live numbers from their Whittier appearance have been widely circulated over the years and were included on the "Stampede" bootleg album released in the 1970s. Though the liner notes erroneously claim Neil's presence on the tracks, the four numbers feature the unmistakable style of Doug Hastings. However, Neil's phoenix was about to rise again.

Amid this period of intense activity, the group was stunned with a bit of news from Dickie: Neil wanted back in. Following the generous publicity surrounding their appearance at the Monterey Pop Festival, the group's profile had been ascending, while Neil's solo career had stalled.

During the intervening couple of months, Neil had retreated to prepare tracks with Jack Nitzsche for a solo album and attempted, unsuccessfully, to negotiate a release from Atco to pursue his career free of any associations with the Buffalo Springfield. With more time on his hands, he and Sunset Sound studio's engineer Bruce Botnick undertook to produce Love's third album, the definitive FOREVER CHANGES, only to have Neil back out after arranging only one song, *The Daily Planet*, an intricate piece involving several distinct passages. Still grist for the teen mags, he was reported in *TeenSet* planning a move to England. But his studio efforts with Jack Nitzsche had yielded little of substance and Neil found himself in limbo.

"I just wanted to get out of all that but I couldn't get Atlantic to let me go," laments Neil. "So it was a choice between not working at all or going back to the group. The managers kept holding me up. Finally, I was starving to death. I didn't have any money. I would have stayed out then if I could have gotten something going." Knowing that he would have to insinuate himself back into the fold, Neil's campaign began by dropping in unannounced on Dickie, inquiring casually how the band was doing, gradually seeking to mend fences. "Neil's sly," suggests Richie. "After Monterey happened, he kinda wanted back in. He didn't get in right then, but shortly thereafter. We got a lot of publicity after Monterey you see."

If Neil was ever to return, Stephen's acceptance was paramount. On August 10th, following an airing of differences and pledges of mutual admiration, Stephen assented and Neil was officially a Buffalo once again. "When Neil came back he was welcomed back by everyone because nobody had wanted him to leave," maintains Dickie. "It was kind of like the prodigal son returns," Richie adds. "We had found we couldn't play without Bruce. He was the only one we could play with. And when Neil left the same thing happened: we found out that we needed Neil. And he found out he needed us. But I'm sure we sensed that after he'd done that to us a couple of times, he'd probably do it again. I just knew Neil always wanted a solo career and the Buffalo Springfield was his security." Dewey is less magnanimous. "He rejoined the band because his career wasn't taking off. He came slithering back and whined his way back into a job." Well versed in such announcements by now, Doug Hastings was summarily dismissed the next day, and Neil made his triumphant return to the stage at the inauspicious Teens and Twenties Club in Huntington Beach.

"It came completely out of the blue," claims Doug. "I got the call in late afternoon and we had a gig that night. Stephen called me up and the conversation went something like, 'Well old budding, Neil's gonna be back in the band. Things just didn't work out so good luck in your future and we'll be seeing ya.' Click. That was pretty much it. I felt like shit. I was disappointed but I never felt that secure in the group, that I was a solid member. One day I was in and two months later I was gone. That was that." Doug suggests that Neil's return was not met with unanimity. "I think Dewey and Richie weren't that sure about letting Neil back in. They were thinking, 'Do we really want this guy back in the band?' He was a part of the Buffalo Springfield persona but obviously they'd had lots of problems between Stephen and Neil that grated on everybody's soul." He also asserts there was a more practical motive to Stephen's embracing his former rival. "Stephen is a very calculating person. I'm sure he added it all up and figured Neil was better for his success than I was. And at the end of the day if the band was more successful, he'd be more successful and if it's going to be more successful with Neil than me then I was outta there. That was it. But I had to agree that when Neil came back, he was the Buffalo Springfield. I didn't quite get the buckskin and all that. I couldn't be Neil and more and more I came to realize that's who Stephen wanted. He wanted Neil but he didn't want Neil. He wanted Neil's presence in the group but he didn't want Neil telling him what to do."

Three days later, on August 14th, the group taped a brief spot for popular television detective drama *Mannix*, appearing fleetingly in a rundown neighborhood bar scene. "We were the band in the bar," states Richie, who found television work unappealing. "I remember being frantic about it because they started at six in the morning and we had to be there real early to start shooting. We had played the night before and I couldn't sing. They played the track but we had to sing live over it — I think we did *For What It's Worth* — and I couldn't sing and I sounded horrible. You couldn't even hear it on the TV anyway." The episode aired October 28th.

With the original five united again, recording sessions were booked with the goal of completing a long overdue second album and recording a follow-up single to *Bluebird*, which by now had descended from its minimal showing on the charts. The group abandoned the fragmented spring and early summer sessions to concentrate on newer material each of the three writers possessed. As was evident when *For What It's Worth* was juxtaposed with the debut album tracks, the group's latest batch of songs revealed a further sophistication distancing themselves from those early 1967 sessions. "That stuff got pushed aside with Neil coming back with new songs and Stephen and I contributing new stuff," attests Richie. "At that point, the hope was, 'Okay, it's all resolved, the family's back together. It's straight ahead.'"

The new line-up without Neil but with Doug Hastings (left) at Columbia Studios, June 1967.

The group heads east on tour.

Neil and Bruce rejoin the Springfield family at their Malibu beach house, August 1967.

EIGHT

Down To The Wire

Take the time to close your eyes,
And look around.
'Cause anyone who helped you out,
Can let you down.
And look out, look out,
The voice is now the choir.
You can feel it getting down,
To the wire.

Down To The Wire (Neil Young)

T he second Buffalo Springfield album was simply yet ironically called BUFFALO SPRINGFIELD AGAIN, for although the band was together again as a "family," domestic accord was short lived and soon again the problems of the previous nine months of 1967 would return. Yet again, despite this discord, the Springfield recorded some of the most innovative songs in the history of rock music.

On August 14th and 18th, less than a week after his return, Neil submitted several compositions and tapes for Springalo Toones publishing, including bits and pieces as well as completed compositions, among them *Extra Extra* (a song dating back to his Toronto days and recorded at that 1965 Elektra demo session as *When It Falls, It Falls All Over You*), *Whiskey Boot Hill*, the year old demo *One More Sign*, as well as a number of recent tunes such as *Round And Round And Round*, later to appear in 1969 as *Round And Round* on his second solo album in a duet with former girlfriend Robin Lane, *Old Laughing Lady*, initially touted as a Stills-Young collaboration though published by Neil alone, and the rather oblique *High School Graduation*.

> The brick jail doors that closed behind are cracking,
> The school boy told the woman in the street,
> "Last night I heard the bells of summer rapping,
> The word vows of a mother incomplete."
> Emptiness of summer must begin it,
> The nagging of the mother of the wild,
> Convinced me that I had no way to win it.

High School Graduation (Neil Young)

Studio logs for June 30th indicate the group also worked on Neil's *Down, Down, Down*, though that seems unlikely. Later that year, Neil copyrighted *Down Down Down*, *Runaround Babe* and *The Rent Is Always Due* (both Toronto-era folk numbers), *I'm Your Kind Of Guy* (derived from an old Squires number *Be My Girl*), *There Goes My Babe*, and the Stills-Young instrumental *Kahuna Sunset*.

Stephen weighed in with *My Angel* (finally appearing eight years later on his 1975 solo release entitled simply STILLS), *Hello I've Returned*, *We'll See*, *Neighbor Don't You Worry*, and *Come On Lover*. Richie included *Nobody's Fool* and *Can't Keep Me Down*. Earlier in the summer on June 30th, the group had recorded another recent composition by Richie, *Nobody's Fool*. The song had been in their stage set for several weeks and was a welcome replacement for Dewey's spotlight, *In The Midnight Hour*. "Dewey thought of himself as a singer who played drums," suggests Doug. "He thought he was as good as Stephen. But he was always pissed off because Stephen wouldn't let him sing." Of this session, Richie concedes, "*Nobody's Fool* was done at a demo session but never got any further. Dewey sang it." Adds Dewey, "That's the time the guys gave me one session to try to produce myself." *Nobody's Fool* lingered as a potential album track over the next six months only to be abandoned; the number made its appearance on the first and second Poco albums in 1969 and 1970, the former as a funky country-rock number with the latter becoming an excuse for an extended studio jam.

In the midst of these sessions, Dewey Martin took time off to marry a former Miss America runner up, Jane Nelson, in another show biz wedding covered by all the teen magazines. This time, however, Neil failed to show up.

On the evening of August 24th, Richie entered Sunset Sound studios to contribute a harmony vocal part to Neil's nearly completed *Expecting To Fly*, with Bruce Botnick engineering. The multi-layered track had originally required tens of hours to record and overdub and was the only tape Neil brought with him from the aborted Jack Nitzsche sessions earlier that summer. No other Springfield members appear on the track with Neil, Jack and pianist Don Randi contributing the instrumentation and Jack the orchestration.

Once again session time was squeezed between commitments, with the group appearing the next night at the Swing Auditorium in San Bernardino, followed by a guest spot at a gig sponsored by KHJ-TV at the Anaheim Convention Center, along with the Nitty Gritty Dirt Band, The Young Men, Sunshine Company, with The Association topping the bill. Sessions resumed on August 30th where Neil contributed to the completion of Stephen's tour de force, *Rock And Roll Woman*, previously arranged and recorded in basic form prior to Neil's return. The session concluded with Richie's country-rock *A Child's Claim To Fame*, the two tracks intended as the A and B sides respectively for their next single release.

The inspiration for the lyrics to *Rock And Roll Woman* derived from Stephen's admiration for the Jefferson Airplane's Grace

Slick, while the music drew on David Crosby's influence. "The idea for *Rock And Roll Woman* came from jamming with David Crosby at his house," affirms Stephen, stopping short of crediting his friend with co-writing the number. "We got hung up on the F to D change in D-modal, which is mountain minor tuning. We kept playing it over and over and over again. So I just made up a melody and finally wrote words. When we went into the studio, David was there and he did what Ahmet did on *Bluebird*. At one point he just said to us, 'Okay, I think you've got it.'"

Opening with a recurring twelve-string guitar riff and cooing harmony singing and progressing through several distinct segments rising to climax with a pounding chord and vibrato sustain, the song is a mini-opera showcasing Stephen's keen sense for arrangement and the group's unparalleled layered vocals. David Crosby guests on the harmony. Stephen takes the lead vocals in his smokey, blues timbre in addition to handling keyboards and lead guitar chores admirably. The song is truly the successor to the masterful *Bluebird*, another example of Stephen's studio savvy and sophistication.

"*Rock And Roll Woman* was a silly lyric next to *For What It's Worth*," states Chris Hillman, "but that song was the essence of that band, that harmony and the drive. When I think of them, I think of that song."

There's a woman that you ought to know,
And she's comin,' singin' soft and low,
Singin' rock'n'roll,
She's a joy to know.
'Neath the shadow of her soothing hand,
I am free there just to make my stand,
Dream of far away lands,
Anything close at hand.
And she will follow me,
Why, do you know?
Familiar places she's been by,
That I know.
Could it be she don't have to try?

Rock And Roll Woman (Stephen Stills)

The inspiration for Richie's tune came a little closer to home. "*A Child's Claim To Fame* was a cynical look at Neil's leaving and coming back," as Richie notes. "I was just tired of that game he was playing." The song was composed during Neil's recent absence.

Well there goes another day,
And I wonder why,
You and I keep tellin' lies.
I can't believe a word you say,
Cause tomorrow's lullaby can't pacify,
My lonesome cryin'.
Well, make believe is all you know,
And to make believe is a game,
A child's rein, you changed your name.
So sadly I watch the show,
Just to see what you became,
Truth is a shame,
Too much fame.

A Child's Claim To Fame (Richie Furay)

The group first attempted to record the song with Doug Hastings but ran into problems. "I wasn't much of a country player," admits Doug. "I tried a solo on it but I was caught with my pants down on that one. Richie was so diplomatic, such a nice guy. I was struggling real hard to try to get something that sounded country, and Richie said, 'Well, yeah, that's kind of like it but maybe it could be a little more country.' He really had something in mind."

It was left to a very special guest to provide the authentic country twang. "It was a real thrill to have James Burton play on the track," Richie comments on the opportunity to have one of the foremost country session players and former sideman to Ricky Nelson play dobro on his song. "Boy, I was excited about that. I had been a huge Ricky Nelson fan as a kid. It was somebody's idea to get James, maybe Steve or Jimmy Messina, who was working at the studio then. James had a big influence on Jimmy Messina personally, he really liked his style." Credit goes to Dewey for the call. "The other guys didn't have the connections for James Burton, I did. So I called him up and he was there in 45 minutes. And he's mentioned to me since then that he never got paid for the session." Obviously not bothered by the sentiment of the lyrics, on his return Neil contributed a harmony vocal and some tasty country pickin' to the track. As with *Rock And Roll Woman*, Doug's part was erased.

Richie's foray into country music would prove to be no mere flirtation. *Go And Say Goodbye* had earlier hinted at the Springfield's country roots, but *A Child's Claim To Fame* was pure Nashville, one of the first examples of country rock a year before The Byrds' seminal *Sweetheart Of The Rodeo*. "The Byrds can't hold anything to us on country rock," laughs Richie. "I think I brought a lot of the country elements to the band, but Neil did, too." Indeed, as far back as 1963 with The Squires, Neil was playing the country and western evergreen *It Might Have Been*. "Even though Dewey played with some country artists," Richie continues, "his influence as far as the way a song would eventually sound didn't have as much effect as the way a song was written and then recorded. I think we all had some country influences. It was daring to do country then, but for me, I never thought about that. That's just what the song sounded like."

On September 1st, the group began work on Stephen's recently written *Hung Upside Down*, a solid rock number that starts off pleasantly enough with Richie handling the lead singing until Stephen takes over, propelling the track into a pounding guitar bridge and solo. The two trade voices back and forth with multi-tracked guitars bringing the song to a driving conclusion. The recorded track omitted an entire second verse from Stephen's original composition and demo:

Yes that's just how I feel,
I'm too unkind for words,
Right says I'm too unreal,
Shouldn't be here,
I find myself by myself.
Stood you up, let you down,
Watch my face hit the ground.
'Cause I'm hung upside down.
And I know that I'm bound,
To be found hangin' round,
Because I love you.

Hung Upside Down *(Stephen Stills)*

A week later, on September 6th, having received an acetate of the single for air play, KHJ's Boss 30 chart tipped *Rock And Roll Woman* as "hitbound." "I thought *Rock And Roll Woman* was a really good song, we all did," confirms Richie. "We were still trying; Steve was still trying. He wasn't going to let all these setbacks completely waste him." The song entered the *Billboard* charts on September 30th, and expectations ran high for a hit record. "You can never tell, it could be the biggest record we've ever had," Neil commented in *Hit Parader*. "All we need is what we always tried to get, a smash hit record. If we have just one that we think is a success, then we'll know that we've actually communicated. If we can survive that without going through changes, then there's no telling what will occur."

Recording sessions reconvened throughout September and early October as the Springfield compiled work for their new album. Overall, the quality of material and production on the album is consistently high, showing the group at the peak of its creative energies with flashes of sheer brilliance from track to track. Clearly evident throughout are three maturing writers moving in different directions, operating as individuals under the group banner. Gone are the unison voicings and triple guitar interplay weaving acoustic and electric guitar lines around a melody that had so characterized the Buffalo Springfield sound, instead replaced by individual solo tracks with various members in support.

"It may have been the family once again, but it wasn't the cohesive unit that made that debut album," attests Richie. "On the second album we drifted off into a lot of our own things and a lot of overdubs were used. The first time we just set up in the studio and played to a four-track machine." Grumbles Dewey of the AGAIN sessions, "Every guy had his songs, his studio time and his frame of mind." As Dickie Davis observes, "They were recording largely on their own rather than as a band."

Band members also produced their own songs, seeking advice on occasion from recording engineers Bruce Botnick and Jimmy Messina. There was a reasonable amount of experimenting with the various knobs on the console at the outset before each member could comfortably take the reins. "It was all hit and miss," notes Stephen, "but it was a great experience." Counters Richie, "We see our names on the records as 'Produced by' but I'm not really sure that meant we sat behind the console and called the shots. I didn't really produce *Child's Claim To Fame*, even though it says that. The engineer on the sessions had a lot to do with it."

No longer content to capture their live sound, a goal they failed to achieve on their debut release, the Springfield now utilized the studio as a creative instrument to construct songs, sometimes piece by piece, replacing spontaneity for pristine production value. "We have to go at it in another way," Stephen elaborated in *Hit Parader* magazine on the album's release. "The way we play live doesn't always work in the studio. We want to get the feeling of the song across. We might take out a guitar or add some strings to get the right effect. Now we don't have to explain to someone what we want to sound like and hope they understand. We wrote the music, we know what it means to us. Now we're learning how to get the feelings across that made us write the songs in the studio."

Besides *Bluebird* and *Rock And Roll Woman*, Stephen's other contribution, *Everydays*, was the only track to be resurrected from the spring sessions supervised by Atlantic's Ahmet Ertegun. *Everydays* remains a neglected gem among an entire album's worth of jewels. Recorded in April at Gold Star with Jim Fielder on bass, the jazz-flavored track illustrates perhaps more than any other cut on the album Stephen's confidence as both a writer and arranger. "It kind of smacks of some early Miles Davis slow tunes and a little bit of Brubeck," muses Stephen. "It just fell out one day when I was riffing in three/four time." Amazingly, the track was recorded live in the studio with no overdubs, Neil providing the sustained fuzz note throughout on his tiny Fender amp. The track reveals, too, what a talented bass player Jim was, as well as hinting at the direction Jim would pursue after leaving the Springfield and hooking up with Al Kooper in Blood, Sweat & Tears.

Jim describes the live session for *Everydays*. "That session was a pretty inspired session. Neil discovered that fuzz tone sound he used by accident. He had an old Fender amp and found you could get that fuzz sound if you plugged the speaker into the extension speaker jack with nothing plugged into the main speaker jack. He got that distortion naturally. He discovered that in the studio that day in his haste plugging the speaker into the wrong jack. He said to us, 'Hey, listen to this!' That's the hum in that song. With the speaker plugged into the extension speaker jack you could crank the volume all the way up and what would come out would be very low volume but all this distortion. He got that massive sustain, and we were all going, 'Wow!' Stephen played piano on the track and I was using my Hofner bass, which I was no longer using on stage and kept at home. On a lark I had pried the frets out of the neck, so I had myself a fretless bass. And that's what I played on that session. Everybody set up right there in the studio and played live. There was very little baffling back then, only on the drums. We ran it down once or twice, then it was take one or take two that we kept. I think Stephen was producing. I was pleasantly surprised to see my name on the second album when it came out six months later. I just figured they wouldn't even bother to give me a credit.''

One of the highlights on the second album is the emergence of Richie from behind the shadows of Stephen and Neil. "In the early days I just couldn't get a tune recorded," smiles Richie on the dominance of the other two in the writing stakes. "They knew royalties would be coming in, and the more songs they had on a record, the better off it'd be for them. I was fairly naive but after the first album, I picked up on the fact that the more songs you have on an album, the more money you make. 'Oh, so this is why you make records. You make money off them.' Those guys were more calculating than I was.''

Richie's *Sad Memory* has an interesting history. "It was one of the first songs I ever wrote when I was still a folkie in New York, about a girl back in Ohio. The only reason it got recorded at all was because I was waiting for those guys to come to the studio one day. They were late and I was sitting there so I just did it. I was all by myself, sitting in a chair with an acoustic guitar. 'Hey, let's get a sound on this guitar. Let's get a vocal sound,' and it came from that. They walked in while I was recording it and Neil thought, 'Hey, I can put this guitar part on it.' And that was it. I had probably showed it to Steve and Neil, but those guys were aggressive and wanted their songs on the album. I was pretty much determined that that was going to be the start of it for me." Contrary to the album notes, Neil's lead guitar on *Sad Memory*, the only other instrument to grace the track, was not recorded across town. That was an inside joke referring to the cavernous reverb echo employed by Neil on the track giving it a sense of distance and depth.

Soft winds blow in the summer time,
Young lovers feel so free.

221

Walking hand in hand down a shady lane,
What happened to me?
Did you ever love a girl,
Who walked right out on you?
You should know just how I feel,
Why I'm so blue.
Well, I made up my mind,
I'd find a new girl,
Who'll love me tenderly.
Forget the past I've left behind now,
It's a sad memory.

Sad Memory (Richie Furay)

Besides *A Child's Claim To Fame*, Richie's other contribution was written specifically with Dewey in mind. Setting *Nobody's Fool* aside, Richie composed *Good Time Boy* about Dewey whose personality and demeanor is epitomized in the line, "It's all right to be a good time boy." That song was a perfect vehicle for 'good ole Dew' to shine on. Bringing in an authentic R'n'B horn section to embellish the track was superb typecasting given Dewey's penchant for soul music. "Dewey loved Otis Redding and the Stax-Volt sound," smiles Dickie. "He used to sing *Good Time Boy* like he was Otis." Though Richie recalls Stephen suggesting the horn arrangement, Dewey remembers it otherwise. "I set up the session and got the horn section," he claims. "I had met the Louisiana Soul Train at the Red Velvet Club. They didn't know us. They were hot so I asked them to come play on my record and they said sure." Dewey received credit on the album as executive producer of the track. Like *A Child's Claim*, *Good Time Boy* marked a sharp left turn musically for the group, its first excursion into soul music, but it found a place among the eclectic mix of tracks. Often cited as the low point of the record by some critics, the song has a buoyancy that livens up the album. Just as *Mr. Soul* characterized Neil, and *Bluebird* Stephen, *Good Time Boy* is pure Dewey Martin.

Neil's three contributions, *Mr. Soul, Expecting To Fly*, and *Broken Arrow*, each stand in marked contrast to the other, revealing Neil's diverging musical paths that year. In *Mr. Soul*, dating back to late 1966 and early 67, Neil is a rock'n'roller, shouting out his oblique tale of the vacuousness of teen adulation over a

Rolling Stones' inspired rock rhythm. By the summer he had fallen under the sway of production guru Jack Nitzsche with *Expecting To Fly*, only to emerge afterwards attempting a Beatles' Sgt. Pepperish sound collage in *Broken Arrow*. But as diverse as they are, what each song shares in common is Neil's uncanny ability to turn out thought-provoking, poetic, almost mystical lyrics.

"I was fascinated with his writing because I hadn't ever really heard the kind of impressions that he wrote," states Richie. "I wrote songs in the same vein as Stephen did, but there was an impression, a person, in Neil's writing that presented a song as a picture in a different way. I learned a lot from Neil. He impressed me so much as a writer and artist." Offers Barry Friedman, "I was always a bigger fan of Neil's songs and of Richie's songs than I was of Stephen's. Neil's songs were just more interesting and Richie's had an innocence, a purity and a kind of Midwestern sensibility that I really liked. Stephen's songs were great, too, they were strong songs, but they weren't my favorites."

In describing *Expecting To Fly* in the liner notes to his DECADE compilation, Neil states, "This record was made by Jack Nitzsche and I. It took a lot of time. I overdubbed my vocal line by line to get it in pitch. Studio singing was still very nervous for me then. Though I was not with the Springfield at the time, I brought this tape to the record when we finally got together." Jack's signature was heavy orchestration, a style used to excess on *Expecting To Fly*, at times obscuring Neil's poetic lyric of love lost. Anyone who has had the rare opportunity to hear Neil perform the song alone seated at the piano will attest to its sheer beauty and poignant lyric.

"*Expecting To Fly* took a long time to write," explains Neil. "It came from two or three different songs that I molded together and changed around to fit together. We spent three weeks recording and mixing it. Some people have said that they can't hear the lyrics too well. I like to hear lyrics and I can hear the words to it. They are buried in spots, but the general mood of the song is there. That's what matters in that particular song. It's not like a modern recording; it's based on an old theory. The new style is to try to hear every instrument clearly. The old way of recording is the Phil Spector idea of blending them all so they all sound like a wall of sound." In order to create that dense quality, Neil and Jack overdubbed extensively, even double tracking acoustic and electric pianos. "The electric piano is playing a melodic figure in the bridge and it sounds almost like a bass. Underneath that, way down, is a concert grand piano adding bottom to it." Neil had also discovered the intricacies of stereo sound, panning the orchestral crescendo at the start of *Expecting To Fly* from channel to channel. On a drum downbeat cue in the middle of the song, the instruments swap channels from left to right. The elaborate production found favor with the others. "I liked Jack Nitzsche's strings and arrangement on *Expecting To Fly* that added a different dimension to it," confirms Richie. "From James Burton's dobro to Jack Nitzsche's strings, there's a lot of space between those songs. But that's who we were at that time."

Of note is the absence of the last two lines of the original composition on the recorded track deleted from the sonorous conclusion:

Sadly, I'll walk into autumn and watch
As the leaves turn gold.
Sadly, I'll wait for the winter,
And long for the day when you're told.

Expecting To Fly remains a masterpiece and serves as a precursor of Neil's first solo album two years later, a style of production he has disparaged in recent years preferring instead a back to basic rock approach.

The ambitious *Broken Arrow*, described by musicologist Pete Doggett as "six minutes of lyrical obscurity and breath-taking musical inventiveness," was a Sgt. Pepper-influenced sound pastiche whose genesis came about during Neil's absence from the group. "I wrote the first verse right away but I couldn't get a refrain," explained Neil in a *Hit Parader* interview that fall, "the part that goes, 'Did you see him in the river.' I finally got it by borrowing from another song I'd written a year and a half ago. Then I mixed it up and came out with the refrain. I had a two minute song with no repetition, so I figured the only way to make it work would be to turn it into a six minute song, repeat the refrain three different times and take it into three different movements. It didn't end up to my satisfaction but the idea is there. I didn't have enough time to complete it the way I wanted to. There's many little things in it that relate to the general feeling. We tried to cut a verse out to make it a single but it just didn't work."

Opening with what sounds like a live take of *Mr. Soul* and then moving into a verse that continues Neil's fascination with the relationship between the artist and his fans, the song also plays on his image as the self-styled Hollywood Indian.

The lights turned on and the curtain fell down,
And when it was over, it felt like a dream,
They stood at the stage door and begged for a scream.
The agents had paid for the black limousine,
They waited outside in the rain.
Did you see them?
Did you see them?

Broken Arrow (Neil Young)

It develops its pastiche quality through three distinct passages linked by interludes identified in the studio logs with titles like "Ball Park" and "Theme Jazz" before concluding with clarinet accompaniment and the beating of a heart.

The refrain in question was lifted from *Down Down Down* written and demoed in 1966.

Come to see her in the river,
She'll be there to wave to you.
In the hope that you'll forgive her,
She'll join you there.

Neil later extracted a further stanza from the unreleased song when he compiled his *Country Girl* medley on Crosby, Stills, Nash and Young's 1970 DEJA VU album. A final verse remains as yet unused.

Now you see how down you've fallen,
Now you hear your conscience call.
Thank yourself alone for stallin,'
I'm not there to call.
Call me a fool 'cause I need her,
And see her but now you're down.
Something inside you will tell you I'm wise,
To what you're spreadin' round.

225

At the time Neil considered this verse in *Broken Arrow* to be the best lyric he'd ever written:

He saw that his brother had sworn on the wall,
He hung up his eyelids and ran down the hall.
His mother had told him a trip was a fall,
And don't mention babies at all.

"It's just an image of being very scared and mixed up," he suggests. "The broken arrow is the Indian sign of peace, usually after losing a war. A broken arrow usually means that somebody has lost a lot." Neil later named his ranch and home studio Broken Arrow.

Constructing the elaborate suite required close to one hundred hours of studio time with Neil relying upon engineer Jim Messina at Sunset Sound. If Neil had a vision of the entire concept mapped out in his head, he kept the rest of the group largely in the dark as the track developed, teaching them their parts only when required. "When we started to record *Broken Arrow*," states Stephen, "Neil was the only one who had heard it. We learned it as we recorded it." With *Broken Arrow*, Neil found his feet as an arranger. "When Neil presented a song, he probably had some ideas for it, and as time went on those ideas became more definite," Richie describes Neil's arrangement style and habit. "At first he was more willing to just throw things out to us, whereas Stephen had more direction on his songs. Stephen was the arranger. When Stephen went into the studio, he was always more interested in the bass and drums. After that, once he'd got the basic track down, he felt confident enough to play the organ or all the guitar parts if Neil wasn't going to be there."

The introductory passage featuring Dewey singing *Mr. Soul* was not, in fact, an actual live recording but fabricated in the studio with a tape of fans screaming for the Beatles at Candlestick Park edited in. "It was never live," confirms Dewey who found the whole concept rather confusing. "It was cut at the end of a session at Columbia. We had a few minutes left and Neil said, 'I wanna slow down *Mr. Soul* and I want you to sing one verse.' So we just pumped it right there in one or two takes. And he put on the screams. He had all this big thing for *Broken Arrow* that I didn't know about and nobody else knew what the hell it was about. It took us three days to cut the song. It was all different tempos." Dewey cites *Broken Arrow* as an example of the expense the group incurred recording. "We were always learning in the studio and that cost us an arm and a leg. The band never rehearsed enough after the first album."

In the liner notes, *Broken Arrow* bears a dedication to Ken Koblun. "I dedicated it to him because he had gone through a rough time," explains Neil. Many believed the song to be about the mysterious "Ken" who loomed large in the Springfield's history; some thought he was the Indian. "Neil dedicated that song to me," explains Ken, "because it's an Indian term for friendship after a war. It's not about me. Probably Neil felt guilty for sending me away from the Buffalo Springfield."

Broken Arrow concludes the album on a powerful note. "I thought it was unique, innovative, very mystical, Beatlish, the George Martin influence/*Strawberry Fields* kind of thing," states Richie of Neil's attempt to create an art piece.

The band rejected the "Stampede" title suggested by Atco, preferring the simplicity, if not the irony, of "Buffalo Springfield Again." Artist Eve Babitz designed the cover, which incorporates a photo of the original group dating from their first photo shot with Ivan Nagy amid an idyllic painting bordered by flowers. What appears to be a cherub or angel reaches out to grasp Bruce's hand in the artwork. The back cover includes an extensive thank you list of names submitted by each member, including not only their musical influences but current close friends and associates as well. Even Mort the hearse is acknowledged. The dedication is directed to Barry Friedman.

Released in mid-November, a full year after their debut album, BUFFALO SPRINGFIELD AGAIN initially sold 200,000 copies, but without a hit single to propel it, sales dropped off after the initial rush. Reviews were mixed as well. In a review in the recently launched *Rolling Stone* magazine on December 14th, the record was deemed a "musically and vocally interesting album. The songs on this album are not always as distinctive as those on their first effort, but they are done well. What BUFFALO SPRINGFIELD AGAIN, though, obviously lacks is cohesiveness." The review went on to cite the diversity among the tracks as a drawback and evidence of disunity within the group. "Together there is no blend, only a rather obvious alienation among the compositions." Kudos were offered for Neil's *Mr. Soul*, but the reviewer leveled criticism at his grand production attempt on *Broken Arrow*, noting that "it becomes tiresome and loses impact." Stephen's contributions, notably *Bluebird* and *Rock And Roll Woman*, were lauded as the highlights of an otherwise uneven album. "Bluebird is a masterpiece of episodic eclecticism that seems to travel backward through history," a critic in *The New York Times* noted. "It starts off like a piece of contemporary west coast rock, and after four and a half minutes of imperceptible mutations, winds up with a back-country banjo solo. . . . Young's *Broken Arrow* has a real mythic quality — not too clear, maybe but mysterious rather than obscure." Writing in the *Detroit South End*, critic Mike Kerman echoed that sentiment stating, "*Rock And Roll Woman* is the best song the band has ever recorded" but scorned Neil as a "production number devotee." As for *Broken Arrow*, he concludes, "Sorry to say, I don't understand the message."

Despite extraordinary promotional efforts by Atco, including handing out Buffalo Springfield lighters, the album stalled at No. 44, much to the surprise of the band. "We all thought it had real potential," says Richie of the AGAIN album. "On that album *Mr. Soul*, *Bluebird*, and *Rock And Roll Woman* were all definite singles. We were still looking for the commercial single but it never happened on that album. This was all a big let down for us. *Bluebird* was a Top Ten hit in Los Angeles but it couldn't get out of town. But that was always a problem with the band. We couldn't get out of town physically or over the airwaves. Had maybe a hit single appeared, it may have been a different story. It was probably at that point when I might have started doubting the whole thing. After the AGAIN album had run its course, we were pretty much at the end of the line."

As recording progressed for the AGAIN album, negotiations were simultaneously underway to break free of Charlie Greene and Brian Stone. Television appearances on the *Andy Williams Show* and Joey Bishop's short-lived late night celebrity gab fest to promote *Rock And Roll Woman*, with Monkee Micky Dolenz making a surprise appearance to say hello to his "close friends The Buffalo Springfield," failed to push the single beyond a disappointing No. 44 in *Billboard*, though once again the group could do no wrong in LA with a No. 2 charting.

The knives were out and the target was management. "They really turned on Charlie and Brian and blamed them for their limited success," suggests Dickie Davis. "Charlie and Brian were waiting for a hit to reap the rewards but the band was starving. Mistakes were made during the Greene and Stone time and it never got whole again. It was like a bad marriage." At Dickie's urging the group turned to Atlantic Records president Ahmet Ertegun, long a supporter of the Springfield, to help them out of their quagmire. Ahmet recommended a lawyer who, after perusing their contract, suggested it could be broken but at a price. "Atlantic Records didn't want to help," Dickie recalls, "so I told the lawyer, 'Okay, fine. If you say we can break the Greene-Stone contract, if you say we have a good case, well, then Atlantic's contract falls too because they have a contract with us through Greene-Stone. You might tell Ahmet Ertegun he's gonna have to pick sides.' The next week Ahmet came in with a great plan as to how we were gonna get rid of Greene-Stone and he was going to give us a certain amount of money to do it."

Atlantic advanced the group $100,000 to buy out Charlie and Brian. In reality, it was the group itself who financed the leverage with the sum applied against future royalties. Atlantic had faith enough in the group's earning potential to finance the deal. "They bought us out with Atlantic's money," confirms Charlie. "Ertegun was the arbitrator. He wasn't taking sides, he was protecting his label. He wanted peace, and I don't blame him. Peace could have been achieved if Stephen didn't rant and rave and carry on." Charlie did not take the ouster well. "I wasn't bitter, I was hurt. Big difference. To this day I love that band. Nobody could touch them."

Greene and Stone remain controversial figures in the Buffalo Springfield story. At the time they took on the group, they had all the connections and hype to dazzle five naive young men. What transpired soon after was the fact that much of what the two boasted was merely smoke and mirrors. As record producers they botched the debut album; as managers they failed to raise the group's profile beyond Southern California. Though there is no doubting Charlie and Brian's motives were sincere, they lacked the means to carry through their talk. "There was a lot of confusing stuff that went on with those guys," muses Richie. "They knew they had something with us but didn't know what to do with it. And they also didn't know what to do or how to bring Steve and Neil together or maybe they were trying not to. They may have been the ones saying, 'Steve you're the guy' or 'Hey, Neil, you're the guy.' I don't remember them coming to me and saying, 'Richie, you're the guy,' but I'm sure I was drawn into siding with one or the other. Greene and Stone do not leave a good memory in my mind."

"The Buffalo Springfield had talent, and in spite of Charlie and Brian, managed to make quite a dent," offers Nurit Wilde. "But they were never as big as they should have been. Nowhere near. If anything, Charlie and Brian kept the Buffalo from becoming as big as they could have been just by virtue of the fact that they didn't know what they were doing. They didn't see the bigger picture. They just wanted some instant fame and didn't care about nurturing the band along. And the band needed it. These were just young guys who were insecure themselves and had problems within the band. What they needed were managers who were understanding and able to resolve things and give them some slack. But Charlie and Brian were pushing and pushing, wanting the immediate success and taking all the glory. They didn't really care about their future, get the money now."

Neil places the group's disastrous financial straits squarely on the shoulders of its managers. "We always owed. We never got out of hock. They'd give us an advance and then when an advance came in from somewhere, they got it. A lot of things didn't add up right or at least we couldn't follow the addition."

With Charlie and Brian out of the picture, Dickie Davis informally assumed managerial duties out of his home on Formosa Avenue, borrowing $300 from his parents to keep the band afloat. With the imminent release of the AGAIN album, he concentrated his efforts at placing the group on an eastern tour. He scored a major coup landing a support slot for the Beach Boys, Strawberry Alarm Clock (*Incense and Peppermints* had been their only hit), and the Soul Survivors, who had recently scored with *Expressway To Your Heart*, on a ten day eastern swing beginning November 17 at the Masonic Auditorium in Detroit. At that moment the Beach Boys were still riding a high with *Good Vibrations* and *Heroes and Villains* having just released their SMILEY SMILE album.

On Saturday, November 4th, the Springfield played the

Earl Warren Showgrounds in Santa Barbara with the Watts 103rd St. Band and Lewis and Clarke Expedition. The following weekend the group appeared earlier in the day at Hamilton High in Santa Monica before the first of two nights at the Shrine Auditorium in Los Angeles along with the Grateful Dead, Moby Grape, and Blue Cheer. *The Los Angeles Times'* Pete Johnson, an ardent Springfield supporter, praised the group as the stars of the show, writing of their opening night performance: "Their sound is rooted in folk-rock, that much abused cliche, but they seem to be able to do almost anything. To prove it, they dished up an endless version of their hit *Bluebird*, which made the best efforts of the Cheer and the Dead sound amateurish and would have been unobtainable by most groups even with the full resources of a recording studio." A review in the *LA Free Press* highlighted the extended workout on *Bluebird*: "It just went on and on and on; every second a more fantastic trip than the previous!" The underground paper *Open City*, in its December 8th issue, dismissed the *LA Times'* review as home town favoritism, contending that the Dead were the undisputed stars of the show. The review claims that the Springfield actually apologized on Saturday for a shoddy performance the previous night. "The Springfield in reality were a bit of a drag both nights," continues the reviewer. "They spent ten minutes trying to freak out the audience with a free improvisation that depended heavily on feedback, fuzztone, and all that." The next night the group returned to familiar territory playing San Bernardino's Swing Auditorium in a concert sponsored by KMEN radio with the Yellow Payges and Canada's Mandala.

Before embarking on the Beach Boys' tour, the Springfield spent time at Sunset Sound on November 14th in an attempt to lay down their next single. Given the unusual title *Telephone Pole*, the song was, in fact, Neil's *On The Way Home*, composed shortly before his return but completed too late for inclusion on the AGAIN album. As Richie recalls, "Neil brought the song in and played it for us, and I remember him saying, 'Richie, I think you should sing this song.'" Work was begun with engineer Jimmy Messina assisting with production duties. The name "Telephone Pole" derived from an incident that same day involving Stephen wrapping his Ferrari around a pole on the way to the studio.

The group was no stranger to car accidents with Bruce cracking up his brand new Corvette Stingray on Old Colony

Road in Malibu that fall. "It was a 90 degree hair pin turn, and when you've got 427 horsepower and you're in a Corvette you figure you can take the turn," recounts Bruce of his next run-in with the law. "I went careening down the highway unconscious after hitting the wall. When I came to, I looked behind me and the back half of my car was about 40 feet behind me. I was strapped in so I only had a small abrasion on my nose but there was blood." The sheriffs arrived at the scene, and as Bruce recalls, spent more time looking for drugs than attending to him and his passenger. "The exact moment the accident happened, the sheriffs were coming around the corner. I'm at Lance's side and I reach into his pocket because his shoulder was dislocated, and I pull out his stash of grass and throw it into the surrounding shrubberies along the side of the road. And I see three or four sheriffs, instead of coming to our aid, run off into the shrubberies in order to search for what I'd obviously thrown away. They didn't find anything, though."

The group left *Telephone Pole* incomplete, intending on finishing up after tour commitments. "The single never got completed," says Richie, "but the tour came and we were off with the Beach Boys to do ten days of good work." Coming on the heels of the release of BUFFALO SPRINGFIELD AGAIN, the group hoped their visibility on the tour would push album sales.

"That Beach Boys tour was a real stable time for the group," claims Dickie. "The five were back together, the second album was getting attention and good reviews, the tour was playing big halls, ten and fifteen thousand seaters, and the Springfield were doing good shows and going down well." For Bruce, sharing billing with the Beach Boys was a thrill and an opportunity for the Springfield to shine. "The Beach Boys at that time were the biggest thing on the planet besides the Beatles," he enthuses. "It was a big deal for us to be on tour with them. They were real lousy musicians but they had terrific harmony and a name. They were a studio group. On stage it was like The Monkees. They would spend weeks and months in the studio with Brian Wilson perfecting harmonies and overdubs but you put them on stage and they stunk. It didn't matter because nobody could hear them over the screaming and yelling. So we blew them off the stage because we were musically better. I later heard that on one of their British tours, they paid us a great compliment by performing *Rock And Roll Woman*."

Beach Boy Mike Love reveals the headliner's affection for the Springfield when he recalled, "It was incredible. We used to go onstage and sit behind their speakers and listen to them." And Dickie remembers another indirect tribute. "The first night in Detroit on November 17th, the Buffalo blew the Beach Boys off the stage. They hadn't toured in awhile and were a bit rusty, but they rehearsed in their hotel room all night and the next day, and on the second show in Buffalo, they blew us off that night."

As the tour progressed along the East Coast playing colleges and theaters, a camaraderie developed between the groups. "Dennis Wilson became one of our closest buddies," recalls Bruce. "We were taking the bus and they flew. One night Dennis wouldn't fly so I took his seat on the plane and he took the bus with the other guys." Richie recalls some of the reverie that went on. "Dennis Wilson would get on the bus with us a few times. Some of the other guys rode with us as well and hung out with us. We were going down the freeway once and Dennis opened the window and had a fire extinguisher and was shooting at cars going by."

On another occasion, Dewey commandeered the chartered Greyhound tour bus the support groups traveled in, much to Stephen's chagrin, and drove around the city with various members of all four bands. "We arrived at the gig and the Greyhound driver and Dick Duryea, the Beach Boys' road manager, went in to check out where to load in," recalls Dewey with glee. "So Mike Love yelled, 'Who knows how to drive this thing?' I said, 'I do.' I had watched Faron Young years earlier. So off we went. All these people were yelling at us as we tooled around. The driver and Dick freaked out when they came out and noticed the bus was gone. When we got back, they came on the bus and growled, 'Who was driving this bus?' And we all shouted, 'We were!' We had all agreed to say that. And Duryea was not pleased. They had the police out looking for the bus."

In White Plains, New York, the group was interviewed prior to their November 21st show at the Westchester County Center where Richie declared *Telephone Pole* to be the group's next single. Bruce took sick during the concert, forcing Stephen to assume the bass duties. As Dickie remembers, this did not sit well with Stephen. "We had Bruce propped up with vitamin C and antibiotics. We had to do two sets and ended the first one with Neil's big number *Mr. Soul*. Bruce had made it through the

233

first set but was too ill to go on. He was pale and drenched in sweat, and we eventually took him to a hospital. Stephen was our backup bass player, so he had to go on for the second set playing bass — and he didn't like it. He went on angry and it just kept building in him. He was getting into more lead playing by that time, so when it came time for *Bluebird* to end the set, he was really agitated. That was his big song to play lead in and he couldn't. Neil took the first solo, and when it came to the second solo, Stephen's solo, his face was beet red and he started flaying away at this bass in a rage. I'd never seen bass playing like that. He was finger-picking the bass rapidly as if it were a guitar. The audience was on its feet and started screaming, and these were college kids not teenyboppers, but Steve was completely oblivious. He was playing so loudly that the amplifier was rumbling and distorting. He finished the song, then threw the bass into the amplifier, walking off in a rage. Steve never knew the audience response because he had been so angry that he couldn't play lead guitar on his song. Several members of the Beach Boys had watched from the wings in awe."

Prior to their appearance on November 23rd in Boston at the Back Bay Theater, members of the Springfield and Beach Boys were invited to attend Thanksgiving dinner at Eaglebrook School in Eaglebrook, Massachusetts as guests of Dickie's father Richard, who was employed as chef at the school. A graduate of Eaglebrook, Dickie was accorded star treatment as the students mobbed the group members for autographs during dinner. Stephen donned a white coat and served as waiter to their table. A few years later on a return trip to Boston, Neil regaled his audience with stories of that first time through, having his fringed jacket stolen and one of their road crew engaging in a fight back stage.

For the tour, the Springfield developed a novel opening to their set. "Stephen had the idea to open the show with *Rock And Roll Woman* by starting the song behind the curtains," explains Dickie. "The band would be announced and they'd start playing the riff so you wouldn't see them, then as the curtain parted it was at the moment Steve hit the microphone for the first verse. He thought that was a cool idea." Richie remembers one concert where Neil tried to leave an impression on an attending police officer. "We were playing somewhere and there were police standing right by the PA speakers. Neil's lead guitar playing was always really shrill. He noticed a cop standing with his ear right by the speaker horn, so he turned up and hit these really high notes and the cop never flinched. I'm sure he was hearing those notes ringing in his head for the next three days."

The tour wound its way through New England and the Middle States, including a concert at West Point Military Academy, before wrapping up in Baltimore on November 26th. Talk of accompanying the Beach Boys on the British leg of their tour was just that. Instead, the group returned to California where, following a couple of days rest and recording, they resumed gigging on December 8th at the Governor's Hall in Sacramento and a benefit the next night for radio station KPFA in Santa Monica.

Scattered recording dates occupied their time until December 19th when they appeared in San Diego at the Community Concourse before 4,200 enthusiastic fans. On the 21st the group began a three night stand headlining at the Fillmore in San Francisco with support from the Collectors and a young southern group named Hour Glass featuring Duane and Gregg Allman. Neil's mother Rassy joined him in California for Christmas, attending one of the Fillmore shows, segments of which were filmed for a television special entitled *The Sights and Sounds of San Francisco* also featuring the Electric Flag and Richie Havens. The show aired in early 1968. The December issue of *TeenSet* featured the group participating in the first annual TeenSet Christmas skating party held at the Topanga Plaza Ice Capades Chalet along with Michael Miller and various members of Hearts and Flowers, the Merry-Go-Round and Giant Sunflower. Having three Canadians, experienced skaters all, gave the Springfield a decisive advantage over the others in the events.

The group saw out 1967 with a gig at the Cheetah in Venice Beach along with the Seeds, Smokestack Lightning, and Lollipop Shoppe in support. With the success of the AGAIN album and Beach Boys tour, the year came to a close on an optimistic note for the Springfield. "The group really seemed together at that point," confirms Richie, echoing his feelings of one year earlier when the Springfield set out to conquer New York. Not surprisingly, many of the same problems that disrupted the band in early 1967 would do so again in 1968.

We wish to thank the following friends, enemies & people we don't know from Adam for their influence and inspiration. The dedication is to Barry Friedman.

Hank/B. Marvin
Otis Redding
Doc Watson
FRED NEIL
Hank Williams
John Herald
Ricky Nelson
Randy Backman
Joe Mara
The Ventures
Roy Orbison
Jane & Sylvia
Jimi Hendrix
Bert Jansh
Jim & Jean
Cyrus Faryar
& Rusty
Gene Pitney
Buddy Miles
Mickey Mickey
Davy Peter
Eric Clapton

The Nurk Twins
& George
Ringo
Phil Spector
Lester B. Pearson
Bobby Harmelink
KEN KOBLUN
Floyd Cramer
The Five Byrds
The Dillards
Robert Johnson
Herbie Cohen
Frank Zappa
Stones
Elmer & Mario
Donovan Leicht
Enid
JIM FRIEDMAN
Rickey James Matthews
The Spoons
Jerry Yester

Chet Atkins
Jefferson Airplane
Peter Noone
Nurit
John Lee Hooker
John Hopkins
Charlie Chin
Jimmy Reed
Flatt & Scruggs
JACK NITZCHE
Jad Diltz
Mickey Most
John Coltrane
Lisa Kindred
Tim Hardin
Ray Brown
Craig Allen
Judy Collins
George Romney
Jim Fielder
Billie Winter
Chip Douglas

BOB GIBSON
Fidel
Jim Messina
Fort William
Robert Zimmerman
Pibehiney Pala
Steve Saunders
Albt. Grossman
Richie Havens
Eddie Miller
Peanuts Willinghan
Pete Seeger
Mort.
Chuck Berry
The Kingston Trio
& John
Felix Pappalardi
The Vanilla Fudge
... and a hundred
thousand more.
(Spelling by The
Buffalo Springfeild

a BUDD FILIPPO Attractions
& SAM GORDON Artists presentation

THE BEACH BOYS

in CONCERT with the

BUFFALO SPRINGFIELDS
The SOUL SURVIVORS

STRAWBERRY
ALARM CLOCK* and   PICKLE BROS

DANDY DAN* of WMCA

Tix: $5.50, $4.50, $3.50**

NOV. 20th at 8:30 P.M.
presented by
FAIRFIELD UNIV. (Gym)
Fairfield, Conn. (203) 259-0926
All Seats $4.

NOV. 21st at 8 P.M.
presented by IONA COLLEGE at
WESTCHESTER CO. CENTER
White Plains, N.Y.
(914) WH 9-8900
Tel: 914 BE 5-6200

NOV. 26th at 2 P.M.
presented by
SETON HALL UNIV.
South Orange, N.J.
Tel: (201) 762-8995
Univ.ConcertProd.—KenRoberts, Ex.Pred.

AMERICAN TALENT MGMT.

Distinguished Guests

glebrook School played host to members of The Beach Boys and the Buffalo Spring-
wo nationally popular singing groups, Thursday at a Thanksgiving dinner. The
stopped at Eaglebrook enroute from Pittsburg to Boston on a concert tour. The
Springfield's manager, Richard Davis, Jr. (at left, behind woman in white sweater)
son of Richard Davis, Sr., Eaglebrook School chef, and a graduate of both Eagle-
and Deerfield Academy. Faculty and local children seek autographs from the song-

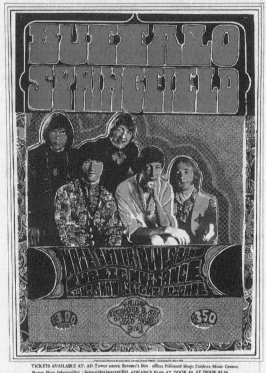

Poster for a performance at University of California at Davis, December 8, 1967.

Performing at the *TeenSet* skating party, Topanga Plaza Ice Capades Chalet, Christmas 1967.

NINE

It's Over

When you see me fly away without you,
Shadow on the things you know.
Feathers fall around you,
And show you the way to go.
It's over.

Birds (Neil Young)

f the title of their second album, BUFFALO SPRINGFIELD AGAIN was unintentionally ironic, the title of the third album, LAST TIME AROUND, was quite deliberate, though equally brilliant. Even as the band broke up during 1968, the Buffalo Springfield found the courage and the creativity to write and record such classics as *On The Way Home, I Am A Child, Kind Woman, Pretty Girl Why,* and *Four Days Gone,* thus enriching their legacy for the bands that would pick up the Springfield's pieces in the next decade.

Yet as the New Year dawned, the Springfield believed there would be many more rounds of concerts and albums. Following further recording sessions at Sunset Sound on January 2, 1968, the band resumed gigging on the 6th in Santa Barbara at the Earl Warren Showgrounds with jazz man Charles Lloyd and newcomers Turquoise. Six days later they appeared at the Purple Haze club in Riverside, selling out the 2,000 seat venue and turning away 350 disappointed fans. The next day, still hopeful of finding a hit off the AGAIN album, Atco released Neil's *Expecting To Fly,* backed by Stephen's *Everydays.* The disk barely scrapped into the *Billboard* Hot 100, peaking at No. 98 for two weeks before disappearing. Like their previous efforts, *Expecting To Fly* was simply too sophisticated for AM radio to comprehend. For Neil, this was a bitter blow that caused him to pause and once again assess his future with the group.

On the same day of the single's release, the Springfield joined a star-studded bill, including, among others, The Turtles, The Byrds (now down to a trio after David Crosby was acrimoniously fired earlier), Stone Poneys featuring Linda Ronstadt, The Box Tops, Jay & the Techniques, Rose Garden, Brenton Wood, and the Classics IV for a day long festival at the San Diego Sports Arena. The groups traveled together to the gig amid a convivial atmosphere via chartered bus. Along for the ride was Michael Miller as well as two aspiring managers who took the opportunity to pitch their wares to the Springfield members. "On the bus was Elliot Roberts and David Geffen," recalls Michael. "Talk about your big time rush; they wanted the band real bad. David was just out of the mail room, and they had one client, Laura Nyro. They were about to sign Joni Mitchell who didn't have a record deal yet, but Joni knew Neil from Toronto. That was the big hustle and it impacted on driving the band apart. 'Who are we going to sign with?' That drove the band apart. Elliot and David drove a wedge between Neil and the rest of the band and that was really what kept it from continuing." Confirms Richie, "I remember Elliot Roberts along trying to pitch himself to us. I think he was still an agent at the time. We thought, 'Well, maybe this guy might be able to help us.' It was always, 'Who can solve our problems?' I think Neil was getting close to Elliot. As far as actually managing the Springfield, he never did. He promised to get us on the Rome Pop Festival but never did and that was it."

Scheduled for February 19th through 25th but postponed until May 11th, the roster of acts for the Rome Pop Festival never included the Springfield. According to Elliot, "Stephen thought the Springfield was his band but Neil had all of these great songs. Yet Stephen and Neil had a great deal of respect for each other. I think that's why the Springfield stayed together as long as it did. But it was just a matter of time before it had to break up."

All was not well with Bruce, whose commitment to the group was beginning to wane in response to the ongoing Stills-Young rivalry and his own drug use. Bruce began withdrawing from the group, even going as far as quitting during their December Fillmore stand. "It was probably true that I was losing interest," he admits. "I was sick and tired of their antics, the dueling that was constant between Stephen and Neil. I was beginning to recognize what the expansion of ego that comes with success and recognition was doing to these two guys. It became disheartening to me. It had gotten to the point where I even quit on stage one night in San Francisco. We were doing three nights. I went back to LA and was riding horses with Michael Clarke up in Topanga Canyon and one of the guys came up the trails in a Mini Minor to coax me to play that night. I flew up to San Francisco to do the gig and in the middle of the set they pissed me off again and I walked off stage. Stephen had to pick up the bass and finish the night. I was fed up with their antics. All it took was a word and I was back in but I was frustrated. To this day, those two guys are still the same."

Dewey considers the incident a turning point. "The Springfield used to waste five to ten minutes tuning up between songs and then they'd play those half-hour things like *Bluebird*. They used super slinky strings and they would go out of tune after every song. And it pissed Bruce off. 'Can't you guys keep those guitars in tune?' He went up to them a couple of times and asked that. Bruce couldn't take it anymore. Finally out of nowhere Bruce looked at them, turned his back on the audience, and slammed his bass down on the stage. It was still plugged in and went blaaaang!! And he walked off stage. Stephen looked up, his eyes as big as silver dollars, and there's Bruce standing in the wings in his monk outfit and purple sunglasses. He wasn't in the group much longer after that. Everybody was through with him by then, including me."

Dewey also vividly recalls the growing animosity between Stephen and Neil flaring up at a gig on January 26th. "These guys would be jamming on one chord for half an hour. We were playing at UCLA Irvine in the auditorium where they played basketball. On stage Stephen was on my left and Neil was on my right. They had these big long curly cords and each guy's way off in the wings. And here they were fighting about who's gonna play the next solo. They kept getting louder and louder at each other. Steve would crank up his Marshall and Neil would be hitting those one note things and no one could hear anything. It got to the point where it was so bad that after we got off stage, these two guys started throwing punches in the dressing room. I got into that one and grabbed each of them and held them apart and chewed them out."

Soon after, the Springfield were rocked once again by the loss of Bruce. Following their appearance at Irvine, Bruce was busted on his way home from the venue, nabbed by the police for speeding in his Camaro without a driver's license. A routine search found Bruce with an open bottle of liquor between his legs and in the company of an under-age girl in possession of marijuana. Bruce was apprehended, detained, and subsequently released on bail pending prosecution. The group's lawyer sent him to the Tropicana Motel, home to the rock music fraternity, to cool his heels, where he was busted again the same night.

Bruce describes the convoluted turn of events that evening and his final exit from the Springfield. "It was another bust. It was at the Tropicana Motel when I called the police about the people downstairs who were really bugging me. The police came to my room instead of their room and figured the girl I was with was the same girl they had stopped me with earlier on Sunset Boulevard, who was sixteen and under the curfew. Her neighbor was a cop and he was in the car that stopped us. Since it was after ten, being the good neighbor, he tells me to send her home in a cab, which I did. I had gone back to the hotel and was with my girlfriend Reine, who later married Peter Tork. The other girl's neighbor, the cop, was one of the policemen who came up to the room, shone a flashlight in Reine's face, realized it wasn't her and apologized. Meanwhile the other cops are snooping around the room and find grass. Busted. So I go to jail, go to court. I figured the fix was in but some lawyer for the group figures that was it for me. I was getting busted too many times. He comes to me and tells me how I'm hurting the business. I had become a liability. He produced a piece of paper with all these conditions on it. I had to forfeit the band, publishing, everything and they'd look after the legal bills. That was it. I was out. I go to jail for marijuana and then immigration got involved. So I'm in El Centro, an immigration camp, for two weeks. I called Peter Tork because the band had abandoned me and Peter got me out of there."

Convinced that Bruce had become an encumbrance threatening the group's reputation and progress, the others reluctantly dealt him out. For Bruce, the decision to leave him to the authorities was cowardly. "I'm sure from his perspective that's the way it looked," concedes Richie. "It's probably an accurate perception that he had that we abandoned him. From ours, I'm sure we were thinking, 'Man, we gotta carry on. We gotta get something that's gonna have some cohesiveness to it. It's not working with Bruce.' It was probably presented to us that he was a liability and we agreed. It's just like the whole thing with Barry Friedman. And it was likely left to someone else to do it, we probably wouldn't have personally done the severing." Bruce was ultimately found guilty and deported back to Canada.

The group limped on without him. "By the time Bruce left," claims Dickie, "Stephen had become unhappy with his playing, attitude, and commitment. He was becoming more difficult to work with. He had also used other drummers like Buddy Miles because Steve wanted to use the best players and liked hanging out with the top musicians." Miles Thomas sums up Bruce's legacy with the group: "He was a frightening musician but he wasn't reliable. He just wasn't around enough. He was a real sweet guy but he would always stand with his back to the audience. I think mainly he was trying to keep Dewey on track. Bruce could play anything. After Monterey he went out and bought a sitar when everyone wanted to play one after seeing Ravi Shankar. Bruce got one in San Francisco and taught himself how to play it."

The scramble was on once again to fill the vacant bass position. Several names were suggested, including Michael Scott, the former bass man with the Au Go-Go Singers and The Company. Michael was flown in for a hasty audition but failed to earn the nod. "They called me out there to play bass for them," remembers Michael on his brief reunion with Stephen and Richie. "I had been playing acoustic bass with The Highwaymen. It was still the New York folk thing dressed in suits, it wasn't the West Coast hippie thing. I arrived in a suit and played an audition for them at the Topanga Corral on electric bass, which I had not been used to playing. It didn't work out so I went back to New York."

The group then turned to a familiar face, Sunset Sound engineer Jimmy Messina. Jimmy had developed a relationship with the group during the AGAIN sessions, moving up to assist in production during sessions in November and December. Told about the vacancy by Neil, Jimmy jumped at the opportunity to try out for the group. "I heard they were looking for a bass player 'cause Bruce was leaving," recounts Jimmy, "so I asked Neil if I could try out and play a few gigs for some extra money. I wanted the money to start a recording studio. He told me to come to a rehearsal and they'd see what happened. But when I got there and we started playing, it felt really good, it felt right, and I knew I wanted to do it."

Born in Maywood, California on December 5, 1947, Jimmy Messina had moved with his family at the age of five to Harlingen, Texas, then returned to California seven years later, settling in the Manhattan Beach area of Los Angeles and attending high school in Colton. He took up the guitar at a young age. "I started playing guitar when I was about five," he attests. "My father was a guitarist and he played in the style of Chet Atkins, so I was impressed and I wanted to learn how to do that too." By the time he was 17, Jimmy was leading his own bands, the best known being surfing and hot rod instrumentalists Jim Messina And The Jesters. "Dick Dale was my hero and I was a surfer then, living at the beach." The group released one album and a couple of singles, including *Drag Bike Boogie* written by Jimmy and credited to The Jesters on the Ultima label. In 1965 he went to work at A&M Records as a studio musician playing

244

on the Parade's *Sunshine Girl* single and *The Rising Sun* by the Deep Six. He went on to apprentice as a recording engineer at both Wally Heider's studio and Sunset Sound, where, as a staff engineer, he crossed paths with the Springfield.

"I didn't even know who they were until I got into the studio with them," he confesses. "I'd heard *Bluebird*, which I really liked. They booked a session that I was an engineer on and that's when I became aware of them." Although not a bass player and lacking Bruce's inventiveness, Neil recommended Jimmy for the remaining tour commitments in early February. Passing the audition, Jimmy became the last in a succession of Springfield bass players.

As Richie recalls warmly, "We were doing a lot of our recording at Sunset Sound, and during one of those periods when Bruce was gone somebody put it out to Jimmy, 'Who can play bass?' and he said, 'I can play bass.' He wanted the job. He still saw that there was a future for the Springfield. I saw in Jimmy another person that I had not only a working relationship with but a friend relationship, and I saw stability. That helped me relax a little bit with what was going on. Jimmy was a lot more dependable and a real likable, up-front guy. I found a friend and a kindred spirit." Observed *TeenSet's* Judith Sims on the choice of Jimmy, "He wasn't involved with the egos, he wasn't trying to get his songs recorded. And he got along well with Furay." Once again the band had been pieced back together.

From late 1967 into February of 1968, the members of the group had been laying down tracks toward a third album, and a tentative running list of tunes was created in January. These included something known only as "Steve's Long Song," of which no one can recall the identity; *Telephone Pole*, listed as a country number; Richie's *I Guess You Made It*, formerly referred to as *Who's The Next Fool*; Neil's *Whatever Happened To Saturday Night*, designated for Richie to sing; *Old Laughing Lady*, identified as written by Stephen and Neil; *Uno Mundo*, Stephen's Latin-flavored jab at world politics; *What A Day* from Richie, which later appeared on the debut Poco album; another one from Richie entitled *Kind Woman*, a country number inspired by Nancy Furay; Neil's bitter rocker *Sell Out*; *Just Can't Seem To Get Movin'* by Richie and Neil, ultimately becoming *It's So Hard To*

Wait; I Am A Child, another country-flavored acoustic number from Neil; *Not Quite Rain*, with lyrics from Mickeala Callen, winner of the KHJ Words contest, set to Richie's music and suggested as a B-side to a possible single of *Whatever Happened To Saturday Night*; and Richie's *Nobody's Fool*, Dewey's lone vocal contribution.

What marked these sporadic sessions was the fact that Neil and Stephen were rarely in the studio at the same time, choosing instead to attend their own sessions and not the other's. One of the few occasions where the two collaborated was for Neil's *Falcon Lake*, named after a popular resort outside Winnipeg where Neil had vacationed as a teen and met a former flame. "*Falcon Lake* was an instrumental," he recalls. "It was a memory of that time at Falcon Lake. It had Stephen Stills and I and Buddy Miles on drums, but we never finished it. I later used the melody from it for *Here We Are In The Years* on my first solo album."

The group had begun working on *Whatever Happened To Saturday Night* on December 9th at Sunset Studios with Jimmy assisting in production. Richie recalls the song as one of Neil's best, characterized by his usual introspective lyrics. In an interview that winter, Neil explained the proposed recording technique for the track, revealing he had not yet abandoned the Jack Nitzsche school of production. "It will be a combination of the two recording styles. Parts of it will be cut in different studios, then put together to get the old big sound and the modern clear sound."

Richie drew inspiration from the band's plight for a couple of his songs that ultimately were more suited to Poco than the Springfield. "*I Guess You Made It* comes from the frustrations we had suffered over the time of the band. *What A Day* was a very optimistic song. After all that we had gone through in the Springfield, we looked at Poco to be the kind of band that had a positive outlook. That's what that song is all about. We weren't going to let the things that were behind us bother us. I'm sure we tweaked it a little in Poco, but the basic idea and melody came from the original writing during the Springfield." An early demo of the song surprisingly featured Stephen on vocals.

Sessions for these and several other numbers continued through February with Jimmy now a full-fledged member. On February 15th, a lengthy list of tracks logged included Stephen's *Four Days Gone, Questions, Special Care*, and *Fa-Fa-Fa*, plus *Merry-*

Go-Round from Richie and Jimmy's own *Carefree Country Day*. This was likely an overdubbing and mixing session in anticipation of their third album. *Can't Keep Me Down*, written by Richie back in 1965 in New York, was attempted during a February 26th session, a song that appeared in 1971 as *Do You Feel It Too* on Poco's fourth album FROM THE INSIDE and was later covered by the Nitty Gritty Dirt Band.

Few tracks involved the five band members playing together. "Everything was very much individualized, what everyone was doing," recalls Richie of the mood that February, "coming in at their own time with their own players and doing their own thing. What we did was try to take what everybody did and put it together as one unit. We were probably trying to buy time and see if we could pull it together or not."

During this same time, Stephen and Dewey recorded with The Monkees, playing sessions on January 25th and 26th for *Do I Have To Do This All Over Again* with Dewey returning two days later for *Can You Dig This*. Richie attended the gala premier of John Lennon's film *How I Won The War*, a benefit held in honor of the LA Free Clinic. On the evening of February 14th, Stephen joined David Crosby for The Hollies' appearance at the Whisky, where he was introduced for the first time to Graham Nash. With no gigs pending and the individual members scattered, the Buffalo Springfield was on hold, treading water amid an uncertain future. "We had all started wondering exactly what was going on and a definite lack of interest developed," suggests Richie.

Neil took the general mood of apathy and inactivity along with the failure of *Expecting To Fly* as his cue to quietly withdraw from the group again in February. No formal announcement had been made of any actual departure; he simply stopped showing up for sessions. "I don't remember Neil being around much then," speculates Richie. Neil's contribution to the tracks recorded that month was virtually nil, choosing instead to submit for the pending album the lone track *I Am A Child*, recorded apart from the group. Retreating to his tiny house in the canyons, Neil used the time to assess his own future, a future that did not include the other members of the Buffalo Springfield.

Jimmy Messina and Richie flew to New York in late February 1968 to oversee sessions at Atlantic Studios to complete tracks for the third album. By that point the Buffalo Springfield existed as a band in name only, though no formal breakup had been announced or even discussed among the members. With Bruce gone and Neil reluctant to commit, Atlantic Records president Ahmet Ertegun, aware of the disintegration and fearing the five individuals would scatter before a suitable album could be cobbled together, intervened. He insisted that an album's worth of material measuring up to the standards of their previous two efforts be completed and turned in prior to an impending tour to allow the company to rush release it by early May. Only Richie and Jimmy had sufficient interest to bother making the trip, boxes of tapes in hand, in an attempt to piece together twelve tracks of mostly unfinished material. As producer, Jimmy submitted the intended album to the label at the end of February, though Atco would find the work unsatisfactory.

"There was a lot of pressure from Atlantic to get the album done," notes Richie. "It was pretty much in everybody's mind that it was over, but we still had dates to do. It was a really fine string holding the group together. There wasn't a good grip on things, that's for sure. When we went to New York, I think we were pretty much under the impression that it was winding down." Returning to LA, a photo shoot was booked with photographer Gene Trindl for a possible album cover featuring the group as a quartet, minus Neil, given that he had contributed little to the sessions and had unofficially abandoned the group. Once re-mixed and partly re-recorded, this album would become LAST TIME AROUND.

In early March it was reported that the Buffalo Springfield would be supporting the Beach Boys once again on a tour through the southeastern states, beginning April 5th, with a possible visit to England to follow. As they prepared for the tour, Neil once again returned to the band. "Neil was gone again and we were going to carry on as a four piece with Jimmy on bass and Stephen carrying the lead guitar load," confirms Richie on the merry-go-round of personnel changes the group rode. "We were planning on carrying on as a quartet, then here comes Neil again. We were getting ready to do a tour with the Beach Boys, and you always need new photos to go before you. With Neil back we had to do the photo session again." Indeed, so soon was the new session after the quartet shoot for the potential album cover that Stephen and Richie are wearing the same clothes — Nehru jacket, turtle neck and scruffy tennis shoes for Stephen, smart pin-stripped suit and cravat for Richie — with Neil now ensconced back among them. The setting was the same as the previous session, the group's massive pile of Fender, Marshall, and Sunn amplifiers, with Dewey perched on his drum kit. Decked out in his black Comanche war jacket, white bell bottom slacks and white cowboy hat, Neil, alongside Jimmy Messina in a Civil War period Union army get-up, reinforced the Old West / Americana image of the group. Closer scrutiny of the publicity shot released to coincide with the tour reveals the original quartet photo tucked in behind Dewey.

The turnaround was quite sudden but not unexpected. "I was going crazy, joining and quitting and joining again," admits Neil on his return to the fold. "So I'd quit, then I'd come back 'cause it sounded so good. It was a constant problem." As Richie explains Neil's ongoing identity crisis with the Springfield,"Neil could not see himself as second fiddle. He couldn't and wouldn't see himself as just a member of the band, one of the five guys."

With Neil back, the group faced another crisis with the defection of longtime associate Dickie Davis. Despite all his efforts on their behalf, the individual members of the group never considered Dickie to be their manager. "I left in a burst of emotion over a fight with Dewey," Dickie admits. "It was simply the culmination of a lot of frustration. We just couldn't get past all the internal problems and I had had it." "Dickie was a road manager and gopher and he managed us when we didn't have anyone," offers Dewey, who shrugs off the altercation. "There was a situation at the airport when he insisted on driving the rental car. And I wanted to drive, so I pitched the keys across the parking lot to the rental car like skipping a rock over a pond. He wasn't happy about that, but I was Dewey and he was Dickie." "Dickie Davis didn't work out as manager because we were always beating him up, literally," Bruce adds. "But we loved Dickie; we gave him one sixth of Springalo Toones." "It wasn't like Dickie was calling the shots for the band," clarifies Richie, "certainly not with Stephen and Neil around. Dickie may have envisioned himself as a manager calling the shots, but I don't recall it that way. I don't see him saying, 'Steve, Neil, Richie, Bruce, Dewey, here's what we need to do . . .' I don't think that happened." Like Barry Friedman and Greene and

Stone before him, Dickie's services were deemed no longer beneficial to the group. With Dickie out of the picture, Beach Boys' manager Nick Grillo acted temporarily on the Springfield's behalf, though no formal contract was signed.

On the weekend of March 15th and 16th, the Buffalo Springfield played two nights at the 5,000 seat Shrine Auditorium in Los Angeles to tumultuous response from the sold out crowd. On March 20th the Springfield returned to the studio to mix their next single, Stephen's Latin-flavored *Uno Mundo* backed by Richie's *Merry-Go-Round*, both recorded in January prior to Bruce's departure, though excluding Neil. Later that day, the five members of the group along with several friends — Stephen's old buddy Chris Sarns, newly installed as road manager, Stephen's sisters Talitha and Hannah, publicists June Nelson and Mary Hughes (ex-girlfriend of the Yardbirds' Jeff Beck), Stephen's girlfriend Susan Hafey and her friends Linda Sontag and Karen Harvey, Nancy Furay and Dewey's wife Jane Martin, plus Cream guitar god Eric Clapton, one of Stephen's idols visiting from Britain — convened at Susan Hafey's residence, 1174 Old Topanga Canyon Road, where she lived with Stephen at the time.

At the house, band equipment and lights had been set up for rehearsals and impromptu jam sessions. With a two night stand at LA's Kaleidoscope that Friday and Saturday launching the opening of that Sunset Strip venue formerly known as the Hullabaloo and now owned by agents John Hartmann and Skip Taylor, the group was rehearsing several new songs to debut. Despite its secluded location set several hundred feet from the road, neighbors had previously complained to Susan of the excessive volume levels at all hours of the day or night. On this particular evening, the neighbors summoned the police. Deputies Andrew Yobuck and Oscar Lowry knocked on Susan's door at approximately 10:15 pm. "When she opened the door," testified Deputy Yobuck, "the marijuana smoke just rolled out." An alert Chris Sarns grabbed the stash of grass and ran to the bathroom in an attempt to flush the goods down the toilet but was apprehended in the process by the deputies. An even more nimble Stephen managed to crawl out a bedroom window to make his escape, leaving the others, minus Dewey and Jane who had bid farewell only moments before the police arrived, to face the music, as it were. Everyone, including Richie, Jimmy, and Neil, was arrested and taken to jail.

"We had all been at Stephen's house," states Richie recounting the details of the much-publicized bust. "We had been rehearsing there off and on and we had been warned by the police the night before to turn it way down if we were playing beyond nine or ten o'clock. That's why we had quit fairly early so we thought we were well within the bounds of being the good guys. I had already left, but Nancy and I returned to get something — Jimmy and I were going to get a stereo. Dewey had left, too. We hadn't been back more than ten minutes, if that. There were cops coming in everywhere, the front and back doors, the windows. It wasn't like a knock at the door and, 'Okay guys, we warned you once, now we're here to arrest you.' They just stormed in like a SWAT team. I don't know how Stephen got out but he did. They caught Chris Sarns with his hand in the toilet trying to stuff the grass down. The police arrested us and took us down to the Malibu Police Station. When we walked into the station, there was this big heavy door and there was this guy who was already in jail and he was singing one of Cream's songs. He didn't know we were there. They booked us and it was an all night thing. They took Nancy to Sybil Brand, the Women's County Prison, along with the other girls, and took us down to the big LA county jail. We sat in this huge holding room almost all night and went through the whole routine of processing which was ugly — spraying us down, delousing us, getting our clothes, and being taken to our cells. We were all together then all of a sudden we were separated, so I don't know what happened to Eric because he was the most prominent name amongst us. I remember walking into my cell, there were two guys in there, and there were four bunks and as I walked in one of the guys looked at me and said, 'That one's yours.' I'll never forget that. I just crawled up on it and lay there. It was early morning by then. Someone had called our lawyers, and they were working on getting us out. I stayed in that cell probably four hours or so until Nick Grillo got us out. He was the closest thing we had to a manager at that time, but we hadn't signed anything with him. I don't know whose house Steve got to but somehow or other Dennis Wilson got involved and word got to Nick. It was in the papers the next day. I was released at about ten in the morning and we had to go to court."

The sordid affair made all the newspapers the next day

under the headline "14 To Face Topanga Pot Party Counts." Says Nancy Furay, "When we got busted it totally crushed my mother. I was a good little girl and would never do anything to hurt her." The group appeared in court on March 26th where the hearing was remanded to a later date to allow the group to fulfill commitments. Eventually all those involved pleaded guilty to disturbing the peace and the drugs charges were reduced to a misdemeanor and small fine. But the damage to the Springfield was irreparable. In the aftermath, Neil once more announced he was leaving the group. No resistance was offered; the others simply threw in the towel. It was all over.

"We were fighting internally," sums up Dewey on the events of the past few months, "and then Neil left the band finally, for a third time. Stephen said, 'I can't go on breaking in new guitar players.' I think it was impossible because of where everybody's head was at. It wasn't just one guy's fault."

"I just couldn't handle it towards the end," confesses Neil regarding his on again, off again relationship with the Buffalo Springfield. "It wasn't me scheming on a solo career, it wasn't anything but my nerves. Everything started to go too fast. I began to feel like I didn't have to answer or obey anyone. I needed more space. That was a big problem in my head. I just wasn't mature enough to deal with it. I was very young. We were getting the shaft from every angle, and it seemed like we were trying to make it so bad and we were getting nowhere."

"We had gone back and started over so many times with guys leaving," sighs Richie regarding Neil's final announcement. "After a couple of them it was like, 'Okay, we've done it once, we'll do it again.' Then, it was, 'Okay, we've done it a couple of times so we can do it again.' But after that it was, 'Who wants to anymore.' We were just broken. How many times can you break up and get back together to break up and try somebody else again and again? It's never the same. That's the whole history of the band, one step forward, two steps back. That's probably why it was so easy in the end to call it quits and say, 'It's over, it's dead. Let's let it die this time.'"

The Buffalo Springfield simply petered out by mutual consent and indifference. "I can't recall that we all sat down together and said, 'It's over,'" Richie recalls. "Neil had been moving more towards his own projects, Stephen was becoming more aloof with some of the people he was associating with. I think everybody just assumed from the talk that it was done. Neil was heading off, Stephen was talking of going off with other people. Jimmy and I were already talking about doing something new. There was some mutual agreement but I don't remember having a meeting and discussing it. We all just knew it was over."

The Springfield's two night stand at the Kaleidoscope that weekend was canceled, Fever Tree filling in for them, as the group sorted out its options. At Ahmet Ertegun's urging, Neil agreed to hang on until the completion of all further engagements through to the end of the Beach Boys tour. It was agreed to split up in early May following a few farewell concerts in and around LA. Atco planned the release of the final album around that time.

A Sunday evening show at the Kaleidoscope, a benefit for striking announcers and other radio personnel at KPPC in Pasadena and KMPX in San Francisco on March 24th organized by Tom Donahue and B. Mitchell Reed, featuring an all star bill with the Jefferson Airplane, Tiny Tim, H.P. Lovecraft, Steppenwolf, Sweetwater, Firesign Theatre, Clear Light, Quicksilver, and the Peanut Butter Conspiracy, went ahead with the beleagured Springfield garnering rave reviews. "Each act seemed to be in top form but the Springfield stole the show," wrote the *LA Times'* Pete Johnson, "which leaves no doubt that it is the best American group to emerge in the last couple of years." Pete declared the event the best rock event ever held in Los Angeles. During their set, the group debuted Stephen's *Questions* and *Uno Mundo* plus Neil's plaintive solo piece *Birds* and the folky *Last Trip To Tulsa*, both destined for inclusion on later solo releases.

"I remember playing *Birds* on those last few shows," recalls Richie. "I thought it was fitting because it was about flying away. Neil played piano on it."

When you see me fly away without you,
Shadow on the things you know.
Feathers fall around you,
And show you the way to go.
It's over.

Birds (Neil Young)

Five nights later the group appeared in Pomona at the Cal

Poly Gym with the Union Gap and October Country. They then retreated in preparation for the Beach Boys tour. In an ironic twist, *TeenSet*, which had inaugurated a series profiling each member of the Springfield beginning with Richie and Dewey, featured a profile of Bruce Palmer in their March issue.

Due to commence in Nashville, Tennessee on April 5th, the Beach Boys' tour was marred at the outset by the assassination in Memphis of civil rights leader Martin Luther King the day before. "We were in the air, somewhere on our way to the South when we heard that Martin Luther King was shot," Richie recalls. Fearing a violent backlash from the black community, Nashville and several dates in North and South Carolina were hastily canceled and the tour picked up on the 9th in Lakeland, Florida. The original package called for an exhausting 33 dates over 17 days, with the Springfield, Beach Boys, and Strawberry Alarm Clock flying from gig to gig. "We were doing two and three shows a day, sometimes in two different cities, flying from one city to the next," Richie confirms. "We'd do our set and hop a plane to the next gig while the Beach Boys were taking the stage at the first gig. Then they'd fly out after their set. We'd be in the air and flying to the next gig while the Beach Boys were taking the stage at the gig we just finished. There were two different planes flying out the equipment and musicians. One concert would be going on and another one starting in another town. Those tours were the most well organized tours and performances I ever experienced. The Beach Boys had the experience of years on the road and everything ran smooth. Dick Duryea, actor Dan Duryea's son, was their road manager and he kept it going tight."

In the months since the last time the groups went out together, the members of the Beach Boys had become converts to the Maharishi Mahesh Yogi's transcendental meditation and expected their touring partners to follow suit. "On the second tour they demanded that we go through the initiation for this whole Maharishi transcendental thing," laughs Richie. "'Okay, you gotta have your piece of fruit, and you gotta have your hanky and your flower, then go and get your mantra'. It was a prerequisite for touring. We didn't take it very seriously. We were somewhere in Florida — I think it was at the university in Jacksonville — and Jimmy Messina and I were in this locker room. We were stoned and had just gone through and gotten our mantra. We turned out the lights, only the two of us, and we're really out there. Then, all of a sudden it got really quiet and spiritual and Jimmy says, 'Richie, are you there?' And we got so freaked out with this mantra thing and being stoned that we just ran outta there as fast as we could."

On the first date of the tour, following sets in Lakeland and Orlando earlier the same day, Neil succumbed to an epileptic seizure at the third performance in Daytona Beach and was taken away in a car driven directly onto the Memorial Stadium field by his brother Bob. His mother Rassy, now residing in Florida, was in attendance that night and carried a supply of his pills. The next day he was fine and the group turned in impressive sets in Jacksonville and Gainesville. From there, the tour proceeded through Georgia, Texas, Oklahoma, Alabama, Tennessee, and Louisiana, before winding down on the 22nd of April at the Civic Auditorium in Little Rock, Arkansas. The cancellation of the earlier dates necessitated a reduction in their agreed upon fee for the tour, leaving the Springfield short. "We had to cancel four dates and the Beach Boys took $7,000 from us because of that," complains Dewey. Adds Stephen, "When we got back, we were bankrupt. We couldn't get airline credit or rent cars or anything. That was one reason we finally had to give up. We were broke."

Upon their return to LA, the group set about a kind of informal farewell tour beginning April 28th with dates in Tarzana at the Valley Music Theater, scene of the CAFF concert the previous year, Peterson Gym at San Diego State College, San Diego on May 3rd, where they were joined by the Electric Flag, and May 4th in Sacramento at the Merchandise Mart in the Old State Fairgrounds along with Quicksilver, HP Lovecraft, and Yukon Daily. The final concert was set for Sunday evening, May 5th at the Long Beach Sports Arena, topping a bill that featured Country Joe and the Fish, Canned Heat, The Hook, and Smokestack Lightning.

The media had announced that the Springfield were to appear earlier in the afternoon of the 5th at a benefit for the American Indian held at The Blue Law club in Torrance in suburban Los Angeles before heading down to Long Beach to close the show. Also featured at the benefit were Buffy Ste. Marie, Big Brother And The Holding Company, the Airplane, Pacific Gas and Electric, Hunger and several members of The Monkees, who made a brief bow. However, the group canceled, choosing instead to focus on the Long Beach gig.

In attendance backstage at the Long Beach Sports Arena were several friends old and new, including Dickie Davis and steel guitarist Rusty Young who had recently come out to LA from Denver at Richie's urging. Up to the last minute, representatives at the William Morris Agency, who had promoted the final dates, were denying the break up, so few fans were aware that Long Beach was to be the group's swansong. Among the 5,000 fans in attendance at the sold out show, word of the Springfield's demise spread through the crowd like a brush fire immediately before the group took the stage. Master of ceremonies John Carpenter, an *LA Free Press* columnist, appeared to announce, "Let's have a big hand for what I think is the best group in America today, the Buffalo Springfield!" With that, the group emerged from the wings, plugged in and greeted their fans. "Hello everyone," said Stephen, tentatively, "We'd sure like to thank you for coming 'cause this is it, gang."

Once the tuning was complete, Richie began the opening riff to *Rock And Roll Woman*, and suddenly hundreds of fans rushed from their seats to the stagefront in an unsolicited show of support for their beloved group. When they were already well into the song's bridge and Stephen's lead guitar solo, one of the police security men leapt on stage and grabbed the microphone from Stephen, bringing the show to a halt while shouting, "You have to get back! You have to get back! You have to get back! The Buffalo Springfield will not perform unless you go back to your seats." Over and over he repeated his exhortation to the throng crowding the front of the stage as the five band members stood by helpless. With order eventually restored, Dewey played a drum roll intro and the group again launched into *Rock And Roll Woman* from the top, offering a spirited rendition of the number, Stephen and Neil trading licks back and forth with Richie holding down the riff on his twelve string. Then came the usual delays while the guitars were tuned again. "We're all so scared up here," offered Neil, mockingly, "just a little tense. But we're gonna try some pickin' and grinnin' for ya, one more time." He then led the group into *A Child's Claim To Fame* with Richie and Stephen embellishing the arrangement with characteristic bluegrass style high harmonies at the end of each verse. Perennial crowd pleaser *Clancy* followed to much applause.

In an unusual move, Dewey relinquished the drum stool to Stephen for *Good Time Boy* as he took center stage barking out what had become his signature tune, punctuated by two blistering solos from Neil. Stephen proved himself worthy on the kit before returning to his guitar to assist Neil in a scorching *Mr. Soul*, Neil spitting out the lyrics with venom and trading solos with Stephen. Up next was *Uno Mundo*, a new tune for the audience, introduced by Stephen as their latest single, with Richie covering the horn parts on his twelve string. Following that came their lone national hit, *For What It's Worth*, and then into the closing number, an extended version of *Bluebird* with Stephen and Neil duelling. Before it was over some twelve minutes later the number had moved from its country rock base to a blues shuffle, and, like a locomotive gathering a head of steam, into one pounding repetitive chord climaxing in a slow bluesy reprise of the verse over a heavy metal Cream-style riff with a fanfare of shrieking guitars. As the final feedback volley died out, Stephen leaned into his mike to wish, "God bless you."

John Carpenter then returned to the stage to eulogize: "The Buffalo Springfield, the last time." It was all over. The crowd called for more, lunging at the stage, toppling microphones but there was to be no encore. The promoters, Gene Harris and Larry Rosenthal, had another concert to oversee across town and wasted little time or sentiment in turning up the lights.

"Backstage at Long Beach was fairly positive," recalls Richie. "We probably hugged one another and all that but it wasn't as if we didn't think we would see each other again. It was more, 'Okay, we did it together, now we'll do it apart.'" It was more an 'Okay, good luck to each one of you.' I didn't have any bitterness, I don't think any of us felt that. I felt a sadness that we never really did accomplish what we could of or should of or what we were destined to. But at that point I was exhausted with all the ups and downs, people in and out. I couldn't keep up with it anymore. I saw stability in being able to put together another band with Jimmy. We didn't know who the players were gonna be yet, but I knew Jimmy and I could do something."

Amid a scrum of reporters backstage, Neil indicated he was already negotiating a solo recording contract, possibly with the Beach Boys' Brother Records. Jimmy said he was returning to record production and engineering, Dewey claimed to be considering going out as a duo with wife Jane, and Richie and

Steve admitted to having no immediate plans. However, both had already entered into tentative discussions with other as yet unnamed parties to pursue a fresh start.

Rusty Young noted a marked difference in the Springfield since first seeing them a year earlier in Colorado. "At the Long Beach gig, I thought the Springfield sounded really good. Again because of the poor quality sound systems in those days you couldn't hear bass, there was no low frequency. But with the three guitars in the Springfield, Stephen played bass parts on his guitar a lot of times, low notes, harmonies, and counter melodies, and you could actually hear those. It gave them more depth than other bands. They blew Canned Heat and Country Joe away that night. It was what you'd expect the Springfield to sound like and not what I'd heard with Doug in Colorado."

Reviewers played up the sentiment of the final performance, lamenting the loss of one of America's best loved if least understood bands. In the *Los Angeles Herald-Review*, Michael Etchison vividly conveyed the spirit of the evening. "Overcoming interruptions by the police to clear the aisles and the dismay of unsuspecting fans, the group got better and better through the set. Their strongest performance was undoubtedly *Bluebird*, in which both Steve Stills and Neil Young achieved perhaps their best guitar solos. The announcer said, 'This is it.' Finally the group finished and the stage was rushed. They left, and the people walked out talking quietly. No more Buffalo Springfield. They never made it. In Los Angeles, they had always been stars, but to the rest of the country they were nothing special. After two and a half years, they had quit trying."

In a *Teen Screen* feature devoted to the final concert, the writer captured the heartbreak of the group's devoted teenybop following. "A very weird wave of emotion hit me as I entered the Long Beach Sports Arena that Sunday to see and hear the fantastic Buffalo Springfield do their concert. As I sat down I was swept up, with what seemed like the whole audience, in a terrible fit of depression. As I looked around people sat numb, staring at the stage, and a whole group of girls were crying. I thought it was just a group of over anxious fans who had gotten excited a little too early, so I shrugged that one off and settled back to watch the pre-concert activities. There was whispering going on all around me and I managed to catch a few inaudible words of protest about something, but that was all. Then the protests began getting louder and I was beginning to put the pieces together. What I came up with was too wild to mention — something about Buffalo Springfield breaking up — that I chose not to listen to anymore. But when I saw the audience reaction to the Buffalo's appearance I knew it wasn't going to be just any concert. When the group got on stage to play, something that was both a little scary and gratifying to them happened: the audience got up out of their seats and flooded down the aisles towards the stage, trying to get a little closer to the group that they loved. It was the kind of last chance rush to the stage that made me realize the whisperings were true. Then the promoters had to stop the show until the house was seated. Steve was visibly shaken and choked up. Girls were crying, some were just sitting dazed as before, a few fainted, and others were cheerily participating by clapping to the music. But everyone was reacting!"

Neil offers a fitting epitaph to the Buffalo Springfield's demise: "It was good, but we didn't know what we were doing so we didn't know how much fun we were having until it was over. Everybody thought, 'Wow, that must have been a lot of fun.' We were just there. I think the Springfield broke up at the right time. I don't think they were improving when they broke up."

Bill Graham pleaded with the group to fulfill an earlier commitment to play a four night Fillmore stand with the Chambers Brothers May 29th through June 1 to no avail. A request from Ahmet Ertegun for a British tour alongside the Beach Boys, too, fell on deaf ears. The Springfield was finished.

It was left to Richie and Jimmy to do the mopping up by delivering to Atco, LAST TIME AROUND. To no one's surprise, Uno Mundo died stillborn, getting no further than No. 105 after a mere two weeks on the Billboard chart. Atco, still looking for a winner to recoup its investment in the group over the years, held out hope that Jimmy and Richie would pull together a more satisfactory effort and delayed release of the album pending more fine tuning. The tracks laid down up to mid-February and presented to Atco were deemed unsatisfactory. Still, there was an assumption that the album would be ready for release around the time of the Long Beach farewell, so much so that during the concert Neil announced that their final album would be released in two weeks. Atco, however, sent the group back to the drawing board to come up with a more polished effort in keeping with their reputation for quality product. But by then no one was interested enough to bother taking the time to rummage through hours of tapes and spend time editing, overdubbing, and mixing tracks. Stephen and Neil washed their hands of the group almost immediately after Long Beach. By default, Jimmy and Richie compiled LAST TIME AROUND.

"The third album, to me, was really disjointed," offers Richie. "It was left to Jimmy and me to collect bits and pieces from everybody and do the best we could. There were songs that either were recorded by a part of the group or given to us by Steve or Neil. Ahmet Ertegun gave us some money to finish up the album. They wanted to keep an eye on us at Atlantic studios I think to make sure they got this album done. By early June the label had everything they needed for the album. We had these packages of tapes, finished and unfinished tracks from various members, and we did some overdubbing, mixing, and putting together to make them into completed songs, though I didn't get credit because Jimmy was the engineer, the technical mind, in the studio. This was a very important time for Jimmy putting the final album together. He and a girlfriend even put the photo collage on the back together. "

Most of the tracks put forth in late December as potential album cuts were abandoned as Jimmy and Richie searched through a mountain of tapes dating as far back as the spring 1967 sessions supervised by Ahmet Ertegun, delving into the group's vaults for *Pretty Girl Why*, the oldest track on the album recorded a year earlier. Though his face and name are both omitted from the sleeve, Bruce appears on several tracks, including *On the Way Home, It's So Hard To Wait, Pretty Girl Why, Uno Mundo, Merry-Go-Round*, and *Questions. Uno Mundo* and *Merry-Go-Round*, though released after Jimmy joined with production co-credited to him, feature Bruce.

It is doubtful that Neil graces more than a couple of tracks; his lone vocal number, *I Am A Child*, was recorded independently. Neil held back several previously recorded tracks such as *Whiskey Boot Hill, Down To The Wire, Whatever Happened To Saturday Night*, and *Sell Out*, as well as recently written material such as *Birds, Last Trip To Tulsa*, and *The Old Laughing Lady*. Obviously, he had other plans for that material. *On The Way Home*, offering Neil's personal reflections on leaving the group in

1967, managed to make it on the album, providing a pleasantly compelling opening track.

According to Richie, "Neil delivered a completed tape of *I Am A Child* to us. That was it. He didn't contribute much to that album other than *On The Way Home. Questions, Special Care, Uno Mundo, Four Days Gone* were not a total band effort. Stephen had gone off and done these. Some of the band may have been on them but not the complete Buffalo Springfield. There was no longer a catalyst to bring the whole thing together. Stephen was tiring of doing that."

Nevertheless, Stephen remained committed and turns in some of his best quality material for inclusion, such as *Four Days Gone*, an understated arrangement and lyric concerning a fugitive's flight from "government madness" that touched a nerve in Vietnam era America; the driving funk of *Special Care; Pretty Girl Why* with its soft, jazzy touch; and *Questions*, which Stephen later borrowed for CSN&Y's *Carry On. Pretty Girl Why* draws inspiration from a girlfriend of Stephen's several years earlier in Greenwich Village. Recalls Jean Gurney, "Nancy Priddy was a model or something in New York. She was one of the first to sport the original Sassoon haircut, which was absolutely the coolest thing. Stephen just fell madly for her, just nuts. Up 'til then he had never expressed an emotional response to a woman other than the usual one night stands. This was during the Au Go-Go Singers. And she broke his heart." Nancy later moved out to California where she continues to model. Her daughter is actor Christine Applegate of the television sitcom *Married With Children*.

Several other outsiders were employed to complete the tracks. Stephen's affinity for Buddy Miles' drumming brought him in for *Special Care*, with Stephen providing all the other instruments on the cut, including the harmony vocals. The song offers Stephen's politically-conscious lyric over Buddy's funky beat with Stephen's organ work dominating the track. The number was later covered adequately by the group Fanny in 1970. Stephen chose session man Jimmy Carstein to drum on *Questions*; he also supplies the beat for *Merry-Go-Round. Four Days Gone* uses an unidentified session man on upright acoustic bass. Neil and Dewey are the only Springfield members playing on *I Am A Child*, the bass handled by the boyfriend of the receptionist at Sunset Sound. Los Angeles-based music arranger Jeremy Stuart scored the orchestration on *The Hour Of Not Quite*

Rain and the carnival sounds in *Merry-Go-Round*, though he did not receive acknowledgement on the album. *Kind Woman* and *The Hour Of Not Quite Rain* use New York session players with steel guitarist Rusty Young guesting on *Kind Woman*.

Rusty recalls how he came to be in Los Angeles to appear on a Buffalo Springfield album track. "Miles Thomas had gone to Los Angeles with The Poor, Randy Meisner's group. They opened for the Springfield at the Whisky and that's how Miles got hooked up with the Springfield. We, of course, kept in touch. He was always trying to get me to come out to Los Angeles. I had a couple of things going and didn't want to leave to do nothing. Miles called up and said, 'I've got this thing set up for you. The Springfield need a steel player on a song they're recording and I've got an audition for you with this guy named Gram Parsons who's putting together a new band and they're looking for a steel player. So come on out.' For a chance to play on a Buffalo Springfield album, it was worth going out there. I idolized that band. That was my favorite band of all time. So I went out and stayed with Miles, got to play on *Kind Woman*, and hang out with the band. Richie picked me up at the airport. I thought, 'All right, a big time pop star,' but he picked me up in this little red Volkswagen. That kind of blew my mind. Neil was driving around in an old Rolls Royce, and Stephen had a Ferrari that he wrapped around a pole and that's what I expected, then Richie shows up in a Volkswagen. Jimmy was pretty much running the session but it was always a partnership between Richie and Jimmy, right from before Poco. Jimmy was an engineer so he knew his way around the technical part, and Richie was more the musical input person. They were a really good partnership. At the same time we were in one studio at Sunset Sound, Stephen was in the other studio working on his tracks for the album. I was struck by the fact that three guys were all doing their tracks with different people in different studios. I don't recall Richie or Jimmy going in and playing or saying, 'Gee, that sounds good' or anything like that. It was Buddy Miles playing drums and a bunch of Stephen's friends. I remember Crosby was hanging around at the time, too."

Kind Woman, the album's closing track, not only marks the end of the Springfield, but also, by its very approach and choice of instrumentation, serves notice of the direction Richie and Jimmy would take soon after. With its smooth pedal steel sound,

Kind Woman is pure country rock even before that epithet had been coined. In fact many musicologists credit the song as not only the last gasp of the Springfield but the first breath of Poco.

"*Kind Woman*, that's about Nancy," smiles Richie. "She's one of a kind."

Got a good reason for loving you,
It's an old fashioned sign.
I kinda get to feelin' like 'mm', y'know,
When I fell in love first time.
Kind woman, won't you love me tonight,
The look in your eyes.
Kind woman, don't leave me lonely tonight,
Please say it's all right.

Kind Woman (Richie Furay)

"We did some of that in New York," he continues. "The bass player on the session was Richard Davis, not Dickie, playing upright bass, and I can't recall the drummer or keyboard player, but he played a Floyd Cramer kind of piano on it. We recorded it in New York and brought it back to California for Rusty to overdub the steel guitar on at a session. *Kind Woman* was more country than *A Child's Claim To Fame*, which was more blue-grass. It had the pedal steel, one of the first rock songs to feature steel guitar. It was kind of like a springboard direction to where we wanted to go. Jimmy and I were doing a lot of talking at that time about doing stuff like this. Then after hearing Rusty, all the wheels started turning in our mind that if things ever did break apart, let's get this guy and do the music that we want to do. We wanted to take what was ultimately to become Poco into the country vein. And as far as I'm concerned Rusty is one of the best. Rusty's an innovator. I didn't need to hear Red Rhodes or Sneaky Pete. Rusty was a young, hip guy."

Indeed, Rusty's steel guitar perfectly complements Richie's tender vocal and soulful country arrangement. However, Richie finds it difficult to listen to the track. "As far as I'm concerned there's a real bad mistake on that track from an aesthetic point of view, a 5/4 measure, that bothers me to this day. It really could have been a covered song by other artists, but if you listen to it, man, the timing in one spot is off. I re-recorded the song later in Poco and corrected it."

Perhaps the oddest track, and the only song in the group's recording career to ever include credit to a non-member was *The Hour Of Not Quite Rain* with lyrics by Mickaela 'Micki' Callen and music from Richie. How this odd collaboration came about was the residue of the Greene-Stone hype machine. In August 1967, KHJ radio launched their "Words" contest announcing in their hit parade chart, "You write the words . . . The Buffalo Springfield writes the music . . . and a hit is born!" — prize is $1000 cash plus publishing royalties — entries must be postmarked by August 20th." Micki Callen, a teenager from suburban Reseda, was chosen the winner on September 6th from a reported 15,000 entries for her poem "The Hour Of Not Quite Rain." The problem was, no one in the group could be bothered setting her lyrics to music.

As KHJ's program director Ron Jacobs recalls, "our promotions manager Mitch Fisher had to follow through on the dirty work on this thing and had to chase down the guys to finish up their end of it. I pitched the idea initially to Charlie that the winner gets their song set to music and goes on their next album. So Charlie says, 'Great, we'll do it!' He hadn't even asked the group. So we went on the air with great promos and the stuff started arriving. We would take the worst one and read it very straight over sappy music every hour. Some of this shit was like 'high school yearbook-on-down' pathetic, just bad rhymes or no rhymes, God knows what they were talking about. We'd go, 'Joe Blow from Thousand Oaks submitted the following: As the moon burst on the scene at night I think of you, Claudia.' Really weird shit. And at the end we'd say, 'That's another finalist in the KHJ Words contest. You could win a chance to be on the next Buffalo Springfield album. If your words win they will be set to music and you'll win a $1,000 and the publishing rights to your song. Enter today at KHJ.' So that went on and we were deluged with stuff. Fifteen thousand entries were received. Somehow through some process Micki Callen's poem 'The Hour Of Not Quite Rain' got selected as the winner. Mitch Reed had to take the finalist to Charlie. It was Mitch's job to get to the group to put it to music and record it. And they were saying, 'What is this?!' So Mitch had to chase them out to their beach house in Malibu. They were all floating out in the water on rubber rafts and Mitch had to swim out or yell or whatever until finally he dragged Richie out and he got stuck with writing the music. That's typical that Steve and Neil would dump on Richie. So Richie writes it and we can't wait to get our hands on the song because it's, 'Here's one of your KHJ fellow listeners'. We played the shit out of it because we were gunning for a number one record nationally that had sprung out of a local radio contest. But it was one notch above *Nowadays Clancy Can't Even Sing* as far as I was concerned. I've often wondered what ever happened to Micki Callen and her publishing. THE LAST TIME AROUND album must have sold more than a half million by now and if she didn't sell out her publishing, she must have made some money from it and all because of the prize from our radio contest."

In the hour of not quite rain,
When the fog was finger tip high.
The moon hung suspended,
In a singular sky.
Deeply and beyond,
Seeing, not wishing to intrude,
Bathed in it's own reflection.
Water mirrored the mood.

The Hour Of Not Quite Rain (Mickaela Callen & Richie Furay)

Richie relates how he was given the onorous task by default. "Bruce picked the song out of all the lyrics sent in, most of them just way out there. You take those lyrics and try to put them anywhere close to any of the songs on the two albums and it just doesn't fit. Steve wasn't gonna write anything for it and Neil certainly wasn't gonna write anything for it; Bruce and Dewey couldn't do it so I ended up kind of being elected to do the music." Orchestrated to the extreme by Jeremy Stuart and recorded in New York, the track does have a redeeming quality and is not out of place on the mixed bag of styles found on the album. Ironically, several reviewers pegged *Not Quite Rain* as the album's standout cut.

Though Jimmy claims overall credit as the album's producer, several tracks were either co-produced or produced independently. Stephen supervised several of his contributions as did Neil for *I Am A Child*. When *Uno Mundo* and *Merry-Go-Round*

were released as a single in April, Stephen and Jimmy were identified as producers of the A side, with Richie and Jimmy the B side.
Given Stephen's penchant for control and growing confidence as
a producer it seems surprising that he would relinquish care of the
final product to someone else, especially the newest member of
the group. "If Steve had it in his mind that it was over," responds
Richie to Stephen abdicating overall supervision of the project as
far back as mid February, "he would have left trusting Jimmy to
pull it together and moved on to his next thing with the attitude
in his mind, 'This is over, it's old news. I'm moving on to the next
thing.' Steve trusted Jimmy as an engineer.".

Rather than a representation of a whole group, then, the
twelve tracks on LAST TIME AROUND are, instead, merely fragments of a group in the throws of disintegration. It is likely that
the five members of the final lineup appear only on Jimmy's sole
contribution, *Carefree Country Day*. Another so-called collaboration, *It's So Hard To Wait*, was anything but. "That one came
from earlier sessions before Messina," notes Richie. "I don't
ever remember Neil and I sitting down and collaborating on a
song like, 'Hey, let's try writing a song together' but I think he
had a fragment and I had a song that fit with it and we put it
together. His part was the bridge, 'I hope that you care, more
than a little for me, it's so hard to wait.'"

"That album doesn't bring back any fond memories for me as
far as who the Buffalo Springfield were and what we did," Richie
concludes. "You can even see in the cover everyone's kind of looking away. We're looking west and Neil's looking east. Even the fact
that Jimmy's there, not to take anything away from Jimmy, but he
was just another one of those guys who wasn't a part of the
band. Now, to his credit, he put a lot of effort and energy into trying to make the best possible representation of what he and I were
left with. Steve was off doing his SUPERSESSION by then and Neil
was figuring out his first solo record. Jimmy and I were thinking
about what was to become Poco. Who knows what Bruce and
Dewey were doing. But I look at this album and feel it's a shame
that Bruce isn't in there somewhere."

Various remixing and overdubbing sessions in June along
with elaborate cover art delayed the release of the album until
mid-July. The cover uses a Gene Trindl photo from the short-
lived quartet session with a shot of Neil peering, appropriately,
in the other direction spliced in. The composite photo is set in

an ornately wood-carved frame. Inside the gatefold, the identical illustration is presented cut into fragments, while the back cover, designed by Derinda Christiansen, a friend of Jimmy's, is a collage of photographs and clippings covering the group's multi-personnel history, burnt into a piece of cowhide. Besides the original five, included in the collage are Jimmy Messina, Jim Fielder, Doug Hastings, Dickie Davis, and Ken Koblun.

By September, LAST TIME AROUND had peaked on the *Billboard* charts at No. 42. *Special Care*, backed by *Kind Woman*, was selected from the album as a single in August but only reached No. 107. The final Buffalo Springfield single, *On The Way Home*, coupled with *Four Days Gone*, peaked at No. 82 in October, their best showing since *Rock And Roll Woman*, but in Los Angeles, ever loyal to their favorites, the single pushed all the way to No. 5 at KHJ.

While several members disparaged the album upon release, critics fell over themselves with praise, citing LAST TIME AROUND as a more cohesive effort than AGAIN. In a *Hit Parader* interview, Neil savaged the record, claiming that he heard it once and declined further listenings, though he admitted to not owning a record player. "It was such a disgraceful mess that I can't bear to listen to it again," he carped. "The mixes are incredibly awful, a very disturbing point." The interviewer did not share his sentiment, nor did many other well-known music critics.

"The best folk-rooted group to emerge since The Byrds . . . brilliant and original," commented the *LA Times'* Pete Johnson, who, noting the imagery of the cover art, went on to state, "but underneath these pictures of disintegration is a first-rate record; a twelve song album which skips across the numerous facets of the group. Within the Springfield were three of the best pop songwriters, singers, and guitarists to be found in any American rock group: Steve Stills, Neil Young, and Richie Furay. It is amazing that all three could be contained in one group and perhaps inevitable that eventually they would fragment. There was too much talent in the Springfield for them to create anything less than excellence. The Springfield never drew sufficient attention to salve the yearnings of three collective egos. Much of the album is, in fact, rather melancholy. None of the songs is haphazard, none of them is included to stretch the album to a respectable size. Everything has subtle flavoring which becomes more pronounced with each listening. I have never seen a group use three guitars as tastefully as they did, weaving a finely detailed fabric whose pattern never blurred from overlapping."

Ellen Sander, reviewing the album in the *New York Times*, lavished on the praise. "In the war of sound the pop revolution has become, the quietly beautiful Buffalo Springfield albums have been consistently overlooked and underrated. The group has always manifested its multitude of talents in straightforward, professional songs, flavored with lithe, sweet country sounds. They have made an art out of music that is unfailingly pleasant; no less moving for its tasteful, understated neatness. Their final album, LAST TIME AROUND is no exception; it is perhaps their finest, albeit their parting, hour. The entire album has a fresh, natural feeling about it, not unlike a soft summer rain."

Rolling Stone deemed the album "the most beautiful record they've ever made," going on to refer to the Springfield as a largely Canadian group, drawing comparisons to that other Canadian contingent, The Band, whose MUSIC FROM BIG PINK·had recently been released. The reviewer, Barry Gifford, noted that the Springfield's approach is "happier sounding, more sweet-country flavored" than The Band's seriousness. Stephen is singled out for individual praise for his five contributions to the album, but Gifford saves his most glowing accolades for Jimmy's *Carefree Country Day* before concluding, "Too bad this isn't the first time around."

LAST TIME AROUND came out within a week of The Byrds' seminal country rock foray SWEETHEART OF THE RODEO and comparisons were inevitable. Minneapolis critic Ray Olson reserves his highest praise for the Springfield's final effort. "In SWEETHEART OF THE RODEO, The Byrds took an imitative approach to country music. By contrast, in their last album, LAST TIME AROUND, Buffalo Springfield have mixed country with other styles to produce the only completely perfect record I've ever heard. LAST TIME AROUND is possibly the best rock album ever made. The only unfortunate thing is that it is the last record by this great group."

From the pieces recorded individually by the band members, Jimmy and Richie had managed to pull together an album that offers a fitting epitaph to the well-earned reputation of the Buffalo Springfield.

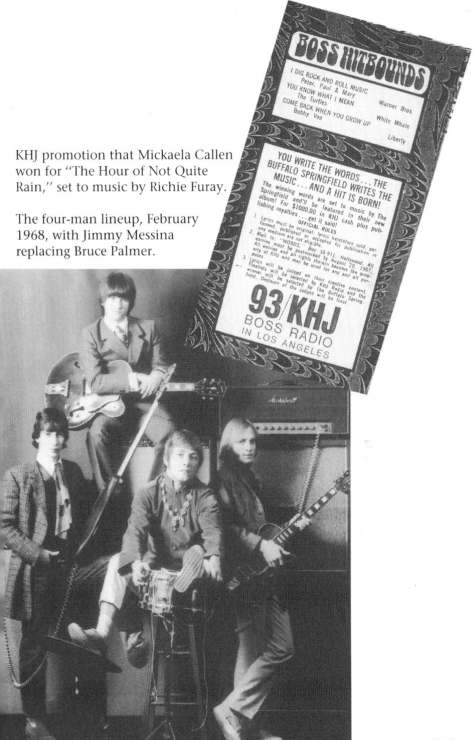

BOSS HITBOUNDS

I DIG ROCK AND ROLL MUSIC
Peter, Paul & Mary
YOU KNOW WHAT I MEAN   Warner Bros.
The Turtles
COME BACK WHEN YOU GROW UP   White Whale
Bobby Vee
                                    Liberty

**YOU WRITE THE WORDS . . . THE
BUFFALO SPRINGFIELD WRITES THE
MUSIC . . . AND A HIT IS BORN!**

The winning words are set to music by The
Springfield and'll be featured in their new
album! For $1000.00 in KHJ cash plus pub-
lishing royalties . . . get it said!

OFFICIAL RULES

1. Lyrics must be original: lyrics heretofore sold, performed, published or accepted for publication in
any medium are not eligible.
2. Mail to: "WORDS," Box 28-911, Hollywood. All
entries must be postmarked by August 29, 1967.
All entries and all rights therein become the property of KHJ and may be used for any and all pur-
poses.
3. Lyrics will be judged on their creative content.
Finalists will be selected by KHJ Radio and the
winner will be selected by The Buffalo Springfield. Decision of the judges will be final

93/KHJ
BOSS RADIO
IN LOS ANGELES

KHJ promotion that Mickaela Callen won for "The Hour of Not Quite Rain," set to music by Richie Furay.

The four-man lineup, February 1968, with Jimmy Messina replacing Bruce Palmer.

Springfield Rock Group Buffaloed

Three members of a popular "folk-rock" singing group—the "Buffalo Springfield" — were among 15 persons arrested on marijuana possession charges last night in a Topanga Canyon home.

Also booked was the "Buffalo" road manager and a member of the "Cream", another singing group.

Sgt. George Kipley of the Malibu sheriff's station identified Eric P. Clapton, 22, as a member of "Cream." The "Buffalo Springfield" members were Neil K. Young, 22, Paul Furay, 23, both of Hollywood,

and James Messina, 20, Burbank.

Also booked was Eugene Sarns, 23, of Malibu, the "Buffalo" road manager.

Kipley said deputies went to the Topanga Canyon house when neighbors complained of a loud party. The officers, he said, found about six ounces of marijuana at the scene. When the front door opened, one of the deputies said, "the marijuana smoke just rolled out."

Also in custody was Furay's wife, Nancy, 21.

Neil Young returns to the band, March 1968.

The last concert,
Long Beach Arena,
May 5, 1968.

The original ph[
shoot for Last
Time Around w[
quartet.

Pickin' Up The Pieces

There's just a little bit of magic,
In the country music we're singin.'
So let's begin.
We're bringin' you back down home,
Where the folks are happy,
Sittin,' pickin' and a-grinnin,'
Casually, you and me'll pick up the pieces.
Oh Lord, I know that the day will come,
When the both of us will sit down and strum,
On our guitars.
And you'll see I really am a lot like you.

Pickin' Up The Pieces (Richie Furay)

Though the Buffalo Springfield failed to sell millions of records, there can be no doubt that the band left an indelible mark on rock music. They left a musical legacy that extends far beyond their two years together. As innovators of what would become known as the California sound, the Springfield opened the folk rock and country rock doors for groups like The Eagles to become one of the most successful rock artists in history. But perhaps the Springfield is best remembered today as the springboard that launched the career of Stephen Stills, Neil Young, and Richie Furay, with Stills going on to superstardom with Crosby, Stills & Nash, Young on to remarkable achievements as a solo artist and with Crazy Horse, and Furay forming Poco with Jim Messina, who in turn teamed up with Kenny Loggins to create one of the most popular duos of the era.

The legacy is rich, even if the band never became so. "Nobody ever really thought we'd break up," muses Dickie Davis. "We thought we'd stay together until we made the million dollars we thought we were entitled to, apiece. We thought the people who wanted to become stars would become stars and those that wanted to be rich would be rich, and the songs would be known and everybody would be famous and happy." For two years, the Buffalo Springfield grabbed for the brass ring, only to fall short several times, plagued by their own demons and undone by their impatience for fame. Perhaps if they had managed to overcome their fractious course and pulled together they might today be spoken of in the same breath as the artists they considered their only competition, the Beatles, Byrds, and Rolling Stones. That they could have remained together as long as their mentors was unlikely, doomed as they were from the start with the envious burden of too much talent. Ahead of their time, unwilling to compromise to the dictates of an industry that has to pigeonhole and categorize, instead they imploded prematurely, leaving us with three albums and a timeless body of music that serves as testament to their immense talent, energy, and enthusiasm.

The musical inheritance left after the break-up of the Buffalo Springfield was wisely and immediately invested by the leading members of the band. Upon parting company following their Long Beach swansong, each member dove into his own activities. Five days later, Neil was in the studio with The Monkees to lay down *You and I* with Davy Jones for their INSTANT REPLAY album, returning on May 30 to work with Mickey Dolenz on the Carole King-Toni Stern song *As We Go Along*, a number destined for their ill-fated *Head* movie and soundtrack. He was also engaged in negotiations once again to break free of Atco-Atlantic, soon after severing all ties to the Buffalo Springfield, ultimately signing with Reprise Records, a West Coast-based label owned by Frank Sinatra and Dean Martin. Elliot Roberts was now handling Neil's affairs exclusively. Of his relationship with his former band mates, Neil revealed in a September 1968 interview, "I don't see Dewey. We never really had much happening. Stephen is out of town so much. If I could just see Stephen, I'd really like to see him. Out of all of them he is the one I like the best, but it's the things he's surrounded himself with that I can't cope with. I'm not in any part of that scene. It really doesn't have anything to do with anything. I guess it's just a way of getting your name in all the magazines. I think for me to go into that scene and pretend I know all those people I really don't know . . . none of them really know each other either because it's impossible to know that many people and be great friends. I think if I did that I'd be a sellout."

In the interview Neil further claimed he was the only one of the five to come out of the Springfield with a nest egg. "I stayed in my room after shows," he declared, going on to boast, "I'm not rich but I could live comfortably if I never worked again." The figure of $100,000 was bandied about on several occasions, to which Richie responds, "I guess I had some money from the Springfield but not much, certainly not $100,000 as Neil claimed. If that's the case, then I got $99,000 less than he did." Commenting on the assertion that Neil left the Springfield financially secure, Stephen stated, "I guess he saved some money. But the rest of us just lived pretty well."

Comfortably settled in a new home he shared with Susan Acevedo in Topanga Canyon and preparing material for his first solo album, Neil also claimed he was considering purchasing land near Winnipeg. With Bruce long out of the picture, Neil drafted Jimmy Messina and Poco drummer George Grantham to play on the sessions recorded over the summer with help from Jack Nitzsche before Jack departed to work on the soundtrack to the movie *Candy*. The self-titled album was released in January 1969 to universal indifference. In a slight, intentional or other-wise, Neil neglected to credit Jimmy and George duly for their work on his solo debut, belatedly rectifying the oversight some 17 years later in the sleeve notes to his countrified OLD WAYS album in 1985.

Amid a flurry of rumors of various affiliations with other well-known artists, including an offer from Blood, Sweat & Tears, Stephen spent the summer of 1968 guesting on other people's records: SUPER SESSION for guitarist Mike Bloomfield and keyboard player Al Kooper (which earned him a gold record and rave reviews), DREAM A LITTLE DREAM OF ME for Mama Cass, WHO KNOWS WHERE THE TIME GOES for girlfriend Judy Collins (inspiration for Stephen's suite *Judy Blue Eyes* on the first Crosby, Stills and Nash album), and John Sebastian's debut solo album. He was reported in the *LA Herald-Examiner* having recorded several tracks, half an album's worth, at Atlantic Studios in New York in mid-May for a possible solo album. While there, Stephen took part in a legendary jam at Steve Paul's Scene club that included Jimi Hendrix and albino blues guitar ace Johnny Winter. In September, the *LA Times* reported him to be forming a new group with David Crosby to be called the Frozen Noses and including "two Englishmen from name groups." As the world learned soon enough, one of those Englishmen was The Hollies' Graham Nash, the identity of the other remaining a mystery, though speculation has generally centered on boy wonder Stevie Winwood, ex of the Spencer Davis Group and Traffic. In the same column, Dewey revealed that he had hired musicians for his own group in which he would be singing lead, his planned duo with wife Jane having died stillborn.

In the final months of the Springfield, Richie and Jimmy had begun to consider their plans for the future, though according to Michael Miller, Jimmy and Stephen briefly entertained thoughts of a collaboration. During the second Beach Boys tour, Richie and Jimmy, having found the *Kind Woman* experience satisfying, hatched their plan to form a country-rock group after the split. Their unanimous first choice for this group was Rusty Young who had impressed them so much earlier. "We were already talking about who was going to be in Poco by the time of the Long Beach gig," asserts Rusty. "I went to that last gig. I didn't do the

Gram Parsons audition because when I went into the studio with Richie and Jimmy, we really hit it off. They knew the Springfield was ending and they weren't sure exactly what they wanted to do, but they wanted to keep playing music. It was a time when everyone was going, 'Holy Mackerel, what are we going to do?' Because we struck up a friendship, we started talking about the kind of music we all liked and wanted to play. So they asked me to stay and get a new band going. There was even talk of us keeping the Buffalo Springfield name, but we decided not to use it. That would have been a real joke." Richie admits that was a fleeting suggestion, one that would not likely have met with approval from the others nor auger well for the launching of a new group.

"We definitely wanted to cross it over between country and rock," offers Richie on the direction he and Jimmy plotted out for their new group, the country-rock pioneering and much beloved Poco. "We had a vision of what kind of sound we wanted. What we wanted to do in Poco had more of a visionary goal-setting direction than the Springfield did. We wanted to be a part of that element that crossed country music and rock'n'roll, but we were never given the privilege of playing the Grand Ole Opry like The Byrds were. We wanted to bring the two together. Gram Parsons was putting together the Flying Burrito Brothers at the time, and Gram and I had conversations about picking and choosing players and making one band. But that never worked because I wasn't gonna give up Rusty for Sneaky Pete, and he wasn't going to give up this guy for that guy, so two bands evolved. Jimmy and I were pretty much in our direction and Gram was in his. But he turned me onto George Jones, who I just thought was the best singer I ever heard in my life, just a great voice. We started putting Poco together in mid to late summer and rehearsed for what seemed like forever. We even tried Gregg Allman when we were trying to put the band together. That lasted maybe a couple of days."

The new group eventually settled on two friends of Rusty's from the Colorado area, bass player Randy Meisner, formerly of The Poor, and Boenzee Cryque singing drummer George Grantham. Says Rusty, "I thought that Jimmy and Richie would know some big time stars to bring into the group, but it took a long time to get Poco together. We tried various bass players and drummers. There were a lot of guys from the LA music scene that Jimmy and Richie knew that we tried but it just kept stalling. It never was right. That's when I suggested Randy Meisner, who I had always wanted to work with. And I told them about George back in Colorado."

Settling on the name "Pogo," the group ran into a legal snag almost immediately. "The Buffalo Springfield Rolling Company supported the use of the name, quite the contrary from what happened a few years later with Walt Kelly," grouses Richie. Walt, cartoonist and creator of the Pogo comic strip, threatened an injunction on the group if they proceeded with the unauthorized use of Pogo. So the group hastily changed the lettering to read Poco and carried on. Rehearsals were held over the summer both at Richie's Laurel Canyon home and the Troubadour. "I remember Neil coming over to Richie's house in Laurel Canyon a couple of times when we were rehearsing Poco," Rusty recalls. "He sat down and played us songs he was going to do on his first solo record and hung out with us. That's where he picked up on Jimmy and George for his solo album."

The group made its debut at the Troubadour in November 1968 to resounding accolades. Pete Johnson, writing in the *Los Angeles Times*, noted, "Poco is one of the tightest groups I have ever seen; a coordination which obviously stems from endless practice and good feelings within the combo. The band seems the natural heir to the originality, diversity and togetherness which marked the beginnings of The Byrds and the Buffalo Springfield, Southern California's two best folk-rooted rock groups so far." Rusty agrees with the comparison to the Springfield. "I think the Springfield and Poco were a lot alike in the fact that I don't think people got it. I don't think people ever understood the Springfield when they were happening nor Poco until after its prime."

Their friendship still intact after his acrimonious departure, Richie enlisted Dickie Davis to manage Poco, with Miles Thomas serving as road manager. Burned by the Greene-Stone experience and determined to eschew the Hollywood star maker machinery, the group entrusted its future to the lesser-known Dickie. The relationship did not last long. Poco was signed to Epic Records, a subsidiary of CBS-Columbia Records, and Dickie ran afoul of president Clive Davis when he insisted that the cover art on the first album be completely redone at the label's expense. Davis' dislike for the diminutive manager was so great that he barred the group from recording their second album until Dickie was replaced. A result of this turmoil was the departure of Randy Meisner. David Geffen stepped in to smooth things over. These early confrontations are often cited as the reason why Poco never attained the success universally predicted for them at the outset.

Prior to signing with Epic, Richie had to settle his contract with Atco-Atlantic. He had expressed concern in the media over attempting to launch a country-rock group on Atlantic, a label that specialized in rhythm and blues. What transpired was akin to a sports trade. With Stephen readying his new group Crosby, Stills and Nash to record for Atlantic, Ahmet Ertegun and Clive Davis agreed to trade Graham Nash, signed to Epic with the Hollies, to Atlantic in exchange for Richie and some minor wrinkles involving Cotillion's publishing. This arrangement left both groups free to record and get on with their careers.

In October 1968, Dewey decided to name his group the New Buffalo Springfield, a mix of LA studio musicians and rookies — guitarist Dave Price, Don Poncher on drums, horn player and future Joe Cocker and Rolling Stones session man Jim Price on horns, bass player Bob Apperson, and Gary Rowles on lead guitar, who soon quit in disgust to join a revamped version of Love. Dewey was now able to exercise his penchant for soul music with a brass section, creating a sound that was a mixture of power rock, rhythm, blues, and jazz. A review of their Hawaiian debut in November termed the group's style "Springfield soul." Other reviews of their shows were less complimentary. Critic Mike Martin, writing about their San Diego show at the Exhibit Hall in the Community Concourse, noted that the group appeared "under the guise of the old Buffalo Springfield, a poor copy with no distinct originality. One was left with the feeling that the whole scene was a cheap ride on the well-earned fame of the Buffalo Springfield. Regretably, someone is making money off the deception."

Dewey believed that, as an original member and since no one else was using it, he was entitled to the name Buffalo Springfield. "I totally thought I had an equal right to use that name," protests Dewey, "because we had all been equal in the band. So I went out and used it." Stephen and Neil disagreed, and what ensued would become one of the first cases of musicians asserting rights to a group name and using the courts to prevent bogus groups from usurping it, an ugly circumstance that would eventually affect The Zombies, Strawberry Alarm Clock, The Byrds, Steppenwolf, The Kingsmen and several other Sixties bands in well publicized legal wranglings. In separate public statements both Stephen and Neil indicated they did not condone Dewey's use of the name and given their higher profile in the media, Dewey perceived his continued ability to find work for his group jeopardized by such public declarations. When the two followed through with an injunction, Dewey retaliated in December 1968. "Neil and Stephen put a cease and desist order on me," he recalls. "So I sued them and I lost. And I lost my royalties."

In the subsequent judgment, Dewey was prohibited from using the name Buffalo Springfield, with Stephen, Richie, and Neil's claim to control of the name confirmed. But according to Bruce, the three did not assume ownership immediately. "Stephen, Richie, and Neil own the name now," Bruce claims, "but that copyright wasn't filed until 1989. They told Dewey in 1969 that they owned the name, sued him, got his royalties, and it wasn't until a couple of years ago that Dewey found out that they didn't file for copyright until 1989. They just said they did." Nevertheless, the three maintain ownership of the copyright and trademark for the Buffalo Springfield name to this day.

Not one to give up that easily Dewey simply shortened the name to New Buffalo and carried on through much of 1969 with a variety of sidemen. In February of that year *Billboard* magazine indicated that Dewey's New Buffalo was set to release an album for Atco-Atlantic Records; however, nothing came of it. By year's end, Dewey had dropped out and signed a solo deal with UNI Records to produce an album. Minus their only connection to the real thing, New Buffalo metamorphosed into Blue Mountain Eagle, relocating to the Seattle area and releasing one forgettable album on Atco in 1970 with help from none other than David Geffen. Earlier that same year Dewey released DEWEY MARTIN AND MEDICINE BALL, the latter being the title of his new aggregation with Dewey serving as vocalist, drummer, and producer. The approach was country rock with Medicine Ball boasting steel guitar on the album played by studio ace Buddy Emmons along with Texan Randy Fuller, ex of his brother's group The Bobby Fuller Four. Bruce Palmer made an appearance on one track, *Recital Palmer*, in which he demonstrated one of his guitar ragas. By the time Medicine Ball debuted at the Troubadour in June, J.D. Maness, who had guested on The Byrds' SWEETHEART OF THE RODEO, was playing steel. Medicine Ball, both the group and album, was met with general hostility and disbanded soon after. "I was in bad shape at the time, drinking a lot and taking uppers," admits Dewey. "I dropped out of the scene after that. I was a bloody drunk. I didn't work."

Bruce managed to negotiate a recording deal of his own in October 1969 with Verve Records, releasing an album of aimless musical meanderings in early 1971 entitled THE CYCLE IS COMPLETE. "MGM approached me, Don Hall and Michael Curb, to do an album," recounts Bruce. "I went in and did a demo for them. It was the first time I had written or sang a song in my life. I wrote it the night before. So I went in, did the song, played several instruments so it sounded like a band, they loved it, signed a contract, and I went in and did two and half hours of instrumental music with Rick James and seven or eight other people. It was spontaneous music, over two hours long so I had to edit it down to 45 minutes. I handed it to them and they dropped their drawers. I gave them what I thought music was all about, not what they thought music was all about. That was what I intended to do. They released it and I retired. I had a laugh at the industry's expense. I did that album and just had enough of the music business. I was seeing my friends turning into beets. Is this what I want to do? Is this what happened to music?" The album died a quick death.

There was still gold to be mined from the Buffalo Springfield. In March 1969, Atco released RETROSPECTIVE: THE BEST OF THE BUFFALO SPRINGFIELD, a compilation of their singles and better known album tracks. The label once again recruited Eve Babitz to design the cover art, but obviously provided her with a limited budget. Replicating the AGAIN format with tranquil rural scenes and the reappearance of the cherub, the design employs cheap black and white xeroxed photographs, front and back, with a short statement on the group from Ahmet. Nevertheless, the album proved a big seller, easily outdoing their previous three studio efforts, going gold and eventually platinum, revealing the band's legacy remained healthy even before the success of CSN, Neil Young, or Poco.

That same year saw the rise of three ex-Buffalo from the ashes. By summer, Crosby, Stills and Nash had the top selling album in America, and with their stripped down acoustic guitar/multiple harmony vocals style, were hailed far and wide as the new direction in rock music. After the failure of his eponymous debut album on Reprise Records, Neil saw the error of his over-produced ways and got back to basics with the marvelously down to earth funkiness of EVERYBODY KNOWS THIS IS NOWHERE credited to Neil Young and Crazy Horse, a group he had met as the Rockets in the early Whisky days. Besides its lengthy guitar jams, the album also boasts a Springfield era number, *Round And Round.*

Neil's star was already rising by the time Stephen came calling to inquire whether his former band mate and rival might like to join his new group, adding a Y to CSN. By the end of the year CSN&Y were the hottest ticket around with favorable comparisons to the Beatles often cited. Indeed, the amalgamation of these luminaries coined the title "supergroup", though in terms of previous success and notoriety, C and N were better known than the one-hit duo from the Buffalo Springfield. Nonetheless, CSN, and later Y, was and remains Stephen Stills' group. He provided the lion's share of material, arranged and produced their recordings, playing multiple instruments. Releasing their debut album *Pickin' Up The Pieces* that same year, Poco inaugurated an effervescent, pleasing pop approach to country rock. Recruiting Timothy B. Schmit to replace the departed Randy Meisner, Poco kept busy on the road, though Richie and Jimmy couldn't help but notice their two ex-band mates flying overhead.

When Neil signed on with CSN, initially to provide more umph to their live sets rather than as an equal writing partner, the foursome, guitar players all, still required a rhythm section. Having already recruited former Clear Light drummer Dallas Taylor during sessions for their debut album, Stephen and Neil turned first to their favorite bass player, Bruce Palmer. Bruce was dispatched from Toronto to rehearse with his two old bandmates in New York prior to joining Crosby and Nash in California in preparation for their inaugural tour. His tenure would prove to be brief.

"Stephen called me, he had talked it over with Neil, and asked me to come on over. We rehearsed in New York, just the three of us and Dallas Taylor without Crosby and Nash, and we were fabulous. But once we got to Los Angeles and started rehearsing at Stephen's house with Crosby and Nash it became real evident that they were nothing more than backup singers. They didn't like it and decided to change it. They couldn't take that; they thought they were too big, too famous, too talented. They weren't talented, they were backup singers. Listen to that first album. It's 95 percent Stephen doing everything and he's got his backup singer boys with him. He's been dragging them around with him for 25 years. I remember there was one day when Graham Nash threw a tantrum about me. He got everybody to leave the room and he talked them into firing me. It had happened once before and Stephen just stood there livid and said, 'Unless everyone in this room remains in the band, then I'm leaving.' So obviously this had been going on for awhile. I was an easy target. They couldn't mess with Neil but they could mess with me. I remember Crosby coming up to me later and saying, 'Even if you played it perfect it wouldn't have mattered.' I should have punched him out right at that point. Then it became real clear. Between him and Graham Nash, there was an incredible conspiracy going on. It looked to them as if it was Crosby and Nash backing up Buffalo Springfield, being nothing more than harmony singers for Stephen, Neil, myself, and Dallas Taylor. That was evident. But it couldn't go that way, Crosby saw to that." Bruce's feelings toward the ex-Byrd remain bitter.

In 1992, Atlantic Records released a lavishly packaged and thoroughly documented four disk box set retrospective chronicling CSN&Y's long career. It was an immediate success. Bruce wasn't even informed by the label or any one of CSN or Y that he played on two of the tracks.

Bruce spent the better part of the 1970s in Toronto doing very little of anything. On a couple of occasions he ventured back to the States to attempt to kick start his career, only to run into dead ends. Financially, Bruce was living hand to mouth, one step ahead of immigration, while his former friends raked in the dough in staggering sums. By the mid 1970s, Stephen and Neil were multi-millionaires, their walls dotted with gold and platinum albums. While Stephen maintained mansions in England and Bel Air and hung with the jet set, Neil, the bigger winner in the monetary sweepstakes with royalty cheques matching the GNP of several third world nations, settled into a sprawling 2,000 acre ranch in Northern California. "If I was in financial difficulty," postulates Bruce on his relationship with his ex-band mates, "the last person I would think to call would be Neil Young. As a matter of fact there was a point back in early 1975 where I had to get out of America real fast. There was another immigration possibility, paranoia thing, and I had no money to get out of the country. I called Neil for the first time ever to ask for enough money for a plane ticket to get out of Los Angeles, and he hung up on me. I called Stephen, he was ill and in New York. He told me to immediately go down to Gold Hill offices, his publishing company, pick up two plane tickets and a thousand dollars in cash and make it on out."

For Jim Fielder, clouds do have silver linings. Following his rather ignominious dismissal from the Springfield in the spring of 1967, Jim managed to land squarely on his feet soon after. Though disparaged by Stephen for his playing ability, Jim would go on to revolutionize bass playing a year later with Blood, Sweat and Tears, becoming one of the most innovative, imaginative and respected players in the business. "The fact that I did get the boot from them is kind of what inspired me to get a lot better real quick," Jim concedes. "So when the offer from Al Kooper came along I was ready. Stephen also played bass and that was sort of his problem in that he wanted to be two people, the singer guitar player and the bass player. If you weren't playing exactly the kind of bass line he would conceive, he wasn't gonna be happy with it. I guess that's why he liked Bruce because Bruce either played naturally the kind of line he wanted or Stephen was able to communicate to Bruce exactly what he wanted to hear."

Jim's timing could not have been better. "It was rather propitious actually. When I got the boot from the Springfield, I had maybe a month left in my house. My next door neighbor was Jim Valley, "Harpo," from Paul Revere and the Raiders. He and Al Kooper were real good friends. During that month that I was sitting in my house, Al came out and stayed with Jim. I had known Al because both the Mothers and the Springfield had done some gigs with the Blues Project. Just by coincidence we were next door to each other and Al said, 'I've got some new tunes I've written. Come on over and let's just jam on them.' So I brought my bass over — he played piano, I played bass — and we worked on all these really neat tunes. I asked him what he was going to do with them. 'I've got this idea to start a band with a horn section.' I thought it sounded cool, and he said, 'Would you be interested in being the bass player if I pull this off?' So I said sure. I did a trio gig with him at the Monterey Folk Festival, not to be confused with the Monterey Pop Festival, where we did these new tunes. Afterwards he said, 'Expect to get a call from me in a very short time to come out to New York and we'll do this thing.' Later that summer I went to New York and we got Blood, Sweat and Tears together. In a way it was a good thing that it happened then because had I still been with the Springfield I would have taken a pass on it. I'm kind of glad my time with the Springfield was mercifully brief and in the long run it worked out better for me.''

Indeed, with their brass section and elaborate arrangements, BS&T virtually defined an entire genre termed jazz-rock, riding the top of the charts from 1969 to the mid-1970s with a dozen gold records — albums and singles — including *You've Made Me So Very Happy, And When I Die,* and *Spinning Wheel,* all propelled by Jim's remarkably fluid bass playing. Jim currently resides in Nashville where he keeps busy as an in-demand session player.

In 1971, Jimmy Messina announced his departure from Poco. Having earned at best a limited success in their first three years and tiring of his multiple duties as lead guitarist and producer, he sought a return to studio production full time. His relationship with Richie had come under some strain as Richie exerted greater control over the writing and direction for the group. With Jimmy serving notice, Poco recruited ex-Illinois Speed Press guitarist Paul Cotton, who Jimmy helped ease into the band. Accepting a position with Columbia as a staff producer, Jimmy's first assignment was a singer/songwriter named Kenny Loggins. The two hit it off so well that Kenny's debut solo effort was renamed KENNY LOGGINS WITH JIMMY MESSINA SITTIN' IN and a duo was formed. During the 1970s, Loggins and Messina scored a number of hits, including *House At Pooh Corner, Danny's Song,* and their best known, *Your Mama Don't Dance,* earning gold records along the way and reaping millions before calling it quits in the early 1980s. Jimmy then attempted to launch a solo career that never got off the ground after a couple of mediocre albums, and by the end of the decade his musical future seemed in doubt.

CSN&Y had gone their separate ways after a particularly

acrimonious 1970 tour ironically titled the Carry On tour. And carry on they did, at each other's throats on and off stage until the four head-strong individuals decided to go the solo album route. Neil ultimately achieved the greatest success of the four. After a couple of so-so outings on his own, Stephen recruited some muscle by calling on ex-Byrd and Burrito Brother Chris Hillman to form the group Manassas. "Funnily enough," offers Chris on receiving the call from Stephen, "when I hooked up with Stephen in Manassas, the first thing he said to me was 'I've never forgotten that you got us that job at the Whisky.' And he gave me this beautiful mandolin. I have great respect for Stephen as a musician. As eccentric as he is, Stephen is a very bright, sensitive musician who really kept me on my toes. He is very driven, very musical. I can relate to him musically more so than anyone I've ever worked with. He made me reach for things. I learned a lot about music from him. There were times of brilliance with him. I learned a lot about leadership from Stephen, too." However, Chris was also witness to the start of Stephen's troubles. "Stephen thought you had to be the tortured artist, the 'I must suffer to create' image. And it doesn't work." Over the next two decades, Stephen would increasingly battle his own demons as his career took a roller coaster ride.

In late 1973, with several of its former members having ascended to the rock stratosphere, Atco-Atlantic again went back to the well and came up with another compilation of previously released tracks, this time a double album simply entitled BUFFALO SPRINGFIELD. Despite possessing a dozen or more unreleased tracks in their vaults, the label chose instead to included the nine minute version of *Bluebird* to snare die-hard fans who had yet to hear it. Eve Babitz was again enlisted to provide the cover art, with the cherub making its third appearance. Unlike its predecessor, RETROSPECTIVE, this double album was not a big seller. Though those unreleased Springfield nuggets would remain in the vaults, in the early 1970s Capitol Records released an obscure album by an equally obscure group named Yellow Hand that included cover versions of several of those gems. *Down To The Wire, Come On Lover, Neighbor Don't You Worry, We'll See, Sell Out,* and *Hello I've Returned* could now be heard in pedestrian arrangements that stayed fairly close to the original demo versions. The album and group disappeared soon after release.

Through the early 1970s, Richie continued to toil away in Poco, a group that could always be counted on to sell out medium sized halls and garner positive reviews. Their album sales, however, stalled. Pouring his heart into the 1972 release A GOOD FEELING TO KNOW, Richie's spirit was broken when both the single, a huge concert favorite penned by Richie, and album failed to make a breakthrough. Soon after, he announced that the next album, 1973's CRAZY EYES, would be his last. Having to sit back while several of his former colleagues, either together or on their own, earned dumptrucks full of money was not easy; Richie determined that it was his turn to reap his just rewards. Even Poco defector Randy Meisner had struck gold with The Eagles. Despite critical praise and decent sales for CRAZY EYES, the title song based on his impressions of a young Gram Parsons, Richie remained resolute, leaving Poco to embark on an ill-fated union concocted by rising mogul David Geffen of Asylum Records. In an effort to emulate the success of Crosby, Stills, Nash & Young, Richie joined up with Chris Hillman (who seemed to be making a career of supporting ex-Springfield members) and Eagles associate, songwriter John David Souther, in the Souther, Hillman, Furay Band.

The idea must have seemed irresistible when floated at some corporate meeting, but the amalgamation never bore much fruit. "The Souther, Hillman, Furay thing was a great idea on paper, but we never jelled as individuals in a group sense," reflects Chris. "It was three individual singer/songwriters. Unfortunately, right at that moment Richie was going through some tough times in his personal life. And I don't think he ever really understood J.D., and I don't think J.D. was a team player. I was almost the mediator between them. I recognized the genius in J.D.'s songwriting and I also recognized this positive, all-American boy Richie Furay. Unfortunately it didn't mesh. There was always a little bit of tension between them. But it wasn't them, the idea just didn't work." Despite earning a gold disk for an impressive debut album, the group, pegged in the media as the CSN&Y minor league, was doomed from the start by the same virus that plagued its mentor CSN&Y through its turbulent years: too many chefs spoil the brew. Throwing three or four names with no shared experience together in a group is no guarantee of success. The association withered from apathy during sessions for a follow-up album, the aptly named *Trouble In Paradise*, and Richie found himself at a crossroads in his personal life.

Separated from wife Nancy and daughter Timmy Sue and frustrated watching from the wings as his former mates gained the success they had all dreamed of, Richie's life was at its lowest point. A conversion to Christianity was his salvation, and reunited with his family in Colorado, he set about rebuilding his life on a solid spiritual foundation. Not long after, Richie became a lay pastor and established the Calvary Chapel of Boulder, Colorado where he continues to minister today. He kept his feet in the music business releasing three solo albums in the late 1970s as well as recording gospel music.

Richie returned to the bright lights in 1989 for the much-publicized though personally disappointing Poco reunion that brought him together with the original lineup of Rusty Young, George Grantham, Randy Meisner, and Jimmy Messina. After leaving The Eagles, Randy Meisner's solo efforts had met with universal indifference, as had Jimmy's post Loggins and Messina recordings. With each of the five participants at loose ends and Randy and Jimmy looking for an appropriate jumpstart to their individual careers, the timing seemed right for a reunion. The affair was brief with Richie pulling out after the first leg of their tour due to conflicts of conscience over lyric content. Richie continues to tend to his congregation and record sporadically, though he no longer needs the limelight to find satisfaction. Observes longtime friend Michael Miller, "The one constant and consistent voice of integrity has always been Richie. That's what shines throughout my experience with the guys in the Springfield then and since. One time Richie and I went to Yellow Springs, Ohio and I met his Mom. She was lovely and it was nice to see that small Midwest kind of life. And you get an understanding of Richie when you see his roots." In 1997, Richie released an album of gospel music on the Calvary label.

The Poco reunion continued to its conclusion without Richie, then the four remaining members went their separate ways. Though their album LEGACY went gold, none of the originals had much desire to push the issue any further. Jimmy resumed his solo career, releasing a new album in the summer of 1996 for the independent River North Records. In an attempt to establish his pedigree as a founding country rocker in the 'New Country' marketplace, a style of music derived directly from

Poco, Jimmy included cover versions of material previously associated with, if not written by, him, including several Poco and Loggins and Messina tunes plus two of Richie's compositions from the Springfield, *Kind Woman* and *A Child's Claim To Fame*. Rusty Young, now residing in Nashville, has a new country band called the Sky Kings, whose debut single on WEA, *Picture Perfect*, came out that same year.

Of the other Springfield associates, Dickie Davis is currently employed in the film industry, as is Nurit Wilde. Unceremoniously bounced from the group in 1966, Barry Friedman returned to promotions working for Derek Taylor and promoting some of Beatles' manager Brian Epstein's acts, including Tommy Quickly and Cilla Black. He later went to work for Elektra and A & M Records as a producer before changing his name to Frazier Mohawk and moving to Canada. He now manages an audio-video production studio and company in Toronto. Miles Thomas is also in the video production business in Los Angeles. Ken Koblun works with computers near San Francisco. After striking gold with Iron Butterfly, another York-Pala Production, Charlie Greene remains active in the music business on the East Coast. Jim Friedman continues to write and perform in lounges in New York. The ubiquitous Brian Stone manages various financial enterprises. Mark Volman still entertains audiences every year with longtime partner Howard Kaylan in The Turtles. After reaping great success on the country music charts leading his group the Desert Rose Band, Chris Hillman released a bluegrass album in 1997. Following his dismissal from the Springfield, Doug Hastings gigged briefly with Clear Light, a shortlived LA-based group featuring future CSN&Y drummer Dallas Taylor, before joining Rhinoceros, brainchild of Elektra Records' Paul Rothchild, who assembled the group in 1968 from a number of well-known second stringers, including ex-Iron Butterfly guitarist Danny Weiss. After two albums that met with critical plaudits and poor sales, Doug split from the troubled group going on to play with Pam Polland and Dr. John before retiring from the music business to return to college. Completing a degree in geology, he currently works in petroleum geology in Alaska.

If anyone was left behind after the Buffalo Springfield, it was Dewey and Bruce. "When you think of the Buffalo Springfield," remarks Mark Volman, "who mentions Dewey or Bruce? They were the guys who got hit the hardest in all this. They didn't get the credibility." After a decade of inactivity, Bruce determined that there was still a living to be made from the Buffalo Springfield legacy, so in 1985 he resurrected the banner, albeit as Buffalo Springfield Revisited, and hit the lucrative nostalgia circuit performing for fans who were less interested in the personnel than in hearing their favorite songs. In order to give Revisited the added credibility it required, Bruce enlisted Dewey, who, though a bit rusty, came out of retirement to beat the skins in the revival effort. Bruce was fortunate to come across Neil Young soundalike Frank Wilks, and with the stalwart support of veteran Toronto guitar ace Stanley Endersby, who had previously worked with Ricky James Matthews and the Kinks' Pete Quaife in his short-lived Maple Oak, along with Bob Frederickson on guitar and Harlan Spector on keyboards, Buffalo Springfield Revisited set out across America gigging fairly consistently over the next two years. The group appeared in night clubs, at fairs and at festivals, including the Vietnam Veterans Benefit at the LA Forum in February of 1986. To their credit, Buffalo Springfield Revisited, though far from the real thing, served up credible if uninspired renditions of the Springfield's better known material and generally went down well with audiences. They were no different than a dozen or more other acts plying the baby boom nostalgia market in the 1980s, boasting one or two original members and rehashing the hits. Indeed, the players in Revisited were skilled players and presented a tight sound.

"It was my inception, my idea," confirms Bruce on the formation of Buffalo Springfield Revisited, "and I brought Dewey up from California. We were playing a resort in Ontario. I neglected to tell him there was another drummer, but he didn't care, it was okay. He wasn't flustered at all. Most drummers would have ranted and raved and stomped off. But we didn't keep two drummers because it got to be too much. The band was working all the time, touring all the time. We had Geordie Hormel's backing, who at one time had the franchise for Silver Eagle tour buses, so we had the best tour buses in the business. We had his recording facilities at hand, he owned

Village Recorders." Heir to the Hormel Meats fortune, Geordie Hormel fancied himself a svengali bankrolling the group with an eye to turning them into the next big thing. Dewey, head-strong as ever, found Geordie's involvement intrusive. "We got tied into a whole thing with Hormel, then he just stopped putting money into the band. There was a lot of crap going on with him. I played hardball with Hormel. I said I wasn't going to sign the contract he had for us. I took it to a lawyer who advised me not to sign it. He told Bruce that Dewey had better sign the contract if he knew what was good for him. Bruce insisted that he had to be the band leader and that pissed me off a little bit. Bruce just isn't a good business man and he made all the wrong decisions." Once Dewey found his feet, the additional drummer, Alan Prosser, was dropped from the band.

Attempts at recording new material, including a credible cover of *Down To The Wire*, faltered after the group failed to land a record deal. "Frank Wilks' songs weren't that strong," claims Bruce. "Everybody recognized that but nobody else in the group was a writer. The playing was there but he wouldn't have been able to sustain a whole album."

On April 15, 1986, Buffalo Springfield Revisited was per-forming at LA's Palomino Club when a familiar face sauntered up to the stage, guitar in hand, looking to sit in. Stephen Stills joined Bruce and Dewey on stage for a spirited run through of old Springfield numbers, straining to remember the chords and riffs but nonetheless providing a genuine treat for club patrons. "Stephen came down to our gig at the Palomino, intentionally brought his guitar, sat in and had a great time," recalls Bruce. "We have that night on video." Said Stephen of the impromptu jam in the papers the next day, "It went pretty well. A lot of the show was just educated guesswork. Some of these songs I haven't even heard in years, and I've got completely different versions of *Bluebird* and *For What It's Worth* for my own four piece band. I actually came by planning to stand back in a dark corner, but I wound up on stage. I'm real happy with what they're doing. These guys are doing a real good job. They've got their act together." The positive experience, well-covered in the LA media, paved the way for a full scale Buffalo Springfield reunion a few months later at Stephen's house in Bel Air.

On several occasions throughout the 1970s, a Buffalo Springfield reunion had been planned but never materialized. In

1974 a proposed extravaganza at the LA Forum involving reunions of the Springfield, the original five member Byrds, and CSN&Y was openly discussed not only in the media but behind the scenes as well. The show was never mounted. In an interview, Neil glowed over the notion of getting together again. "Everybody in that group was a genius at what he did," he freely asserted. "That was a great group, man. I'd love to play with that band again just to see if the buzz was still there." Talk of a reunion again surfaced in 1982 when the five were alleged to have met in a hotel room to consider the possibility. With Neil tied up, the idea never got off the ground, but in a gesture to his old friend, Neil brought Bruce into his Trans Band for a one-off world tour. As one of the principals in the 1982 Us Festival, Michael Miller gave serious consideration to approaching the Springfield to reunite for the massive outdoor event before letting the idea drop.

However, in early July 1986, the five originals met up at Stephen's house armed with guitars and drums, all old animosities forgiven, to make some music. Convening in the basement music room lined with Stephen's gold records, the group got down to working on several new tunes. The *joie de vivre* that permeated the room belied the wrinkles and paunchy physiques. After exchanging pleasantries, Neil and Stephen took the lead, calling all the shots. After all, according to the golden rule, he who has the gold records makes the rules. Neil directed the rehearsals. Richie maintained a low profile. "When we got together for that reunion," he concedes, "I really wasn't prepared. I hadn't done a lot musically or hadn't been playing a lot. I'm more prepared now since the Poco reunion with new songs. I felt a little awkward, too. My life had changed quite a bit differently from the other guys and that's why I probably did kind of hang back." Despite that, he has fond memories of the event. "It was fun when we tried to get together and just see if we could still actually play together. The original five of us playing those songs after 15 years of none of us sitting in the same room together."

With a film crew on hand to record the moment for posterity and Revisited band keyboard player Harlan Spector noodling away intrusively in the background, the five ran through some new songs from Neil, including *Road Of Plenty*, still a work in progress that would materialize a couple of years later as the Spanish-flavored *Eldorado* on his 1990 FREEDOM album, and an unidentified boogie of Stephen's in which he mumbled his way through some unfinished verses. The five then posed for photographs, laughing over the suggestion that they try to recreate their album covers, to which Stephen responded, "I quit," throwing his hat down at Neil's feet and feigning choking his wayward colleague. The reunion was broken up when Dewey, who had been working as a mechanic in the ensuing interval between Medicine Ball and Revisited, attempted to repair his Cadillac, which had died in Stephen's driveway, as the others, camera crew and all, watched bemused. "Everybody was trying to treat each other as equals," waxes Dewey on the dynamics of the personalities at the reunion, "but Neil was trying to be the one in charge. Even Stills bent to him. But both of them kept praising Richie's singing."

"It was totally wonderful, magical, a total revitalization," gushes Bruce who had much at stake in any possible longevity for the venture. Not everyone shared the sentiment. "Everybody needed it. But somebody didn't and that was Neil. He was incredibly irresponsible. I still get mad over it." Following the basement jam, the five assembled in Stephen's living room to lay out their options. It was at that point that Neil balked at making the reunion more than a one-off event. "This was after our day of playing together," states Bruce on the letdown that followed, "We were all so pleased with everything. We meet in the living room to discuss things. My management had received a commitment from Fort Worth, Texas for our first live show, a binding contract. Neil sits there and looks at us and says, 'You guys think I've got a lot of money but I've just got a lot of things. I don't want to do this because we don't have to do this now because it's too soon. I know I'm taking money out of your pockets, but we don't have to do this so soon. We can do this every two years.' In other words, putting himself in the kingship, being the decision guy. But there was no other way around it. So okay, we'll do it in two years, fine." The five then went their separate ways, agreeing to reconvene two years later.

In 1988 the stage was once again set for a reunion at Stephen's house. Discussions regarding a possible 1987 reunion had fallen apart almost immediately when Richie indicated his unavailability due to a planned trip to Israel. However, the next year seemed feasible for everyone. In an attempt to determine

Neil's depth of commitment, Bruce visited him. "I went up to Santa Cruz two weeks before the second reunion was supposed to take place," he grouses. "Crosby, Stills, Nash & Young got back together for a gig, and I asked Neil whether he remembered that on the 27th we were going to get back together to do this thing. Stephen walks out of another dressing room and Neil looks at him and says, 'Let's keep the ball rolling. We'll be at your house on the 27th.'" Buoyed by his response, four members arrived on the appointed date, but Neil failed to show.

Bruce angrily recounts the woeful tale of the doomed second reunion. "The next rehearsal is set, I remind him in Santa Cruz, and he agrees to keep the ball rolling. So we get to Stephen's, Richie flies in from Colorado and his guitar is broken in freight. We sit around waiting for two hours. Where is he? We find him in town, in LA at a recording studio in Hollywood, ten minutes away. His excuse was that he forgot. 'I really screwed up, man. I forgot. I'm really sorry, man.' My blood pressure was rising by the nano-second. I couldn't take that excuse. So we say, 'Well, come on over here now.' 'I can't, I've got 16 musicians, I've got Jack Nitzsche, I can't do it now.' Bingo. I immediately realized that I was still dealing with the same self-righteous son of a bitch, cold hearted, that doesn't give a damn about anybody other than himself. I handed the phone over to Richie who's a minister and he talked to Neil for a little while and hung up saying, 'It's not going to happen'. My shoulders sagged. Richie walked out the front door. I was really angry. There was no alternative action. 'Let's do it tomorrow' didn't even come up. We weren't going to sit around and wait for him to relinquish his time to condescend to be with us. The commitment was made beforehand and he forgot? Crosby and Nash show up at the door because they want to be there for the trip. They walk in and go, 'What's going on?' 'Neil isn't going to show up.' And Crosby says, 'Well, that's why we call him Shakey.' Enough said. A moment in musical history went out the window. People's lives were adversely affected. And he forgot. He knew that Richie was flying in and the rest of us were sitting there. Those four people were, in effect, essentially responsible for putting him on the musical map."

Richie remains philosophical about the whole affair. "I don't believe you can go back," he admits. "It's not the same. There is something about recapturing it, but does anybody ever? It would be more satisfying just for the five or the six of us." As is his nature, Richie retains an optimistic outlook. "If there was an opportunity, I'd love to sit down and really create something with those guys one more time. But maybe because of the mystique surrounding the band or all that's gone down, maybe it doesn't need to be done. But it would be fun just for personal satisfaction because I think I've grown a lot musically since then." Just such an opportunity came in 1997 when the Buffalo Springfield was inducted into the Rock'n'roll Hall of Fame.

Members of Buffalo Springfield remain active in the rock music world. Stephen Stills continues to tour and record with CSN, who were also inducted into the Rock'n'Roll Hall of Fame in 1997. He has also done a solo acoustic album entitled STILLS ALONE for his own Gold Hill Records label. Neil Young continues to reinvent himself every few years, winning new converts along the way. His recent incarnation as the godfather of grunge rock, the Seattle-based, back-to-basics alternative music characterized by groups like Nirvana and Pearl Jam, has brought him a new lease on life. For Neil, change is a way of life. The one consistency throughout his long and winding career has been his inconsistency, though he is always in control. In the summer of 1995, Richie accepted an invitation to perform at an outdoor venue in San Diego opening for old friends Chris Hillman and headliner Stephen Stills. Accompanied by songwriting partner Scott Sellen, Richie's spirited acoustic set was liberally peppered with the familiar — songs from the repertoires of the Springfield and Poco — even pulling out *On The Way Home*, a number he had not performed since the group's split in 1968.

In early 1987, Dewey bowed out of the Revisited group. Though back in fighting form the road was proving too long and he grew weary of the grind. "I just couldn't take it anymore. All these bad decisions were being made. I was almost 50 and I didn't want to live in a band house any more with a bunch of guys." Bruce carried on, incurring some wrath over the continued use of the name fronted by only one ex-member. He and Dewey had won the tacit approval of Stephen and Neil under the proviso that as long as they both were in the group, it was okay to use the name. "If one of us leaves then the band can't exist," Dewey remarked to writer Pennye Nelson. A year later he, too, threw in the towel. "It was, if not financially rewarding, a good few years," assesses Bruce on the Revisited band's run. "But it just got to the point where I couldn't play another note again, night after night. I found myself in Las Vegas, we were doing the Hilton, and I was in the dressing room pounding the walls, telling them, 'I just can't do this anymore. I don't want to do this anymore. Enough is enough.' So that was it for that band." Bruce subsequently returned to Toronto.

Dewey revived the Buffalo Springfield banner one more time in 1991 in a bid to earn a living. Recruiting Mike Curtis, Robin Lambe, and Billy Darnell, he billed the group this time as Buffalo Springfield Again. "I had to make some money, so I put a pretty good band together," he asserts. But he quickly ran afoul of Richie who had taken up the cause of misrepresenting the name. "That's when Richie ordered a cease and desist on me. The letter from his lawyer said I was pawning myself off as Buffalo Springfield, which was not true. We were with the Bellamy Brothers and the promoter knew he could get me in trouble. We get to the gig and all the signs are up: 'Bellamy Brothers and Buffalo Springfield.' Richie got word of that, saw the picture, and got pissed off at me. But it wasn't me that was doing it." The legal action was precipitated by an unscrupulous promoter in Colorado seeking to scam unsuspecting audiences by claiming publicly that the group was, in fact, the Buffalo Springfield, adding further fuel to the fire by asserting that Richie Furay would be performing with the group at a club engagement in Boulder. By this time, Dewey had hooked up with Steve Green, a promoter of revival versions of name acts, whose clientele over the years has included members of Three Dog Night, Nick St. Nicholas and Goldy McJohn of Steppenwolf, and Dewey.

"They came and played a club here in Golden called the Buffalo Rose," recounts Richie on the deception that took place in his own backyard. "I phoned the club — I didn't tell them who I was — and asked who was in the band. After a bunch of mumbling around, the club owner blurted out, 'Dewey Martin is the only original member.' They were taking liberties with the public and making things up like I was playing with them." Richie remains adamant over Dewey's violation of the Buffalo Springfield name and defends his actions in protecting it. "I'm not too crazy about that. In recent years I have really taken more of the initiative to try to get him to just stop it. I never have wanted to see Dewey and Bruce do that. I was furious. Dewey felt he had the right to do it and had a right to make some money from the name. Every time he went out it was like a thorn to me. It irritated me. I took legal action the last time. And I think they very reluctantly stopped. But he'll do it again and we'll have to stop it again. I feel that if that band is ever to stand for anything, anything that anybody does apart from the five of us has taken away from what people remember of the Buffalo Springfield and what it was. I don't care how well people sing the songs or how well produced it is, it's not Buffalo Springfield. My personal feelings are, stop it. It's not fair to the group."

In the early 1990s, following a prolonged illness and convalescence during which time he claims to have become a born again Christian, Dewey managed to negotiate his share of royalties back from Neil, though Stephen remains intransigent. "Neil and I are getting along better now than ever, Dewey claims."

Bruce continues to collect checks a couple of times a year, which provide him with enough to live on, turning up for the occasional gig around Toronto. "What pisses me off," says Dewey, "is that the guy is just vegetating away. I love him. We've always stuck together." Dickie Davis sold out his one sixth stake in Springalo Toones in 1972 to Stephen, and Neil for a tidy though hardly staggering sum. "What I got from the sell out wasn't much compared to what was earned later when *For What It's Worth* was revived in *Forrest Gump*," laments Dickie. "I wish I had a piece of that now."

With the advent of compact discs for re-issuing albums, classic rock and oldies radio formats, and Sixties nostalgia, the Springfield pot was enhanced significantly. For a time in the 1980s you couldn't turn on a television documentary or watch a movie about that much hyped decade without hearing, "There's something happenin' here," accompanying it. Currently, Stephen, Neil, and Richie retain control of Springalo Toones administered by Warner-Tamerlane Publishing. Stephen managed to parlay *For What It's Worth* into a vehicle for selling beer for a rumored six figure deal, re-recording the song as opposed to employing the original track. But the big windfall came with *Forrest Gump*, whose soundtrack album featuring two dozen oldies, including *For What It's Worth*. As a result, there were a few bloated bank accounts lending further credence to the Gumpism that life is like a box of chocolates. Offers former KHJ program director Ron Jacobs, "That song has shown up in movies, commercials and, to me, really represents the Sixties era. It's as immortal as a rock song can be."

With the popularity and financial viability in recent years of the multi-disk CD box set retrospective, the Buffalo Springfield seem a natural for such career immortalization, an idea considered but abandoned by Atlantic Records. Far lesser artists have been granted such an accolade, yet chances remain remote that such a package will ever materialize. Ownership of Springfield songs and master tapes has been complicated by the fact that several members and associates hold control, some more tenaciously than others, and there is considerable reluctance to allow their past to be revealed without their direct input into the final product. Over the years both Stephen and Neil have been quietly acquiring the rights to their past compositions. In the late 1980s Neil embarked on a vigorous campaign to collect, catalog, and stockpile virtually anything and everything associated with his past, an obsession that reached near religious zeal in pursuit of tapes, photographs, and all manner of memorabilia bearing his name, with the intended goal of releasing his own archives box set. Such a compilation does indeed exist, lovingly compiled, remixed, photographed, digitized and whatever by longtime employee Joel Bernstein, whose work shepherding the CSN box set was a praiseworthy effort. Charlie Greene, too, possesses his own vault of tapes, as does Atlantic Records, and would likely relinquish them for the right price. Neil tapped Charlie's resources a few years back in his archival pursuit. "If we did have a box set," states Richie optimistically, "I'd like to see us include some new material from the five of us."

Recognition of another sort, induction into the Rock'n'Roll Hall of Fame in Cleveland, too, continued to elude the band. Nominated twice only to be passed over, the Springfield was finally honored with acceptance in May 1997, the induction taking place for the first time at the newly opened museum in Cleveland. Their pioneering work in the history of rock music has been suitably recognized. The legacy of the Buffalo Springfield is indeed rich. "There was so much talent in the band that never got tapped the way it could have," Richie Furay remarks. "Even though it was a struggle for us, as I look back on that group, I have only the fondest of memories of what we created in that brief period. It was amazing what the five of us uniquely brought together to make the music we did." Smiles Richie, "I was just glad to be there."

Poco, December 1968: (left to right) Randy Meisner, who would join The Eagles, Rusty Young, Jimmy Messina, George Grantham, Richie Furay.

CSN&Y, 1974: (left to right) Stephen Stills, Graham Nash, David Crosby, Neil Young.

Buffalo Springfield Revisited: (left to right top) Bruce Palmer, Bob Frederickson, Dewey Martin; (bottom) Stan Endersby, Frank Wilks, Harlan Spector. Stephen Stills jamming with Stan Endersby at the Palomino Club.

EPILOGUE

On The Way Home

Three's the charm. After two previous nominations, the five members of the Buffalo Springfield were finally inducted into the Rock 'n' Roll Hall of Fame in May 1997 at a ceremony held for the first time in the Hall of Fame's hometown, Cleveland. Despite a life span that barely ran two years and despite never selling a million records, the group's rich legacy and profound influence was undeniable. As one pundit suggested, "Without them the entire LA music scene wouldn't have existed." The group was in illustrious company that year with Joni Mitchell; the Bee Gees; Rascals; Jackson Five; Parliament-Funkadelic; Crosby, Stills and Nash; bluegrass pioneer Bill Monroe; and gospel great Mahalia Jackson all being honored. With the five original Springfield members still alive it was anticipated that the entire group would attend the event. There were even strong hints that the quintet might perform together for the first time in almost thirty years.

"How do you put something like that into words?" muses Richie on the import of the tribute. "To be recognized like that? It was such an honor simply to be nominated and then to be inducted was a real thrill. When I left Ohio in the early sixties, I just wanted to make music and who could ever know that I would fulfill those dreams and all those years later have my name written in the Rock 'n' Roll Hall of Fame alongside all those great artists. To have made an impact on peoples' lives and be appreciated by so many people, it's really kind of cool."

Two months before the event, the five exchanged faxes and e-mails weighing the possibility of performing. Neil took the initiative in a communiqué to the others soliciting suggestions for a possible mini set. Richie's list consisted of *For What It's Worth, Mr. Soul, On The Way Home, Rock & Roll Woman,* and *Sit Down I Think I Love You.* The intent was to find three or four songs they could all agree on and rehearse in Cleveland two days prior to the ceremony. Richie was excited to play again. Then, just before leaving, came another fax from Neil stating that he was boycotting the ceremony over excessive ticket prices ($1,500 a seat) and gratuitous television coverage of the event on VH1. "When we got there," Richie recalls, "obviously a lot of attention or focus was on Neil's decision, 'What do you think about it?' over and over. So it became a wonderful moment that shouldn't have been shared with that. But that's just the way it went down."

Neil's no-show cast a pall over the night; however, the others were determined not to let it undermine the occasion. "Neil had some good points on why he stayed away and made the protest," notes Richie. "I just think he just chose the wrong time and the wrong year to do it. This should not have been the year to distract from the Springfield. One of his complaints was that you couldn't bring your kids. For him it wouldn't have mattered that much in terms of money but there wasn't room for kids. I could have brought four or five kids but I couldn't afford to nor would there have been room."

"He's Neil," Richie shrugs. "This is who he is. It's just what he felt he needed to do and we all know basically that's what Neil does. But I like him. You just have to learn that this is who he is."

Speculation ran rampant that Neil's absence may have been sparked by the fact that his old Springfield rival, Stephen Stills, was being fêted not once but twice that night—as a member of the Springfield and Crosby, Stills and Nash—and it would have been too much for him to handle.

Following a retrospective video montage, Tom Petty stepped forward to induct the Springfield. His speech captured the essence of the group:

Buffalo Springfield was born in 1966.
They were blonde and brunette,
They were fringe and paisley.
They were the city and they were the canyons,
They were the Sunset Strip and the Whisky A Go-Go.
There were three great voices and they were poets.
They were electric and they were an absolutely new acoustic.
They were ominous and they were a country morning.
They were Cuban heels and moccasins,

And they were Gretsch guitars and Fender amps.
They were dueling guitar solos, one bluesy, the other fuzzy and angry.
They were beautiful harmonies and they were a psychedelic orchestra.
They sang of children's claims to fame, of broken arrows, and for what
it was worth.
They were immeasurably influential and they begot many more
groups that would make more silver and gold music throughout the
decades to follow.
They were most of all Stephen Stills, Richie Furay, Neil Young, Dewey
Martin, and Bruce Palmer.

With that, Stephen, Richie, Bruce, and Dewey came out one by one. Looking much heavier than his Springfield days and sporting a kaftan, Bruce addressed the issue the media had been running with all day: "You probably notice that there is one of us missing tonight. You all know what I'm talking about. And I'm pissing off a lot of people. If you can get all that off of your mind, this is a wonderful thing." He then launched into an incoherent monologue that left many in the audience, and those onstage, fidgety.

Richie followed Bruce. After giving thanks to God, he effused, "To be honored tonight with the musicians here, I'm just absolutely blown away." He then thanked Nancy and all four daughters, even managing to squeeze in the name of his brand new grandson, Jackson Thomas. Dewey was his amiable self, though the weight of the occasion did temper him slightly. He alluded to his recent health problems and to the fact that he was fortunate to be there at all.

It took Stephen to ease the tension surrounding the four. "So Rich, he quit again!" he quipped, bringing the house down. In his speech Stephen paid special tribute to Ahmet Ertegun and the entire Atlantic Records family, closing with, "The class of '97 is a heck of a bunch and I'm honored to be with them."

"It was great to see Steve," beams Richie. "He was quite pleasant and certainly recognized the significance of the event. I saw Dewey for a few moments but I didn't see Bruce until the dinner that night. He was as weird as ever."

But the question of Neil's nonappearance just wouldn't go away. "At the press gathering after the induction itself it really got embarrassingly out of hand," Richie chuffs, "and finally it was time to step in and remind everyone that the event wasn't about Neil but about the honor we had come to receive."

"Things were going by so fast and we were so hurried once we got up there," he recalls. "I thought Tom Petty did a marvelous job of introducing us with that wonderful speech. And he was so nervous it was kind of cute. But I guess in his nervousness Tom had left his notes on the podium. When Bruce got up to speak he was rambling on and on and a heaviness had fallen over the whole audience. I was trying to lighten up the mood so I grabbed Tom's notes and said 'Here, Bruce, you forgot your notes.' I can't believe I gave those notes, that terrific speech, to Bruce. I have no idea if he kept them or not but I sure wish I had."

The opportunity to perform was lost when Neil bailed out. "I was disappointed that we didn't play," Richie opines, "because we had all talked about it and it would have been fun. But after hearing the Rascals play I thought they left a lot to be desired. The voices just weren't there. Then when the Bee Gees played it was like 'Oh, my gosh!' They were just phenomenal. So maybe it was a blessing in disguise that we didn't play. I don't know how cohesive it might have been. I would have hoped we would have done as well as the Bee Gees but I just don't know how we would have sounded. If we had the opportunity to sit down and rehearse it might have been okay. But in my heart, yeah, I was disappointed. I think it might have been fun to get up onstage and play a few songs. People would have enjoyed it."

Crosby, Stills and Nash followed their induction with a live performance. After a stirring *Wooden Ships*, which featured Stephen's blistering lead guitar work, CSN hosted the inevitable jam with Tom Petty joining in on *For What It's Worth*. At one point in the song, David Crosby leaned into his mike to inquire, "Richie, are you out there?" His request went unanswered. It was well past midnight and Richie and Nancy had returned to their hotel room. "I got food poisoning that night. I had been down to Canton, Ohio, to see my old friend Bob Harmelink. I was speaking at his daughter's school that afternoon but I was feeling real queasy all day. I even went back to bed afterwards. So at the ceremony I did what I had to do and left because I wasn't feeling well." There was some suggestion of bad blood between Richie and the others but that was hardly the case. "We all got along fine. Crosby, Stills and Nash were kind of like the band that played the rest of the evening but I just didn't want to be a part of it. So I left."

Perhaps in an effort to bury the hatchet, Neil recorded a song entitled *Buffalo Springfield Again* on his April 2000 release BROKEN ARROW. "I'd like to see those guys again and give it a shot; maybe now we can show the world what we've got," sang Neil, hinting at a possible reunion, or at least a public reconciliation following the Hall of Fame debacle. The song was one of the weaker tracks on an otherwise impressive album. While the sentiment may have been present, the execution wasn't. "I saw Neil after he released that song but he didn't comment on it at all," recalls Richie. "Nothing. It wasn't one of his better songs and it kind of let me down. I didn't think too much of it." Neil did take a tentative step in that direction by inviting Dewey and Bruce up to his ranch for a day of recording, though nothing came of it.

However, Neil was hardly about to abandon the Springfield cause. Having already spearheaded the re-release of the group's three albums (including the debut album in both stereo and mono mixes) in digitally enhanced HDCD high-definition format, rendering the old recordings crystal clear and pristine, he was tipped by the media to compile a comprehensive four CD box set of the group's entire recorded output featuring released, unreleased, and alternate tracks. Under the direction of longtime Young associate and employee Joel Bernstein, who had done a marvelous job with the CSN box set, Neil spared no expense in a relentless search for long lost tracks, photos, and Springfield memorabilia. Given the group's tangled recording and song publishing history it was a Herculean effort.

"Neil was the one who was financially able to do it and had the time to do it," suggests Richie. "Stephen may have been involved but I think it was a thing of the past for Steve. I don't think he's one to look back much." Richie received a last-minute invitation from Neil back in August 1998 to visit his ranch and preview the tracks along with Stephen, but the timing was not suitable, coming on the weekend of Richie's daughter's wedding. At that point he believed the package was complete and Neil was simply seeking Richie's tacit approval.

A few months later he did make the trip. "It was a bit overwhelming. The whole thing was heavily orchestrated. Neil and I hadn't really seen each other in a long time. So I flew out to San Francisco, he had a guy pick me up at the airport and take me to the ranch. I had never been to his ranch before. We had our twenty minutes of 'Hi, how are you? Nice to see you? How's the family?' And from there it was time to listen to the tracks and I listened to all of them in one sitting, most I hadn't heard in over thirty years. Neil stood and listened to them with me but didn't say much. He was grooving to some of the songs that he was particularly fond of. There wasn't much interaction between us. When I listened to all the tracks, I heard so many things I hadn't heard in so long that it made me kind of not think about some of the things I should have critiqued a little harder. Then when I was done it was time to get back on the plane and go back to Colorado. It was all so orchestrated. Fly in, listen to the tracks, then leave."

The final product, several years in the making, was released to much fanfare in the summer of 2001. Critics, Springfield aficionados, and music lovers alike gushed over the box set, which boasted eighty-eight tracks chronicling the group's evolution and disintegration in chronological order, with a stunning thirty-six unreleased demos or alternate takes. The set reveals the prolific recorded history of the short-lived group. "It's like revisiting your childhood neighborhood and being awash in memories, only this is in IMAX," enthused Stephen Stills to *USA Today*. "You can really hear us learning how to play and how to make records."

For die-hard fans who had spent decades speculating on the wealth of treasures hidden in Atlantic Records' tape vaults, the simply titled BUFFALO SPRINGFIELD BOX SET was the Holy Grail of compilations. Having contented themselves with poor quality bootleg copies of a handful of Springfield outtakes, to finally hear fully recorded gems like *Whatever Happened to Saturday Night, We'll See, No Sun Today,* and *Down Down Down* was a joy beyond words. That the latter track, recorded in the fall of 1966, was left off the group's debut album is bewildering given its compellingly moody air and rare three lead vocals. The box set is testimony to the profusion of talent the group possessed. Many of their outtakes stand head and shoulders above legitimate releases by their contemporaries. But the heart of the box set is the demo recordings, most simply acoustic guitar and voice. "I think those early demos are awesome," gushes Richie. "We were just sitting there singing. There was no digital stuff and no studio tweaking, just the two of us, Stephen and I, and you can really hear that we had a very distinctive vocal blend and we did it very well, the harmonies we were singing and the parallel lines. I was quite impressed hearing those tracks again. *Go And Say Goodbye* remains one of my favorite songs that Steve ever wrote. *What A Day* blew me away, hearing Stephen sing it. I had forgotten about it. That was the only one of my songs I ever remember him singing."

But while reviewers raved over the package with its elaborate booklet of clippings and rare photos, they were unanimous in criticizing what was termed an incomprehensible decision by Neil to repeat the group's first two albums track by track intact (in a couple of cases for the third time) on the fourth disk. "The set's only real flaw," wrote *Rolling Stone* reviewer Ben Edmonds, echoing the sentiment of others, "is the redundant Disc Four, which reprises the first two albums." In doing so Neil chose to omit several Springfield tracks, including demos of *Clancy* and *Sit Down I Think I Love You*, unreleased gems like *Sell Out*, *Extra Extra*, and *I Guess You Made It*, the nine- and eleven-minute versions of *Bluebird*, and, perhaps more telling, a full five tracks from the group's final album, LAST TIME AROUND—the familiar string and horn arrangement of *On The Way Home*, the band's jazz-flavored take of Stephen's *Four Days Gone*, the final version of *Pretty Girl Why* (represented instead by an earlier Jim Fielder take), latter-day member Jimmy Messina's loping *Carefree Country Day*, and Richie's elegant *The Hour Of Not Quite Rain*. Indeed, his disregard for the group's swan song release is clearly evident in the box set. As far as Neil is concerned, the group released only two albums, the third being an illegitimate offspring. A decision, given the group's reputation for stellar live performances, to avoid the dozen or more live tapes that were uncovered, including a rare rehearsal tape of the group barely a month old working their way through songs at the Hollywood Center Motel, is further baffling. For these reasons, the box set remains incomplete. A widely circulated three CD bootleg entitled THE MISSING HERD culled together many of the absent tracks to complete the picture. One can only hope that with the eventual release of Neil's massive 10 to 12 CD career retrospective SELECTIONS FROM THE NEIL YOUNG ARCHIVES, already delayed several times with no release date in sight, many of the missing pieces to the Springfield saga will finally be filled in.

"I am very proud of the box set and I compliment Neil for doing it," offers Richie. "He worked on it a long time." However, in hindsight, he feels Neil imposed too much of his own personal agenda on the final track selection. "Stepping back from it now and looking at the whole package I think it was a mistake not to have included all the songs from LAST TIME AROUND. Even though it was Neil's personal take on it, or maybe if Stephen agreed that the third album wasn't really a Buffalo Springfield album, I just think that there were some songs that should have been included simply because they were a part of the group's recordings. Really the only album that was truly a Buffalo Springfield album by the group was the first album. But the band released three albums. Why some songs were picked and others were not I don't know. Neil was the one who was really driving the whole thing and only he knows. I had several people tell me, people like Ken Viola, who wrote the liner notes to the set, 'You need to bring this up to Neil. *The Hour of Not Quite Rain* should be on that album.' Frankly it wasn't one of my favorite songs but it's unique and it is a Springfield track." Jimmy Messina concurs. "I'm disheartened that Neil felt so poorly about that third album," he recently opined, "because I did put a lot of energy and effort into it for his sake, and for Stephen's sake, and Richie's. Perhaps he didn't want it to be successful without him and it was subconscious self-sabotage. I can't say."

Despite being the errant member of the group during its lifetime, Neil's stamp is all over the box set. In a bold move, it is *his* photo and profile featured first before the others, most notably preceding Stephen who, more than Neil, set the vision and direction for the group and remained to the end. "It was Stephen's band from the day we started," Richie told a *Rolling Stone* interviewer.

The extensive booklet that accompanied the box set offered little in the way of new information about the group and its recordings, a frustrating point for longtime fans. However, it did unearth one previously forgotten fact. While the group members and musicologists have always pegged the Byrds tour in mid-April 1966 as the Springfield's public debut, in fact the group made its first appearance four days earlier, on April 11, at the Troubadour, a mere five days after their star-crossed Sunset Strip traffic jam meeting. "I can't remember the gig but that blows me away that we were performing within just a few days of getting together," marvels Richie. "I know that there was not much time before we started playing."

With the release of the box set, the question of a full-fledged Buffalo Springfield reunion was inescapable. Indeed, Neil took tentative steps in that direction in the wake of his Hall of Fame abstention. On his trek to Neil's ranch to preview the box set tracks in early 1999, Richie believes Neil was hinting at some sort of reunion. "Right before I left, Neil said to me 'You can't go until you hear this jam that Dewey, Bruce, and I did when they were up here.' I don't know if he just wanted me to hear that they could still play or if he was leading towards getting us all together again. I let him take the lead on that but nothing happened. It was just some old rock 'n' roll song they were jamming on."

In the midst of compiling the Springfield box set, Stephen and Neil rekindled their friendship. From that emerged a new CSNY album, LOOKING FORWARD, along with two massive North American tours. The group was even rumored to have cut a version of *Rock & Roll Woman*. Dewey remains in retirement living off an insurance settlement and claims to have invented a new type of drum hardware. Bruce has retreated to a farm north of Toronto, where he is writing his memoirs. Richie continues to minister at the Calvary Chapel in Boulder, Colorado, and performs occasionally. He and Jimmy Messina are talking of recording together again. "I really still have this music thing in me," he smiles, "but haven't had the chance to record. If Jimmy and I did do something together it would be a lot of fun. No pressure, just have some fun."

Does Richie feel a future reunion is in the cards? "I doubt it," he sighs. "I think we missed the moment. Obviously the time to have done it would have been at the Hall of Fame induction or around the release of the box set. There was a Crosby, Stills, Nash and Young tour going on then and it probably would have been a little too much but that would have been a good time for it. I've always felt that if it's going to happen, it'll be Neil who instigates it. But I personally don't think it will ever happen. It would be difficult for some of the guys and we would almost have to get other players to go along as backup musicians to make it work. But then it wouldn't be the Springfield, would it?

"If it's not going to be the same, if we couldn't really put a spark to the memory that everybody has of us, then I think we would be defeating the purpose. People remember us in their minds or have heard the records so they remember us for what it was. And if it isn't the same then everyone would be disappointed. I just don't think it will ever happen."

Whether the Buffalo Springfield reunites or not is a moot point. Their position in rock history remains secure and their recorded legacy continues to delight and inspire further generations.

DISCOGRAPHY

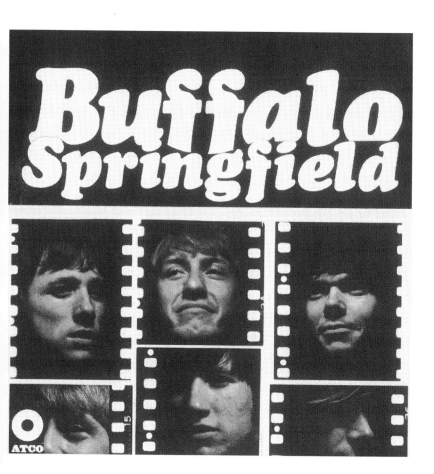

A. Pre-Buffalo Springfield

THE SQUIRES
(with Neil Young)

Single
The Sultan / Aurora —
V Records V 109 (1963)

AU GO-GO SINGERS (with
Richie Furay and Stephen Stills)

Album
THEY CALL US AU GO-GO SINGERS
— Roulette R / SR 25280 (1964)

*San Francisco Bay Blues, What If,
Gotta Travel On, Pink Polemo-
niums, You Are There, Oh Joe
Hannah, Miss Nellie, High Flying
Bird, What Have They Done To
The Rain, Lonesome Traveler,
Where I'm Bound, This Train*

Single
*San Francisco Bay Blues / Pink Pole-
moniums —* Roulette 4577 (1964)

JACK LONDON AND THE
SPARROWS (with Bruce Palmer)

Single
*If You Don't Want My Love / It's
Been One Of Those Days Today —*
Capitol 72203 (1964)

SIR RALEIGH AND THE
COUPONS (with Dewey Martin)

Singles
*White Cliffs Of Dover / Somethin'
Or Other —* A&M 757 (1964)

*While I Wait / Somethin' Or Other
—* A&M 764 (1964)

*Tomorrow's Gonna Be Another
Day / Whitcomb Street —*
Jerden 760 (1965)

*Tell Her Tonight / If You Need Me
—* Tower 156 (1965)

I Don't Want To Cry / Always —
Tower 220 (1966)

Album
ONE BUFFALO HEARD — Picc-A-
Dilly / First American PIC 3483
(1982)

*I Don't Want To Cry, I Don't Have
To Worry About You, Tell Her
Tonight, It Took A Long Time, I'll
Understand, White Cliffs Of Dover,
While I Wait, Always, Somethin'
Or Other, Things We Said Today,
If You Need Me, Tomorrow's
Gonna Be Another Day*

THE MOTHERS OF INVENTION
(with Jim Fielder)

Album
ABSOLUTELY FREE —
Verve 5013 (1967)

TIM BUCKLEY
(with Jim Fielder)

Albums
TIM BUCKLEY —
Elektra EKS 74004 (1966)

GOODBYE AND HELLO —
Elektra EKS 74028 (1967)

THE DAILY FLASH
(with Doug Hastings)

Singles
*Queen Jane Approximately /
Birdses —* Parrot 308 (1965)

French Girl / Green Rocky Road —
UNI 550001 (1967)

JIMMY MESSINA AND THE JESTERS (with Jimmy Messina)

Singles

Panther Pounce / Tiger Tail — Feature 101 (1964)

Drag Bike Boogie / A-Rab — Ultima U-705 (1964)

The Breeze And I / Strange Man — Audio Fidelity 098 (1964)

Side Track / Sherrie — Viv 1000 (1964)

Album

THE DRAGSTERS — Audio Fidelity DFM / DFS 7037 (1965) (re-released on Thimble TLP 3 (1973)

Honky Tonk, Raunchy, The Breeze and I, High Voltage, Yang Bu, Chiuahua, The Jester, Hollywood Sound, Masatlan Rally, No Name Dragster, The Cossack, Tamale Wagon

B. BUFFALO SPRINGFIELD

Singles

Nowadays Clancy Can't Even Sing / Go And Say Goodbye — Atco 6428 (1966)

Burned / Everybody's Wrong — Atco 6452 (1966)

For What It's Worth / Do I Have To Come Right Out And Say It — Atco 6459 (1967)

Bluebird / Mr. Soul — Atco 6499 (1967)

Rock And Roll Woman / A Child's Claim To Fame — Atco 6519 (1967)

Expecting To Fly / Everydays — Atco 6545 (1968)

Uno Mundo / Merry-Go-Round — Atco 6572 (1968)

Kind Woman / Special Care — Atco 6602 (1968)

On The Way Home / Four Days Gone — Atco 6615 (1968)

Pretty Girl Why / Questions — Atco 226 006 (UK 1969)

Bluebird / Mr. Soul / Rock And Roll Woman / Expecting To Fly — Atlantic K 10237 (UK 1972)

Albums

BUFFALO SPRINGFIELD — Atco SD / 33-200 (1966)*

Go And Say Goodbye, Sit Down I Think I Love You, Leave, Nowadays Clancy Can't Even Sing, Hot Dusty Roads, Everybody's Wrong, Flying On The Ground Is Wrong, Burned, Do I Have To Come Right Out And Say It, Baby Don't Scold Me, Out Of My Mind, Pay The Price

*re-released in 1967 with *For What It's Worth* replacing *Baby Don't Scold Me*†

BUFFALO SPRINGFIELD AGAIN — Atco SD 33-226 (1967)†

Mr. Soul, A Child's Claim To Fame, Everydays, Expecting To Fly, Bluebird, Hung Upside Down, Sad Memory, Good Time Boy, Rock & Roll Woman, Broken Arrow

LAST TIME AROUND — Atco SD 33-256 (1968)†

On The Way Home, It's So Hard To Wait, Pretty Girl Why, Four Days Gone, Carefree Country Day, Special Care, The Hour Of Not Quite Rain, Questions, I Am A

Child, Merry-Go-Round, Uno Mundo, Kind Woman

RETROSPECTIVE —
Atco SD 33-283 (1969)†

For What It's Worth, Mr. Soul, Sit Down I Think I Love You, Kind Woman, Bluebird, On The Way Home, Nowadays Clancy Can't Even Sing, Broken Arrow, Rock And Roll Woman, I Am A Child, Go And Say Goodbye, Expecting To Fly

EXPECTING TO FLY —
Atlantic 2462 012 (UK 1970)

For What It's Worth, Expecting To Fly, Special Care, Hot Dusty Roads, Everybody's Wrong, Pay The Price, Flying On The Ground Is Wrong, Burned, Do I Have To Come Right Out And Say It, Leave, Out Of My Mind, Merry-Go-Round

BUFFALO SPRINGFIELD —
Atco SD 2-806 (1973)

For What It's Worth, Sit Down I Think I Love You, Nowadays Clancy Can't Even Sing, Go And Say Goodbye, Pay The Price, Burned, Out Of My Mind, Mr. Soul, Bluebird*, Broken Arrow, Rock And Roll Woman, Expecting To Fly, Hung Upside Down, A Child's Claim To Fame, Kind Woman, On The Way Home, I Am A Child, Pretty Girl Why, Special Care, Uno Mundo, The Hour Of Not Quite Rain, Four Days Gone, Questions

*previously unreleased nine minute extended version

C. Unreleased Springfield-Era Songs Recorded On Related Albums

NEIL YOUNG (1969)† — Neil

Young: String Quartet From Whiskey Boot Hill, Last Trip To Tulsa, The Old Laughing Lady

PICKIN' UP THE PIECES (1969) —
Poco: What A Day, Nobody's Fool,

EVERYBODY KNOWS THIS IS NOWHERE (1969)† — Neil Young: Round And Round

AFTER THE GOLD RUSH (1970)† — Neil Young: Birds

DEJA VU (1970)† — Crosby, Stills, Nash & Young: Whiskey Boot Hill, Down Down Down

POCO (1970)† — Poco: Nobody's Fool

DELIVERIN' (1970)† — Poco: I Guess You Made It

FROM THE INSIDE (1971)† — Poco: Do You Feel It Too (Can't Keep Me Down)

JOURNEY THROUGH THE PAST (1972) — Neil Young: For What It's Worth, Mr. Soul, Rock And Roll Woman (live from TV)

STAMPEDE (1973) — (bootleg):

Neighbor Don't You Worry, We'll See, Down To The Wire (#1), Down To The Wire (#2), Do I Have To Come Right Out And Say It, Raga One, Raga Two, My Kind Of Love, Come On, Baby Don't Scold Me (#1), Baby Don't Scold Me (#2), Pay The Price*, Nobody's Fool*, Nowadays Clancy Can't Even Sing*, Rock And Roll Woman*

*recorded live at Whittier College, August 1967

STILLS (1975)† — Stephen Stills: My Angel

316

DECADE (1977)† — Neil Young: *Down To The Wire*

NEIL YOUNG MEETS BUFFALO SPRINGFIELD AND THE SQUIRES (1989)† — (bootleg) :

Nowadays Clancy Can't Even Sing, When It Falls It Falls All Over You [Extra Extra], Down To The Wire, Do I Have To Come Right Out and Say It, There Goes My Babe, One More Sign

THE FORGOTTEN TRAIL (1990)† — Poco: *My Kind Of Love, I Guess You Made It*

THE LEGACY OF... NEIL YOUNG & BUFFALO SPRINGFIELD (1991)† — (bootleg):

There Goes My Babe, One More

Sign, Mr. Soul, Do I Have To Come Right Out And Say It, Down To The Wire (#1), Down To The Wire (#2), Neighbor Don't You Worry, We'll See, My Kind Of Love, Come On, For What It's Worth*, Nowadays Clancy Can't Even Sing*, Rock And Roll Woman*, Bluebird*, A Child's Claim To Fame*

*live recordings from the Monterey Pop Festival, June 1967

PICKIN' UP THE PIECES (1996)† Poco: *What A Day, Nobody's Fool, Do You Feel It Too (Can't Keep Me Down)**

* alternate take

† currently available on compact disc

BUFFALO SPRINGFIELD BOX SET—Atco/Elektra/Rhino R2 74324 (2001)†

DISC ONE: *There Goes My Babe, Come On, Hello I've Returned, Out Of My Mind, Flying On The Ground Is Wrong, I'm Your Kind Of Guy, Baby Don't Scold Me, Neighbor Don't You Worry, We'll See, Sad Memory, Can't Keep Me Down, Nowadays Clancy Can't Even Sing, Go And Say Goodbye, Sit Down I Think I Love You, Leave, Hot Dusty Roads, Everybody's Wrong, Burned, Do I Have To Come Right Out And Say It, Out Of My Mind, Pay The Price, Down Down Down, Flying On The Ground Is Wrong, Neighbor Don't You Worry*

DISC TWO: *Down Down Down, Kahuna Sunset, Buffalo Stomp, Baby Don't Scold Me, For What It's Worth, Mr. Soul, We'll See, My Kind Of Love, Pretty Girl Why, Words I Must Say, Nobody's Fool, So You've Got A Lover, My Angel, Everydays, Down To The Wire, Bluebird, Expecting To Fly, Hung Upside Down, A Child's Claim To Fame, Rock And Roll Woman*

DISC THREE: *Hung Upside Down, Good Time Boy, One More Sign, The Rent Is Always Due, Round And Round And Round, Old Laughing Lady, Broken Arrow, Sad Memory, On The Way Home, Whatever Happened To Saturday Night, Special Care, Falcon Lake (Ash On The Floor), What A Day, I Am A Child, Questions, Merry-Go-Round, Uno Mundo, Kind Woman, It's So Hard To Wait, Four Days Gone*

DISC FOUR: *For What It's Worth, Go And Say Goodbye, Sit Down I Think I Love You, Nowadays Clancy Can't Even Sing, Hot Dusty Roads, Everybody's Wrong, Flying On The Ground Is Wrong, Burned, Do I Have To Come Right Out And Say It, Leave, Out Of My Mind, Pay The Price, Baby Don't Scold Me, Mr. Soul, A Child's Claim To Fame, Everydays, Expecting To Fly, Bluebird, Hung Upside Down, Sad Memory, Good Time Boy, Rock And Roll Woman, Broken Arrow*

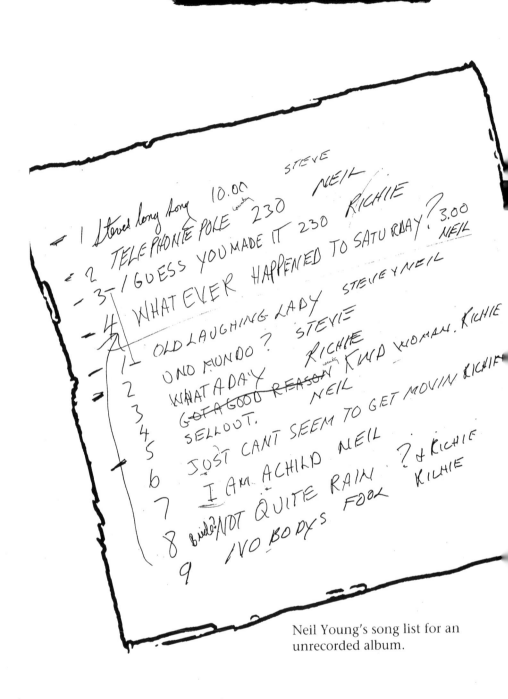

Neil Young's song list for an
unrecorded album.

ACKNOWLEDGEMENTS

I would like to extend my sincere thanks to all those people who kindly consented to be interviewed for this book and whose names appear throughout. Warmest thanks go to Richie and Nancy Furay along with their family for their gracious hospitality, patience, and generosity over the past two years. Special recognition is due to Buffalo Springfield and Poco historian extraordinaire Jerry Fuentes of Stockton, California, whose assistance and ongoing dialogue with me throughout the research and writing process was invaluable. A special thanks to you Jerry for your pioneering work in charting the Springfield story and for your friendship.

In addition, I would like to cite the following for either support above and beyond the call of duty, helping break through the various log jams encountered in putting this book together, or simply for lending a sympathetic ear: Michael Heatley (for his encouragement), Mark Ferjulian, Nurit Wilde (for her positive encouragement and network of contacts), Stan Endersby (an all round nice guy who opened several doors for me; thanks for the photos, Stan), Gail Jones, Richard 'Dickie' Davis, Jean Gurney, Scott Sather and his Moby Grape web site (http://www.geocities.com/SunsetStrip/1256/), Fred Redekop (for loaning the album), John and Jutta Kay, Canadian musicologist Bill Munson, Carny Corbett, Mike Stelk, Neal Skok, Pete Long (meticulous Neil Young archivist and author of *Ghosts On The Road*), Marc Skobac, Dieter Ostrowski (thanks for the tapes), Alan Jenkins (Neil Young Appreciation Society, 2a Llynfi Street, Bridgend, Mid Glamorgan, CF31 1SY, Wales, UK), Howard Mandshein (for planting the seed several years earlier on a radio special together), and Scott and Carolyn Sellen (for their warm hospitality and marvelous green chili).

The following served as invaluable resources: *The Rock Story* by Jerry Hopkins (Signet Books); *Summer Of Love* and *Monterey Pop* by Joel Selvin (Chronicle Books); David Zimmer's biography of Crosby, Stills and Nash (Sierra Books); and the impressive series of British magazines entitled *The History Of Rock* (Orbis Publishing).

As always, I would like to thank my family — my wife Harriett and children Matt and Lynsey — for their continued love and support of my work.

JOHN EINARSON
Winnipeg, Manitoba

CREDITS

Lyrics

Buffalo Springfield songs quoted to illustrate and document this history of the band are copyright and published by Springalo Toones - Warner Tamerlane.

Photos

All photos are from the private collection of Richie Furay with the exception of the following:

Courtesy of Gene Trindl: pp. 210 (top), 269 (bottom), back cover

Courtesy of Gail Jones: p. 64 (bottom)

Courtesy of Norbert Jobst: p. 182

Courtesy of Annabel Bonds: p. 302 (bottom)

Courtesy of John Einarson: p. 63

Courtesy of Bob Harmelink: p. 40